Grow Your Money!

Grow Your Money!

101 Easy Tips to Plan, Save, and Invest

Jonathan D. Pond

Collins

An Imprint of HarperCollinsPublishers

This book is meant to provide general investment and financial advice. It is not designed to be a definitive investment guide or to take the place of advice from a qualified financial planner or other professional. Given the risk involved in all investments, there is no guarantee that the investment methods suggested in this book will be profitable. Thus, neither the publisher nor the author assumes liability of any kind for any losses that may be sustained as a result of applying the methods suggested in this book, and any such liability is hereby expressly disclaimed.

GROW YOUR MONEY! Copyright © 2008 by Jonathan Pond. All rights reserved. Printed in the United States of America. No part of this book may be used or reproduced in any manner whatsoever without written permission except in the case of brief quotations embodied in critical articles and reviews. For information, address HarperCollins Publishers, 10 East 53rd Street, New York, NY 10022.

HarperCollins books may be purchased for educational, business, or sales promotional use. For information, please write: Special Markets Department, HarperCollins Publishers, 10 East 53rd Street, New York, NY 10022.

FIRST EDITION

Designed by Jaime Putorti

Library of Congress Cataloging-in-Publication Data

Pond, Jonathan D.
   Grow your money! : 101 easy tips to plan, save, and invest / Jonathan D. Pond. — 1st ed.
      p. cm.
   Includes index.
   ISBN 978-0-06-112140-1
   1. Finance, Public.   2. Investments.   3. Retirement income—Planning.
I. Title.

   HG179.P555574 2007   2007024071
   332.024—dc22

08 09 10 11 12 WB/RRD 10 9 8 7 6 5 4 3 2 1

For my wife, Lois, and our three Puddles,
Elizabeth, Laura, and Emily

Contents

Acknowledgments   *xv*

Introduction   *xvii*

CHAPTER 1: ACHIEVING YOUR FINANCIAL DREAMS   *1*

Idea 1   Program Your Financial Navigation System   *2*

Idea 2   Time Is Your Ally   *4*

Idea 3   Getting Rich Is Boring   *9*

Idea 4   Millionaire Success Secrets   *11*

Idea 5   Go Forth and Let Your Money Multiply   *15*

CHAPTER 2: PROFITING FROM A FABULOUS CAREER   *19*

Idea 6   The Ingredients of Career Success   *20*

Idea 7   Advice for Those Who Have Taken
               a Career Sabbatical   *23*

Money Tip   Continuing Your Education—For
               Consumption or Investment?   *25*

Idea 8   Considering a Career Change?   *26*

Money Tip   Leave Your Job on Good Terms   *29*

Idea 9   Buck the Odds by Starting and
               Succeeding in Your Own Business   *30*

Money Tip   Pension-Plan Advisory   *33*

Idea 10	Your Career Doesn't Have to End When You Reach Retirement Age	35
CHAPTER 3:	**ACCUMULATING REAL WEALTH**	37
Idea 11	How Great Wealth Is Created	38
Idea 12	The Miracle of Tax Deferral	43
Idea 13	Devising a Plan to Reconcile Your Gross Habits with Your Net Income	46
Money Tip	Help Yourself and the Economy by Practicing "Reverse Keeping Up with the Joneses"	50
Idea 14	Out, Out, Damned Budget	51
Money Tip	Chump No More: Using Online Coupon Codes	53
Idea 15	Save Your Raise	54
Idea 16	Deciding What to Do with a Financial Windfall	55
CHAPTER 4:	**USING DEBT TO YOUR ADVANTAGE**	59
Idea 17	Borrow for Things That Will Appreciate in Value	60
Money Tip	Establishing Your Good Credit for the First Time	62
Idea 18	Getting Richer with Borrowed Money	63
Idea 19	Manage Your Home Equity Loan Like a Business	65
Idea 20	Pay Off Your Credit Cards Later Rather Than Sooner	66
Money Tip	Managing Your Student Loans	68
Idea 21	Getting Out of Debt Problems	69
Idea 22	Buffing Up Your Credit	73
Money Tip	Need a Short-Term Loan? Borrow From Your IRA	75

CHAPTER 5: PUTTING MONEY AWAY FOR
A PROSPEROUS FUTURE   *76*

Idea 23   The Tortoise Beats the Hare:
Getting Rich Slowly   *76*

Money Tip Both a Saver and an Investor Be   *78*

Money Tip Advice for Those for Whom the Lottery
Is Their Primary Retirement Plan   *79*

Idea 24   Making the Most of Money You're Going to
Need Within a Few Years   *80*

Idea 25   Preparing for a Financial Emergency
Can Cost You Thousands   *82*

Idea 26   The Best Ways to Invest for Retirement   *83*

Idea 27   Saddled with a Lousy 401(k) Plan? Roll Your
401(k) Plan Into an IRA After You Turn 59½   *87*

Money Tip Investing in Your Employer's Stock? Stock
Purchase Plan, Okay; 401(k) Plan, Not   *87*

Idea 28   Should You Make a Roth IRA Conversion?   *88*

Idea 29   Yes, Virginia, You Do Qualify for
an IRA Contribution   *92*

Idea 30   Retirement Plans for the Self-Employed
Simplified   *93*

Idea 31   Smart (and Painless) Ways to Add
to Your Investments   *96*

Idea 32   Free at Last: Deciding What to Do
with Your Retirement Savings Plan
When You Change Jobs   *98*

Money Tip What's Your Number?   *101*

CHAPTER 6: BECOMING A SAVVY INVESTOR   *102*

Idea 33   Create a World-Class Investment Portfolio
with Just Six Investments   *102*

Idea 34   Making the Most of Your Mutual Fund
Investments   *107*

Idea 35   Idle Cash Need Not Earn Paltry Returns   *110*

Idea 36   What Kind of Investor Are You? Take the Quiz   *111*
Idea 37   Investing When You're Just Starting Out   *115*
Money Tip   Shun Those Who Think They Can Predict
              the Future of the Investment Markets   *120*
Idea 38   When It Comes to Investing, Average Is
              Pretty Good   *121*
Idea 39   Putting Your Investments on Autopilot   *125*

CHAPTER 7:   SUPERCHARGING YOUR INVESTMENTS   *128*
Idea 40   There's Something Nice About Being
              a Contrarian   *129*
Idea 41   Investment Returns Make a Big Difference   *133*
Idea 42   Four Can't-Miss Investments   *135*
Idea 43   A Rich Recipe: Adding Individual Securities
              to Your Mutual Fund Portfolio   *139*
Idea 44   The Truth and Nothing but the Truth   *143*
Idea 45   Investing Profitably in Sector Funds   *144*
Idea 46   Sayonara: Deciding When to Sell an Investment   *147*
Idea 47   Surviving a Market Decline   *151*
Idea 48   Quick Ways to Evaluate a Real
              Estate Investment   *153*
Idea 49   Why Not Be Lord or Lady of the Land?   *156*

CHAPTER 8:   BUYING AND MAINTAINING A HOME   *159*
Idea 50   Tricks of the Home-Buying Trade   *159*
Idea 51   Save for a House or Save for Retirement?   *163*
Idea 52   Should You Pay Off Your Mortgage Early?   *165*
Idea 53   Appeal Your Property Tax Bill   *169*
Idea 54   Move or Improve?   *171*
Money Tip   Find Out If You're Still Required to
              Pay for Private Mortgage Insurance   *175*
Idea 55   Surviving a Home Improvement Project   *176*
Money Tip   Think Thrice Before Buying an
              Appliance Service Contract   *179*
Idea 56   Vacation Home Follies   *180*

CHAPTER 9: **PAYING FOR COLLEGE AND OTHER**
BIG-TICKET ITEMS 185
Idea 57 Big-Ticket Items Tell a Lot 186
Idea 58 Why College and Cars and Other
Costly Necessities Are So Expensive 189
Idea 59 Saving for College 190
Idea 60 Preparing for Annoying but Inevitable Expenses 193
Idea 61 Create a Homemade 529 Plan Without
the Hefty Expenses 195
Idea 62 Save for College and Retirement in the
Same Account 197
Idea 63 Cutting College Costs 198
Money Tip The Peril of Sacrificing Retirement Savings
to Save for College 199
Idea 64 If You Hate Cars, Buy New; If You
Love Cars, Buy Used 200
Idea 65 Ten Money Savers That Will Save You
Thousands of Dollars in Car Ownership Costs 203
Idea 66 Dr. Jonathan's Car-Loan-Addiction Elixir 205

CHAPTER 10: **GIVING UNCLE SAM HIS DUE, AND NOT**
ONE CENT MORE 207
Idea 67 Ten Top Tax-Savings Ideas 208
Idea 68 News Flash: Congress Isn't Going to
Tinker with Your Tax Breaks 212
Idea 69 Increasing Investment Returns by
Decreasing Taxes on Investments 214
Money Tip Many Tax-Saving Strategies Aren't Worth
the Effort 217
Idea 70 Getting a Tax Refund Is Bad News 218
Money Tip Prepare Your Own Income Tax Returns 220
Idea 71 Managing Your Tax Bite After You Retire 221
Money Tip How Long Should You Keep Your Tax Returns? 224
Idea 72 Last-Minute Tax-Savings Ideas 226

**CHAPTER 11: SECURING THE FUTURE FOR YOU
AND YOUR LOVED ONES** *230*

Idea 73   Filling Gaps in Your Property
Insurance Coverage   *231*

Idea 74   Surprise: You're Probably Overinsured   *233*

Idea 75   The Straight Scoop on Life Insurance   *235*

Idea 76   Is It Time to Trade In Your Term Life
Insurance Policy for a Newer Model?   *240*

Idea 77   Long-Term-Care Insurance? Not for Everyone   *242*

Idea 78   Insurance to Avoid   *244*

Idea 79   Estate Planning—Ignore This If You
Dislike Your Heirs   *247*

Idea 80   Do You Really Need a Living Trust?   *249*

Money Tip   Where Should You Store Your Will?   *252*

Idea 81   Helping Older Family Members Cope with
Their Finances   *253*

**CHAPTER 12: MAKING SMART MONEY DECISIONS A
FAMILY AFFAIR** *257*

Idea 82   Picking the Right Professionals to Advise You,
If You Really Need Their Advice   *258*

Idea 83   Domestic Financial Felicity Need Not Be an
Impossible Dream   *263*

Idea 84   Advice for Twentysomethings: Something Your
Parents and Grandparents Know for Sure   *267*

Idea 85   Dual-Career Parents of Youngsters: Does
That Second Paycheck Really Help the
Family Budget Very Much?   *269*

Idea 86   Teach Kids About Money   *271*

Idea 87   IRAs for the Younger Set   *274*

Idea 88   Avoiding Financial Scams   *278*

CHAPTER 13: ENJOYING A GREAT RETIREMENT *282*

Idea 89   Can You Get There From Here?
Finding Out Where You Stand   *283*

Idea 90   Achieving Early Retirement   *287*
Idea 91   It Will Probably Cost You Less When
              You Retire Than You Think   *290*
Idea 92   Last-Minute Ways to Boost Your
              Retirement Income   *293*
Idea 93   It's a Mistake to Collect Social Security Early *297*
Idea 94   Changes You Should Make in Your Finances
              When You Retire   *302*
Idea 95   Making Sure You Never Run Out of Money   *305*
Money Tip   The New Breed of Variable Annuity   *311*
Idea 96   The Reverse Mortgage: Less Than Meets the Eye *312*

CHAPTER 14: SAVORING THE GOOD LIFE—
NOW AND LATER   *316*
Idea 97   Simplifying Your Financial Life   *317*
Money Tip   Always Keep the Basics in Mind   *321*
Idea 98   Financial Security in Thirty Minutes a Month *323*
Money Tip   Never Underestimate the Value of
              Common Sense   *326*
Idea 99   Invest in Your Good Health   *327*
Idea 100   Taking Advantage of the Best Financial
              Opportunities   *331*
Idea 101   It's Time to Indulge Yourself   *334*

Appendix   *Grow Your Money!* To-Do Calendar   *337*

Index   *345*

Acknowledgments

Grow Your Money! has benefited from the contributions of several capable and enthusiastic people who share my belief that a book that provides unbiased and understandable guidance will help you achieve financial security. I gratefully acknowledge their dedication.

Steve Ross, president and publisher, and Margot Schupf, associate publisher, oversee a team that is second to none in the publishing industry.

The people involved in the copyediting and production of the book are consummate professionals who are also far too kind when pointing out this author's grammatical deficiencies. I admire and thank you all, particularly Helen Song, senior production editor, Sarah Brown, assistant editor, Diane Aronson, senior copy chief, and Cecilia Hunt, copyeditor. You really are the saviors of those of us whose academic records could politely be described as "inconsistent." Rather than graduating in the top half of our high school and college classes, we made it possible for our classmates to graduate in the top half, and our writing skills reflect that.

Despite ignoring my advice to avoid taking financial responsibility for things that eat, Angie Lee, marketing director, has earned my admiration for her insights. Good luck with your new tax exemption, Angie. Chase Bodine, my HarperCollins publicist, is handling the promotion with aplomb. *Grow Your Money!* has also benefited greatly from the skills of Richard Ljoenes, senior art director.

My editor, Ethan Friedman, has once again shown a marvelous understanding of how to communicate effectively to readers. He always comes up with suggestions that greatly enhance the work, and I am sincerely grateful for his perspicacity, a word that he probably wouldn't allow me to use elsewhere in this book.

Alan Lavine and Gail Liberman, a writing duo par excellence, provided many ideas for *Grow Your Money!* as did Betsy Petersen. The encouragement and insights of the many people with whom I have worked at AARP is much appreciated as well, particularly Al Sommers and George Blooston. Thanks as well for the advice and support of Peter Ginsberg, my automobile-loving agent.

My associates John Annino, Joan Lohr, and Richard Merrill were and will continue to be very helpful as we maintain the *Grow Your Money!* special reader Web site to provide timely and helpful updates to the book's content.

I would also like to acknowledge the contributions of many people I've spoken with across the country over the past decade—in person and on television and radio. Your questions, concerns, and insights have been indispensable in shaping this book.

Authors' families suffer immensely. The spouses inevitably think they've made an error in matrimonial judgment. The children must feel it's an accident of birth. I'll leave it to other authors to chronicle the travails that inevitably befall their loved ones. I'll just thank my family yet again for their patience, including my 93-year-old mother, whose words of encouragement are always forthcoming and welcome.

Introduction

Now's the time. *Grow Your Money!* will help you get serious about achieving your financial dreams by giving you my favorite ideas and tips so that you can

- ✦ Ameliorate any shortcomings in the way you handle your investments and other important family financial matters.

- ✦ Employ ideas and strategies that will help you make the most of your money now and in the future. Many will surprise you because they refute conventional wisdom.

The following chapters contain my 101 favorite money ideas with a smattering of tips for good measure. Rather than burdening you by covering every last area of your financial life, *Grow Your Money!* focuses on the most important topics, those that can make a big difference in your lifelong financial success. Be sure to take advantage of the special reader Web site introduced on page xliii, so that you can keep up to date on the ideas discussed here.

Growing your money requires paying attention to a lot of financial matters—from living beneath your means to wisely investing what you save, from keeping your debt under control to insuring against the unknown to avoid financial setbacks. Most of us do a reasonably good job in some areas, but aren't so savvy in others. Attaining and maintaining financial security, however, requires attention to many different areas. After all, what's the use of building up a princely investment stash if you risk losing it by carrying inadequate insurance coverage?

Little oversights can have long-term consequences. Part of getting serious about your financial future is making sure you've covered important matters and avoided putting yourself in a situation that can take a long time to resolve.

✦ For lack of a $250-a-year umbrella liability insurance policy, a surgeon lost most of his assets and a good portion of his future income.

✦ Chasing hot stocks and neglecting to diversify their investments caused many investors to lose more than half of their money during the tech-stock bust that began in 2000.

✦ Waiting many years before beginning to set money aside for retirement has made it necessary for many people to retire late or settle for a lower standard of living after retirement.

✦ For many running up credit card and other loans has put a big dent in their ability to make retirement-plan contributions for years—even decades.

Just because you think something's okay doesn't mean it can't be better. Contentment is good for the soul, but may not be good for the pocketbook.

✦ You've got plenty of insurance but don't realize you could save a thousand dollars or more on premiums.

✦ You're delighted that your stock investments grew 8 percent last year, but is that really so good when the market indexes gained 14 percent?

✦ You're contributing a goodly sum to your retirement savings plan at work, but those savings don't grow due to the dreadful performance of the funds you selected in the plan.

✦ You've been very successful with your investments over the past several years, but should the stock market plummet, your investments are a disaster waiting to happen.

✦ You're making headway reducing a mountain of debt, but you don't realize that some minor changes in your debt-reduction strategy could lop years off the time it takes you to eliminate the loans.

A guide for all ages. *Grow Your Money!* will help you get on track to achieve your retirement dreams. Whether you're twenty-two or ninety-two or somewhere in between, whether you're single, partnered, betrothed, or married, *Grow Your Money!* will help you smooth out the rough edges in your financial life and give you ideas to help you make the most of your money. Lifetime financial peace of mind is easily within your grasp, despite what the media would have you believe.

. . . even for those with big financial responsibilities. The easiest way to achieve your financial dreams is to avoid taking financial responsibility for anything that eats. But even if in a moment of emotional abandon that caused you to temporarily lose sight of the financial implications of your actions, you (in order of increasing costliness)

✦ acquired a pet,

✦ married or partnered, and/or

✦ had kids (ouch!),

you can still attain and maintain financial freedom. After all, your parents have probably done okay financially, despite the financial demands you and, perhaps, your siblings imposed on them. Life has a way of balancing things out anyway. At least that's what my ninety-three-year-old mother implies when she says, "Whenever I die, let it be known that had it not been for you boys [your author and his similarly obstreperous brother, Roger], I would have lived five years longer." If she's correct, then kids and those other responsibilities shorten our lives, which in turn means we don't need as much money when we retire as do those happy-go-lucky souls (or so we think, since the grass is always greener on the other side) who haven't been similarly encumbered.

The lay of the land. Here's a rundown of what's ahead in *Grow Your Money!*

> **Chapter 1—Achieving Your Financial Dreams.** Despite news reports that portray Americans as hopelessly inept at preparing financially for the future, no matter what your age or financial condition, you can definitely achieve a sound financial future. You just need to get serious about your financial life. It doesn't take a lot of time, but if you take easy steps to correct any shortcomings and do even better in the areas that are already under control, you'll be able to approach the future with confidence and enthusiasm.
>
> **Chapter 2—Profiting From a Fabulous Career.** Your career is by far your most important investment (with the possible exception of marrying someone worth $25 million). Are you making the most of your current job, or should you be moving on to greener pastures or obtaining more education? At the least, you should be making sure you're career is on the income-maximization track.
>
> **Chapter 3—Accumulating Real Wealth.** Taking control of your finances isn't as difficult as you may have been led to believe. (It's also not as easy as the late-night infomercials breathlessly attest.) Accumulating real wealth simply requires getting serious about a few techniques that will put you on the road to true financial security.

Chapter 4—Using Debt to Your Advantage. You probably think that debt is bad. After all, debt is a lot easier to amass than it is to pay off. But wisely used, debt can be an important tool to enhance your lifetime wealth.

Chapter 5—Putting Money Away for a Prosperous Future. The list of places where you can put your money looks like alphabet soup—IRAs, 401(k)s, SEPs, etc., etc. Making the right selections can spell the difference between a so-so financial future and a great financial future.

Chapter 6—Becoming a Savvy Investor. Investing need not be complicated. By adhering to a handful of important, but not well understood ideas, you can put your money to work for you to achieve excellent results in all market conditions. These techniques work even if you're just starting to invest.

Chapter 7—Supercharging Your Investments. You don't have to be a millionaire to use straightforward strategies to increase your investment returns. Paying a little extra attention to your investments can yield much richer returns. Better investment returns could double your retirement income.

Chapter 8—Buying and Maintaining a Home. For most of us, home ownership is a crucial part of our long-term financial success. Whether you're already a homeowner or aspire to buy a home, you will learn in this chapter how to make the most of your biggest lifetime investment.

Chapter 9—Paying for College and Other Big-Ticket Items. There's nothing like college, cars, and other big-ticket items to disrupt the most carefully devised financial plans. But there are ways to cope with these inevitable expenses that don't require that you work an extra ten years to pay for them.

Chapter 10—Giving Uncle Sam His Due, and Not One Cent More. Most people overpay their income taxes and don't realize it. Every dollar you save in income taxes is a dollar you can put to much better use, unless you think the government can do better with it. The suggestions in this chapter could help you reduce your tax exaction by thousands of dollars a year.

Chapter 11—Securing the Future for You and Your Loved Ones. Over the course of our lifetime, we are periodically dealt some tough cards, but adequate preparation can ameliorate the effects. This chapter will show you ways to protect what you now have and not jeopardize what you accumulate in the future.

Chapter 12—Making Smart Money Decisions a Family Affair. Running a family is like running a small country and costs about as much. Sometimes, it's beneficial to seek professional (financial and, maybe, mental) help in addressing these challenges. Helping family members become financially responsible can reap rewards in the future, such as not having to support them in your dotage.

Chapter 13—Enjoying a Great Retirement. Sound financial planning doesn't end at retirement. In fact, planning for a great retirement is something you should do throughout both your working and retired years. Whether you're still working or retired, this chapter will provide important suggestions for making retirement as wonderful as it can be.

Chapter 14—Savoring the Good Life—Now and Later. The process of reaching your financial aspirations needn't condemn you to a life of deprivation for the duration. After all, you work hard for your money and you deserve to enjoy it. The ideas in this chapter will empower you to enjoy life with a minimum of financial hassles as you prepare for a great financial future.

Appendix—*Grow Your Money!* To-Do Calendar. Your calendar will remind you of important things to do throughout the year to keep your investments and other financial issues in fine fettle.

Pronoun pronouncement. *Grow Your Money!* is rife with quotations for your inspiration and amusement. Many originated decades, if not centuries, ago when the male noun and pronoun predominated. For example:

> ■
>
> *If a man dies and leaves his estate in an uncertain*
> *condition, the lawyers become his heirs.*
> —EDGAR WATSON HOWE (1853–1937)

My use of these is in no way intended to slight women. As the only male in a household of five, I can assure you that any intentional affrontary would be addressed sternly at home.

What's Your Pleasure?

While I encourage you to read *Grow Your Money!* from cover to cover, you may prefer to focus on your areas of particular interest. The following indexes will help you quickly identify areas of importance to you:

1. **Master List of 101 Ideas.** The first section is a list of all 101 ideas with check boxes so that you can highlight ideas that are important to your unique financial circumstances.

2. **Age-Specific Checklists.** Starting on page xxxiv, you'll find lists of ideas that are of particular interest to people at various life stages. For example, if you're a Generation Yer—a mere stripling—there's an age-specific checklist for you, and there are also checklists for those of us with higher mileage.

3. **Your To-Do Summary.** The to-do summary on page xliii is a convenient place to write down the most significant matters that merit your attention.

As much as I would like you to mark up this book so that it can't be resold, the following checklists are also in downloadable format on the *Grow Your Money!* special reader Web site described on page xliii.

1. Master List of 101 Ideas

NEEDS   I'M OKAY
ATTENTION   OR N/A

CHAPTER 1—ACHIEVING YOUR FINANCIAL DREAMS

❏ ❏ 1. Program Your Financial Navigation System (page 2)

❏ ❏ 2. Time Is Your Ally (page 4)

❏ ❏ 3. Getting Rich Is Boring (page 9)

❏ ❏ 4. Millionaire Success Secrets (page 11)

❏ ❏ 5. Go Forth and Let Your Money Multiply (page 15)

CHAPTER 2—PROFITING FROM A FABULOUS CAREER

❏ ❏ 6. The Ingredients of Career Success (page 20)

❏ ❏ 7. Advice for Those Who Have Taken a Career Sabbatical (page 23)

❏ ❏ 8. Considering a Career Change? (page 26)

❏ ❏ 9. Buck the Odds by Starting and Succeeding in Your Own Business (page 30)

❏ ❏ 10. Your Career Doesn't Have to End When You Reach Retirement Age (page 35)

NEEDS   I'M OKAY
ATTENTION   OR N/A

CHAPTER 3—ACCUMULATING REAL WEALTH

❏   ❏   11. How Great Wealth Is Created (page 38)

❏   ❏   12. The Miracle of Tax Deferral (page 43)

❏   ❏   13. Devising a Plan to Reconcile Your Gross Habits with Your Net Income (page 46)

❏   ❏   14. Out, Out, Damned Budget (page 51)

❏   ❏   15. Save Your Raise (page 54)

❏   ❏   16. Deciding What to Do with a Financial Windfall (page 55)

CHAPTER 4—USING DEBT TO YOUR ADVANTAGE

❏   ❏   17. Borrow for Things That Will Appreciate in Value (page 60)

❏   ❏   18. Getting Richer with Borrowed Money (page 63)

❏   ❏   19. Manage Your Home Equity Loan Like a Business (page 65)

❏   ❏   20. Pay Off Your Credit Cards Later Rather Than Sooner (page 66)

❏   ❏   21. Getting Out of Debt Problems (page 69)

❏   ❏   22. Buffing Up Your Credit (page 73)

CHAPTER 5—PUTTING MONEY AWAY FOR A PROSPEROUS FUTURE

❏   ❏   23. The Tortoise Beats the Hare: Getting Rich Slowly (page 76)

❏   ❏   24. Making the Most of Money You're Going to Need Within a Few Years (page 80)

NEEDS   I'M OKAY
ATTENTION   OR N/A

❏   ❏   25. Preparing for a Financial Emergency Can Cost You Thousands (page 82)

❏   ❏   26. The Best Ways to Invest for Retirement (page 83)

❏   ❏   27. Saddled with a Lousy 401(k) Plan? Roll Your 401(k) Plan Into an IRA After You Turn 59½ (page 87)

❏   ❏   28. Should You Make a Roth IRA Conversion? (page 88)

❏   ❏   29. Yes, Virginia, You Do Qualify for an IRA Contribution (page 92)

❏   ❏   30. Retirement Plans for the Self-Employed Simplified (page 93)

❏   ❏   31. Smart (and Painless) Ways to Add to Your Investments (page 96)

❏   ❏   32. Free at Last: Deciding What to Do with Your Retirement Savings Plan When You Change Jobs (page 98)

CHAPTER 6—BECOMING A SAVVY INVESTOR

❏   ❏   33. Create a World-Class Investment Portfolio with Just Six Investments (page 102)

❏   ❏   34. Making the Most of Your Mutual Fund Investments (page 107)

❏   ❏   35. Idle Cash Need Not Earn Paltry Returns (page 110)

NEEDS   I'M OKAY
ATTENTION   OR N/A

❑   ❑   36. What Kind of Investor Are You? Take the Quiz (page 111)

❑   ❑   37. Investing When You're Just Starting Out (page 115)

❑   ❑   38. When It Comes to Investing, Average Is Pretty Good (page 121)

❑   ❑   39. Putting Your Investments on Autopilot (page 125)

CHAPTER 7—SUPERCHARGING YOUR INVESTMENTS

❑   ❑   40. There's Something Nice About Being a Contrarian (page 129)

❑   ❑   41. Investment Returns Make a Big Difference (page 133)

❑   ❑   42. Four Can't-Miss Investments (page 135)

❑   ❑   43. A Rich Recipe: Adding Individual Securities to Your Mutual Fund Portfolio (page 139)

❑   ❑   44. The Truth and Nothing but the Truth (page 143)

❑   ❑   45. Investing Profitably in Sector Funds (page 144)

❑   ❑   46. Sayonara: Deciding When to Sell an Investment (page 147)

❑   ❑   47. Surviving a Market Decline (page 151)

NEEDS   I'M OKAY
ATTENTION   OR N/A

❏   ❏   48. Quick Ways to Evaluate a Real Estate Investment (page 153)

❏   ❏   49. Why Not Be Lord or Lady of the Land? (page 156)

CHAPTER 8—BUYING AND MAINTAINING A HOME

❏   ❏   50. Tricks of the Home-Buying Trade (page 159)

❏   ❏   51. Save for a House or Save for Retirement? (page 163)

❏   ❏   52. Should You Pay Off Your Mortgage Early? (page 165)

❏   ❏   53. Appeal Your Property Tax Bill (page 169)

❏   ❏   54. Move or Improve? (page 171)

❏   ❏   55. Surviving a Home Improvement Project (page 176)

❏   ❏   56. Vacation Home Follies (page 180)

CHAPTER 9—PAYING FOR COLLEGE AND OTHER BIG-TICKET ITEMS

❏   ❏   57. Big-Ticket Items Tell a Lot (page 186)

❏   ❏   58. Why College and Cars and Other Costly Necessities Are So Expensive (page 189)

❏   ❏   59. Saving for College (page 190)

❏   ❏   60. Preparing for Annoying but Inevitable Expenses (page 193)

NEEDS   I'M OKAY
ATTENTION   OR N/A

❏   ❏   61. Create a Homemade 529 Plan Without the Hefty Expenses (page 195)

❏   ❏   62. Save for College and Retirement in the Same Account (page 197)

❏   ❏   63. Cutting College Costs (page 198)

❏   ❏   64. If You Hate Cars, Buy New; If You Love Cars, Buy Used (page 200)

❏   ❏   65. Ten Money Savers That Will Save You Thousands of Dollars in Car Ownership Costs (page 203)

❏   ❏   66. Dr. Jonathan's Car-Loan-Addiction Elixir (page 205)

CHAPTER 10—GIVING UNCLE SAM HIS DUE, AND NOT ONE CENT MORE

❏   ❏   67. Ten Top Tax-Savings Ideas (page 208)

❏   ❏   68. News Flash: Congress Isn't Going to Tinker with Your Tax Breaks (page 212)

❏   ❏   69. Increasing Investment Returns by Decreasing Taxes on Investments (page 214)

❏   ❏   70. Getting a Tax Refund Is Bad News (page 218)

❏   ❏   71. Managing Your Tax Bite After You Retire (page 221)

❏   ❏   72. Last-Minute Tax-Savings Ideas (page 226)

NEEDS   I'M OKAY
ATTENTION   OR N/A

CHAPTER 11—SECURING THE FUTURE FOR YOU AND YOUR LOVED ONES

❑ ❑ 73. Filling Gaps in Your Property Insurance Coverage (page 231)

❑ ❑ 74. Surprise: You're Probably Overinsured (page 233)

❑ ❑ 75. The Straight Scoop on Life Insurance (page 235)

❑ ❑ 76. Is It Time to Trade In Your Term Life Insurance Policy for a Newer Model? (page 240)

❑ ❑ 77. Long-Term-Care Insurance? Not for Everyone (page 242)

❑ ❑ 78. Insurance to Avoid (page 244)

❑ ❑ 79. Estate Planning—Ignore This If You Dislike Your Heirs (page 247)

❑ ❑ 80. Do You Really Need a Living Trust? (page 249)

❑ ❑ 81. Helping Older Family Members Cope with Their Finances (page 253)

CHAPTER 12—MAKING SMART MONEY DECISIONS A FAMILY AFFAIR

❑ ❑ 82. Picking the Right Professionals to Advise You, If You Really Need Their Advice (page 258)

❑ ❑ 83. Domestic Financial Felicity Need Not Be an Impossible Dream (page 263)

NEEDS   I'M OKAY
ATTENTION   OR N/A

❏   ❏   84. Advice for Twentysomethings: Something Your Parents and Grandparents Know for Sure (page 267)

❏   ❏   85. Dual-Career Parents of Youngsters: Does That Second Paycheck Really Help the Family Budget Very Much? (page 269)

❏   ❏   86. Teach Kids About Money (page 271)

❏   ❏   87. IRAs for the Younger Set (page 274)

❏   ❏   88. Avoiding Financial Scams (page 278)

CHAPTER 13—ENJOYING A GREAT RETIREMENT

❏   ❏   89. Can You Get There From Here? Finding Out Where You Stand (page 283)

❏   ❏   90. Achieving Early Retirement (page 287)

❏   ❏   91. It Will Probably Cost You Less When You Retire Than You Think (page 290)

❏   ❏   92. Last-Minute Ways to Boost Your Retirement Income (page 293)

❏   ❏   93. It's a Mistake to Collect Social Security Early (page 297)

❏   ❏   94. Changes You Should Make in Your Finances When You Retire (page 302)

❏   ❏   95. Making Sure You Never Run Out of Money (page 305)

NEEDS   I'M OKAY
ATTENTION   OR N/A

❏   ❏   96. The Reverse Mortgage: Less Than Meets the Eye (page 312)

CHAPTER 14—SAVORING THE GOOD LIFE—NOW AND LATER

❏   ❏   97. Simplifying Your Financial Life (page 317)

❏   ❏   98. Financial Security in Thirty Minutes a Month (page 323)

❏   ❏   99. Invest in Your Good Health (page 327)

❏   ❏   100. Taking Advantage of the Best Financial Opportunities (page 331)

❏   ❏   101. It's Time to Indulge Yourself (page 334)

2. Age-Specific Checklists

Ideas of Particular Interest If You're a Generation Yer (Born After 1980)

While you will find important ideas throughout *Grow Your Money!* pay close attention to the following:

IDEA

❏ 1. Program Your Financial Navigation System (page 2)

❏ 2. Time Is Your Ally (page 4)

❏ 6. The Ingredients of Career Success (page 20)

❏ 7. Advice for Those Who Have Taken a Career Sabbatical (page 23)

❏ 8. Considering a Career Change? (page 26)

❑ 9. Buck the Odds by Starting and Succeeding in Your Own Business (page 30)

❑ 11. How Great Wealth Is Created (page 38)

❑ 13. Devising a Plan to Reconcile Your Gross Habits with Your Net Income (page 46)

❑ 15. Save Your Raise (page 54)

❑ 17. Borrow for Things That Will Appreciate in Value (page 60)

❑ 20. Pay Off Your Credit Cards Later Rather Than Sooner (page 66)

❑ 21. Getting Out of Debt Problems (page 69)

❑ 22. Buffing Up Your Credit (page 73)

❑ 23. The Tortoise Beats the Hare: Getting Rich Slowly (page 76)

❑ 25. Preparing for a Financial Emergency Can Cost You Thousands (page 82)

❑ 26. The Best Ways to Invest for Retirement (page 83)

❑ 28. Should You Make a Roth IRA Conversion? (page 88)

❑ 32. Free at Last: Deciding What to Do with Your Retirement Savings Plan When You Change Jobs (page 98)

❑ 37. Investing When You're Just Starting Out (page 115)

❑ 48. Quick Ways to Evaluate a Real Estate Investment (page 153)

❑ 49. Why Not Be Lord or Lady of the Land? (page 156)

❑ 50. Tricks of the Home-Buying Trade (page 159)

❑ 51. Save for a House or Save for Retirement? (page 163)

❑ 52. Should You Pay Off Your Mortgage Early? (page 165)

❑ 58. Why College and Cars and Other Costly Necessities Are So Expensive (page 189)

❑ 75. The Straight Scoop on Life Insurance (page 235)

❑ 76. Is It Time to Trade In Your Term Life Insurance Policy for a Newer Model? (page 240)

❑ 81. Helping Older Family Members Cope with Their Finances (page 253)

❑ 90. Achieving Early Retirement (page 287)

Ideas of Particular Interest If You're a Generation Xer (Born Between 1965 and 1980)

While you will find important ideas throughout *Grow Your Money!* pay close attention to the following:

IDEA

❑ 1. Program Your Financial Navigation System (page 2)

❑ 2. 4 Time Is Your Ally (page 4)

❑ 6. The Ingredients of Career Success (page 20)

❑ 7. Advice for Those Who Have Taken a Career Sabbatical (page 23)

❑ 8. Considering a Career Change? (page 26)

❑ 9. Buck the Odds by Starting and Succeeding in Your Own Business (page 30)

❑ 11. How Great Wealth Is Created (page 38)

❑ 13. Devising a Plan to Reconcile Your Gross Habits with Your Net Income (page 46)

❑ 15. Save Your Raise (page 54)

❑ 17. Borrow for Things That Will Appreciate in Value (page 60)

❑ 20. Pay Off Your Credit Cards Later Rather Than Sooner (page 66)

❑ 21. Getting Out of Debt Problems (page 69)

❑ 22. Buffing Up Your Credit (page 73)

❑ 23. The Tortoise Beats the Hare: Getting Rich Slowly (page 76)

❑ 25. Preparing for a Financial Emergency Can Cost You Thousands (page 82)

❑ 26. The Best Ways to Invest for Retirement (page 83)

❑ 32. Free at Last: Deciding What to Do with Your Retirement Savings Plan When You Change Jobs (page 98)

❑ 37. Investing When You're Just Starting Out (page 115)

❑ 48. Quick Ways to Evaluate a Real Estate Investment (page 153)

❑ 49. Why Not Be Lord or Lady of the Land? (page 156)

❑ 50. Tricks of the Home-Buying Trade (page 159)

❑ 51. Save for a House or Save for Retirement? (page 163)

❑ 58. Why College and Cars and Other Costly Necessities Are So Expensive (page 189)

❑ 75. 235 The Straight Scoop on Life Insurance (page 235)

❑ 76. Is It Time to Trade In Your Term Life Insurance Policy for a Newer Model? (page 240)

❑ 84. Advice for Twentysomethings: Something Your Parents and Grandparents Know for Sure (page 267)

❑ 90. Achieving Early Retirement (page 287)

Ideas of Particular Interest If You're a Baby Boomer (Born Between 1946 and 1964)

While you will find important ideas throughout *Grow Your Money!* pay close attention to the following:

IDEA

❑ 1. Program Your Financial Navigation System (page 2)

❑ 6. The Ingredients of Career Success (page 20)

❑ 7. Advice for Those Who Have Taken a Career Sabbatical (page 23)

❑ 8. Considering a Career Change? (page 26)

❑ 9. Buck the Odds by Starting and Succeeding in Your Own Business (page 30)

❑ 10. Your Career Doesn't Have to End When You Reach Retirement Age (page 35)

❑ 11. How Great Wealth Is Created (page 38)

❑ 13. Devising a Plan to Reconcile Your Gross Habits with Your Net Income (page 46)

❑ 15. Save Your Raise (page 54)

❑ 17. Borrow for Things That Will Appreciate in Value (page 60)

❑ 20. Pay Off Your Credit Cards Later Rather Than Sooner (page 66)

❑ 21. Getting Out of Debt Problems (page 69)

❑ 22. Buffing Up Your Credit (page 73)

❑ 25. Preparing for a Financial Emergency Can Cost You Thousands (page 82)

❑ 26. The Best Ways to Invest for Retirement (page 83)

❏ 27. Saddled with a Lousy 401(k) Plan? Roll Your 401(k) Plan Into an IRA After You Turn 59½ (page 87)

❏ 28. Should You Make a Roth IRA Conversion? (page 88)

❏ 32. Free at Last: Deciding What to Do with Your Retirement Savings Plan When You Change Jobs (page 98)

❏ 48. Quick Ways to Evaluate a Real Estate Investment (page 153)

❏ 49. Why Not Be Lord or Lady of the Land? (page 156)

❏ 50. Tricks of the Home-Buying Trade (page 159)

❏ 51. Save for a House or Save for Retirement? (page 163)

❏ 52. Should You Pay Off Your Mortgage Early? (page 165)

❏ 58. Why College and Cars and Other Costly Necessities Are So Expensive (page 189)

❏ 75. The Straight Scoop on Life Insurance (page 235)

❏ 76. Is It Time to Trade In Your Term Life Insurance Policy for a Newer Model? (page 240)

❏ 77. Long-Term-Care Insurance? Not for Everyone (page 242)

❏ 81. Helping Older Family Members Cope with Their Finances (page 253)

❏ 90. Achieving Early Retirement (page 287)

❏ 91. It Will Probably Cost You Less When You Retire Than You Think (page 290)

❏ 92. Last-Minute Ways to Boost Your Retirement Income (page 293)

❏ 93. It's a Mistake to Collect Social Security Early (page 297)

❏ 94. Changes You Should Make in Your Finances When You Retire (page 302)

❑ 95. Making Sure You Never Run Out of Money (page 305)

❑ 96. The Reverse Mortgage: Less Than Meets the Eye (page 312)

Ideas of Particular Interest If You're Just About to Retire (Within Five Years of Retiring)

While you will find important ideas throughout *Grow Your Money!* pay close attention to the following:

IDEA

❑ 10. Your Career Doesn't Have to End When You Reach Retirement Age (page 35)

❑ 13. Devising a Plan to Reconcile Your Gross Habits with Your Net Income (page 46)

❑ 27. Saddled with a Lousy 401(k) Plan? Roll Your 401(k) Plan Into an IRA After You Turn 59½ (page 87)

❑ 28. Should You Make a Roth IRA Conversion? (page 88)

❑ 32. Free at Last: Deciding What to Do with Your Retirement Savings Plan When You Change Jobs (page 98)

❑ 52. Should You Pay Off Your Mortgage Early? (page 165)

❑ 71. Managing Your Tax Bite After You Retire (page 221)

❑ 76. Is It Time to Trade In Your Term Life Insurance Policy for a Newer Model? (page 240)

❑ 77. Long-Term-Care Insurance? Not for Everyone (page 242)

❑ 79. Estate Planning—Ignore This If You Dislike Your Heirs (page 247)

❑ 80. Do You Really Need a Living Trust? (page 249)

❑ 81. Helping Older Family Members Cope with Their Finances (page 253)

❑ 90. Achieving Early Retirement (page 287)

❑ 91. It Will Probably Cost You Less When You Retire Than You Think (page 290)

❑ 92. Last-Minute Ways to Boost Your Retirement Income (page 293)

❑ 93. It's a Mistake to Collect Social Security Early (page 297)

❑ 94. Changes You Should Make in Your Finances When You Retire (page 302)

❑ 95. Making Sure You Never Run Out of Money (page 305)

❑ 96. The Reverse Mortgage: Less Than Meets the Eye (page 312)

Ideas of Particular Interest If You're a Recent Retiree (You Have Retired Within the Past Five Years)

While you will find important ideas throughout *Grow Your Money!* pay close attention to the following:

IDEA

❑ 10. Your Career Doesn't Have to End When You Reach Retirement Age (page 35)

❑ 24. Making the Most of Money You're Going to Need Within a Few Years (page 80)

❑ 28. Should You Make a Roth IRA Conversion? (page 88)

❑ 35. Idle Cash Need Not Earn Paltry Returns (page 110)

❑ 54. Move or Improve? (page 171)

❑ 69. Increasing Investment Returns by Decreasing Taxes on Investments (page 214)

❑ 71. Managing Your Tax Bite After You Retire (page 221)

❑ 74. Surprise: You're Probably Overinsured (page 233)

❑ 77. Long-Term-Care Insurance? Not for Everyone (page 242)

❑ 79. Estate Planning—Ignore This If You Dislike Your Heirs (page 247)

❑ 80. Do You Really Need a Living Trust? (page 249)

❑ 94. Changes You Should Make in Your Finances When You Retire (page 302)

❑ 95. Making Sure You Never Run Out of Money (page 305)

❑ 96. The Reverse Mortgage: Less Than Meets the Eye (page 312)

Ideas of Particular Interest If You're a Veteran Retiree (Retired Over Five Years Ago)

While you will find important ideas throughout *Grow Your Money!* pay close attention to the following:

IDEA

❑ 24. Making the Most of Money You're Going to Need Within a Few Years (page 80)

❑ 35. Idle Cash Need Not Earn Paltry Returns (page 110)

❑ 54. Move or Improve? (page 171)

❑ 69. Increasing Investment Returns by Decreasing Taxes on Investments (page 214)

❑ 71. Managing Your Tax Bite After You Retire (page 221)

❑ 74. Surprise: You're Probably Overinsured (page 233)

❑ 78. Insurance to Avoid (page 244)

❑ 79. Estate Planning—Ignore This If You Dislike Your Heirs (page 247)

❑ 80. Do You Really Need a Living Trust? (page 249)

❏ 94. Changes You Should Make in Your Finances When You Retire (page 302)

❏ 95. Making Sure You Never Run Out of Money (page 305)

❏ 96. The Reverse Mortgage: Less Than Meets the Eye (page 312)

3. Your To-Do Summary

As you read *Grow Your Money!* use the following to list your most important to-do items—those that require your attention sooner rather than later. Once you have resolved them, just cross them off and reward yourself with something nice, but not too expensive.

1. _____

2. _____

3. _____

4. _____

5. _____

6. _____

7. _____

8. _____

9. _____

10. _____

Special *Grow Your Money!* Reader Web Site

The investment markets and the entire financial-planning environment are a moving target. The economy and investment environment change, tax regulations are modified, the financial industry is constantly introducing "new" products (albeit not necessarily "improved"), and new and sometimes worthwhile financial ideas are uncovered. If you are intent on growing your money, the special *Grow Your Money!* reader Web site will keep you up to date on important money matters.

You'll notice a special Web icon appearing throughout the book:

w w w

The Web icon is a reminder that updated and additional information pertaining to the subject is available on the *Grow Your Money!* Web site. You can link to it from this Web address: http://www .jonathanpond.com

Click on the special *Grow Your Money!* link on the main page. You'll want to check out this site periodically, because information contained in it will be updated regularly.

The *Grow Your Money!* Web site also includes customizable to-do lists, identical to those appearing on pages xxvi to xliii.

For your convenience, here is a summary of the areas that are kept up to date on the special reader Web site:

Web References

	PAGE	TOPIC
❑	xxvi	Customizable to-do lists
❑	23	Resources on ways to advance in your career
❑	29	Guidance for career changers
❑	33	Resources for those considering starting their own business
❑	35	News on pension plan regulations and trends
❑	41	Guidance on tax-advantaged investment strategies
❑	45	Tax-deferred-investment illustrations and regulations

❏ 49 Suggestions and resources for reducing your living expenses

❏ 53 The best coupon code Web sites

❏ 68 Managing your credit cards

❏ 72 Dealing with debt problems and finding a legitimate credit counselor

❏ 75 Suggestions for improving your creditworthiness

❏ 82 Making the most of short-term investments

❏ 86 Information on qualification rules and contribution limits for the various retirement savings plans

❏ 91 Current Roth IRA conversion rules

❏ 92 Current IRA qualification rules

❏ 95 Guidance and current tax regulations an retirement plans for the self-employed

❏ 97 Information on automatic investment, including Internet resources

❏ 106 Mutual fund recommendations

❏ 109 Internet sites and information of interest to mutual fund investors

❏ 111 Current interest rates on short-term investments

❏ 115 Examples of investment diversification

❏ 119 Information and recommendations for investors who are new to investing

❏ 127 Recommended lifestyle-fund and target-date funds

❏ 132 Information for contrarian investors and an illustration of portfolio rebalancing

❑ 138 Recommended emerging-market, real-estate, commodity, and multisector-bond mutual funds

❑ 142 Recommendations on adding individual securities to your investments

❑ 146 Sector-fund tips and recommendations

❑ 156 Guidance and rules of thumb for investing in income-producing real estate

❑ 163 Homebuyer's checklist

❑ 164 Rules for retirement-plan withdrawals or loans

❑ 168 Explanations and illustrations of ways to prepay your mortgage

❑ 174 Internet resources to help you evaluate a contemplated remodeling project

❑ 175 Guidance on ridding yourself of private mortgage insurance

❑ 180 Important matters to consider when reviewing an appliance or automobile service contract

❑ 192 Update on college savings alternatives

❑ 196 Low-cost investment alternatives for a homegrown 529 plan

❑ 211 Tax-savings ideas and Internet resources

❑ 216 Resources to help you minimize taxes on your investments

❑ 221 Information on tax-preparation services

❑ 228 Guidance on last-minute ways to reduce your income taxes

❑ 233 Guidelines and information on closing gaps in insurance coverage

❏ 239 Securing the right kind of life insurance coverage

❏ 249 Preparing and keeping up to date the various estate-planning documents, and a summary of current estate-tax regulations and strategies

❏ 262 Guidance for selecting and working with financial professionals and Web sites for do-it-yourselfers

❏ 266 Working amicably with your spouse or partner on family money matters

❏ 277 Updates on the use of IRAs for children

❏ 286 Tips on preparing retirement-income and expense projections, including Web sites and a retirement-budget work sheet

❏ 290 Strategies for those who want to retire early

❏ 292 Worksheets and tips for preparing a retirement budget

❏ 301 Social Security update

❏ 305 Guidance on the important changes facing retirees

❏ 311 Examples of balancing annuities and self-management of retirement resources

❏ 312 Annuity update

❏ 315 Reverse-mortgage update and Internet resources

❏ 321 Worksheets and tips to help you simplify your financial life

CHAPTER 1

Achieving Your Financial Dreams

It's time to get serious about growing your money and achieving your financial dreams. It isn't very complicated, despite the relentless efforts by the financial services industry to make it appear that you're a money dummy. But the road to financial security does require taking small steps in the direction of improving your finances, no matter what your age or money situation is. You first need to think about what you want your money to do for you now and, more important, in the future. This requires careful thought and decisions, including making the inevitable tradeoffs between satisfying immediate needs and indulgences and preparing for longer-term and inevitably more costly financial needs. Having more time to accomplish your financial goals is a real advantage, thanks to the miracle of compound investment growth. But whatever your age, if you devote some attention to your financial life and make sensible decisions along the way, your financial dreams will become a reality.

IDEA 1

Program Your Financial Navigation System

Before delving into the nitty-gritty of your financial planning, you should spend a moment dreaming about what you want your money to do for you. Accumulating enough money to be able to retire comfortably is certainly a goal for all working-age people. Everyone should be concerned with retirement, even if you are young and retirement is a long way off. But your financial aspirations are probably not limited to retirement. You may yearn for something more immediate, such as buying a car or taking a vacation. A house or college for the kids are other common objectives. If you're retired, you are undoubtedly concerned about having enough income to live comfortably and keep up with inflation. You may also want to have enough to pass on an inheritance, although I would encourage you to consider otherwise. After all, if you're retired, why have ground chuck when you deserve tenderloin? Your heirs will concur.

Here are a couple of suggestions to help you program your own financial navigation system:

+ On the following table, write down all the financial goals that you can think of, from the obvious (retirement) to the self-indulgent (climbing Mount Everest or space travel). Be sure to include your spouse or partner, if you have one, in this exercise. Hopefully, you will agree on most of the goals. If you don't agree, Idea 83, on page 263, will explain why and offer you both some words of solace.

+ Some goals are more important than others, so it's important to set priorities. Generally, your longer-term goals are more important than those that you want to achieve in the near future.

ESSENTIAL	IMPORTANT	NICE, BUT NOT ESSENTIAL	MY (OUR) FINANCIAL GOALS
❏	❏	❏	_____
❏	❏	❏	_____
❏	❏	❏	_____
❏	❏	❏	_____
❏	❏	❏	_____
❏	❏	❏	_____
❏	❏	❏	_____
❏	❏	❏	_____
❏	❏	❏	_____
❏	❏	❏	_____

"I want it now." Did you have some difficulty prioritizing your financial goals? That's what gets many people into a pickle. Delayed gratification is, well, so un-American. We'd rather enjoy life now, because that's one of our financial dreams, after all. The future is a long way off, and we can always hope that the future will take care of itself. But it's important to balance both the present and the future, and that requires making tradeoffs in the way we deploy our money. Consider, for example, the tradeoff between buying a more expensive car versus putting the money away for retirement.

Don't let short-term indulgences impede your long-term goals. Here's how a short-term money fling could affect your long-term financial security.

Short-term need: a new car (a suitable car will cost $20,000, but a wonderful car is $40,000)

Long-term goal: a nice retirement

In play here is $20,000, the difference between the ho-hum car and the great car. Here's how much more our car buyer would accumulate by buying the cheaper wheels and investing the $20,000 "savings" for the future, assuming a 7 percent annual return:

NUMBER OF YEARS	$20,000 WILL GROW TO:
10	$ 40,000
20	75,000
30	150,000
40	400,000

> You can't get there (to financial security) from here without programming your financial navigation system.
>
> ■
>
> *To write songs, I usually need a reason. Like not having any money.*
> —WILLIE NELSON

IDEA 2

Time Is Your Ally

Put time on your side when investing for the future. There's nothing like the luxury of time to help you meet your most important—and most expensive—goals. Work toward the less important goals only after the more important ones have been attended to.

The miracle of compound growth. Compound growth happens when the earnings on your investments—dividends, interest, and capital gains—are reinvested to earn more investment income. Getting earnings on your earnings helps turn a small amount of money into a lot of money over time.

THE EIGHTH WONDER OF THE WORLD
The Miracle of Compounding

The longer you have until you need to begin withdrawing your money, the more you'll reap the benefits of compound growth. Consider the following table that compares the amount of money saved with the amount of growth over varying periods of time, assuming annual savings of $10,000 and average annual investment returns of 7 percent. While compound growth of course works in shorter savings periods, the early bird gets a heck of a lot more than worms.

TIME PERIOD	TOTAL AMOUNT SAVED	TOTAL COMPOUND GROWTH	GRAND TOTAL
10 years	$ 100,000	$ 40,000	$ 140,000
20 years	200,000	210,000	410,000
30 years	300,000	650,000	950,000
40 years	400,000	1,600,000	2,000,000

For example, over a thirty-year savings period, you would have saved a total of $300,000 but the compounded earnings on that money is $650,000, more than twice the amount you saved.

Start early, save often. The two keys are to start early and plan for the long term. Younger people understand this, but they don't necessarily do it. Too often, it turns into a decision between, say, putting $500 into a retirement savings plan or using that money to buy a nice set of clothes. Clothes are a necessity (unless you reside on certain European beaches), but life is a series of tradeoffs. The longer you choose current consumption over long-term investment, the shorter the time period in which you will be able to create the necessary savings to achieve your financial dreams. But like many financial decisions that will be addressed in later chapters, the $500-clothes-versus-savings conundrum need not be viewed as an either/or decision. Perhaps our hypothetical clotheshorse could split the $500 between raiment and savings. Now, $250 might not sound like much money, and it's easy to conclude that there's plenty of time to put money away for the future, but if that money won't be needed for thirty-five years and is invested so that it earns 7 percent per year on average, it will grow more than tenfold. If you wait five years to put the money aside, it will require $350 to grow to the same amount thirty years later.

The following table offers another illustration of how effective starting early, sticking to your plan, and letting compound growth do its thing can be.

THE EARLY—AND PERSISTENT—BIRD GETS THE DOUGH

Four people were born the same year and each contributed $4,000 to an IRA, but each started at a different age; some quit contributing, while others made contributing an annual habit. Each earned 7 percent on their IRA lucre. Here's how much each accumulated at age sixty-five:

	AMOUNT IN THE KITTY AT AGE 65
1. Started at age 20, contributed for ten years, and then stopped contributing	$ 600,000
2. Started at age 30, contributed for ten years, and then stopped contributing	300,000
3. Started at age 40 and contributed every year until age 65	250,000
4. Started at age 20 and contributed every year until age 65	1,150,000

Special note to parents and grandparents: The single best financial lesson you can impart to younger-generation family members is the importance of saving for retirement when they get their first real job. If you can spare the change, help them fund their retirement plans when they're just starting out and perhaps can't otherwise afford it. (See Idea 87, on page 274.) That's a damn sight better financial lesson than passing on a bundle of money to them after you pass on.

Start small. Even a small amount of money grows well, if invested smartly. It grows a lot more if you can regularly increase the amount you save, which should be achievable as your work income increases.

EXAMPLE: Someone who is twenty-five years from retirement has finally concluded that the time has arrived to start saving, initially at a modest level, but subsequently increasing the amount saved. Here's the plan: Save $1,500 this year and raise the amount saved 10 percent each year thereafter for twenty-five years. Therefore, next year's saving would be hiked by $150 to a total of $1,650. A 10 percent annual increase sounds like a lot, but the additional savings rise so gradually that you shouldn't miss the money—particularly upon learning how much you'll accumulate. If you stick with the plan for twenty-five years and the money earns an average of 7 percent a year, how much do you think you'll have at the end of twenty years?

❑ $100,000

❑ $150,000

❑ $200,000

That was a good try, but your answer is incorrect, as are the other two. This is the only time I will trick you, I promise. At the end of twenty-five years, you'll have saved $300,000. Time is indeed your ally.

The miracle of compound growth will be your best ally on the way to achieving your financial dreams.

■

A Quick Course on Investment Jargon

Confused about investment terminology like "gain," "yield," and "return"? They are easily and often confused. Here are some definitions so you can leave the land of the befuddled.

◆ *Gain*. This is shorthand for *"capital gain,"* which means how much the value of an investment, primarily stocks, bonds, and real estate, has increased or, as you probably know all too well, has lost resulting in a *"loss"* or *"capital loss."*

◆ *Yield.* This is income earned from an investment through interest paid by bonds and temporary interest-paying investments like money market funds as well as dividends paid by some stocks. Yield is usually expressed as a percent. For example, if a stock selling for $30 per share on the stock market pays an annual dividend of $1.20 per share, it has a dividend "yield" of 4 percent ($1.20 ÷ $30).

◆ *Return*. This is shorthand for *total return* and combines both *gain* or *loss* and *yield*. Total return, rather than simply the *yield* of an investment, is the best way to compare different types of investments and to evaluate how your investments have performed.

EXAMPLES:

	WINNER	LOSER
Gain	+7%	-5%
Yield	+2%	+3%
Return	+9%	-2%

Here are explanations of two other terms that the investment community loves to use:

+ *Equity or equities.* That's synonymous with "stock," since stock represents ownership—or equity—in the corporation, in much the same way you have equity in your home if you're a homeowner. For example, if you own a $300,000 home with $100,000 remaining on your mortgage, you have $200,000 equity in your home. (Special example for residents of California and the Northeast U.S.: If you own a $2,800,000 home and owe $2,785,000 on it, you have $15,000 equity in your home.) Similarly, if you own $5,000 of ExxonMobil stock, you have $5,000 equity (ownership) in ExxonMobil, which isn't a whole lot, but it's a whole lot better than nothing.
+ *Fixed income investment.* That's a fancy term for "bond" since a bond pays a fixed amount of interest. If you own a $10,000 bond that pays 5½ percent interest, you will receive $550 interest each year until the bond matures (and the issuer pays you back the $10,000).

■

The safest way to double your money is to fold it over once and put it in your pocket.
—KIN HUBBARD

IDEA 3

Getting Rich Is Boring

Despite all of the infomercials and wealth seminars that purport to tell you the secrets of getting rich quickly in the real estate business or with gold coins or by llama farming, the truth is that getting rich is boring, and it takes time to get rich—decades for most of us. You already know that the surest route to wealth is to spend less than you earn and invest those savings wisely. It's boring to be sure, but it's also almost a certainty that you will accumulate a sizable amount of money over the years. Moreover, as you are amassing your fortune, you'll be able to sleep well, knowing that you'll have the financial wherewithal to meet any financial challenges that arise along the way.

It's your choice. Some people would rather get rich quickly. Otherwise, the infomercials and the millionaire seminars would cease to exist. If that's your preference, more power to you. But the odds of that kind of success are long. A lot of people who try end up worse off financially, although when they get back on their feet, they usually try again.

If you'd rather choose a more reliable way to wealth, take the boring route, which involves (you may already be in the midst of this plan):

1. Eliminating any debt that doesn't provide long-term benefits. That's just about everything but a home mortgage and student loans.

2. Always maintaining adequate insurance coverage, leaving no potential peril uncovered.

3. Finding out ways to reduce your spending. You may not need a total money makeover; cutting expenses just a smidgen is a good start.

4. Working to increase your income by becoming a star at your job.

5. Building up and diversifying your retirement investments. If you have to start small, that's fine. There's time to increase your contributions later on.

6. Buying a home—which is for most people, but not all, a wise financial move, as is paying off the mortgage before retirement

and resisting the temptation to trade up to a more expensive home.

These above steps are **boring**, but if you adhere to them, you'll end up being the envy of your less-disciplined counterparts. The goal is very simple: to eventually have enough money to live on, plus some extra.

Getting rich the old-fashioned way isn't very exciting, but the results will be.

■

There are more things in life to worry about than just money—how to get hold of it, for example.
—ANONYMOUS

IDEA 4

Millionaire Success Secrets

There's a certain amount of wisdom in the old adage: "If you want to be a millionaire, find some millionaires and just do what they do." Certain characteristics that are common to many if not most of the well off have been well documented. It could pay to incorporate them into your own life and the lives of your children. But if your children get rich as a result, don't expect them to support you in your dotage.

While one of the surest ways to become a millionaire is to have parents who are multimillionaires, you might be surprised to learn that most of today's millionaires grew up in very modest circumstances. Based on interviews of millionaires, the findings of which appear in *Rags to Riches,* by Gail Liberman and Alan Lavine (Authors Choice), here are some characteristics they commonly displayed.

✦ Millionaires typically set some type of goal, which may not necessarily be to make large amounts of money. It might start with trying to put food on the table or eliminate a mortgage.

✦ They often had strong encouragement from a family member. Keep this in mind if you have kids. Encourage them to be successful and to follow their dreams.

✦ Instead of being defeated by a challenge or failure, they picked themselves up and regained control of their lives.

✦ They didn't mind making sacrifices to achieve goals. They were very willing to make sacrifices in exchange for longer-term financial success. They practiced "reverse keeping up with the Joneses." See page 50 for an explanation.

✦ They weren't afraid to take risks. This may have meant keeping money invested in stocks when their prices were plummeting, starting a business, or investing in real estate. As I have long said: "The biggest risk in investing is taking no risk at all." Taking a risk need not mean risking it all, but you do have to take prudent risks to reap financial rewards.

✦ They had great sales skills. The millionaire entrepreneurs had the ability to sell someone on a good idea. Why not come out of your shell and cultivate those skills in yourself?

✦ They followed their passions. They gave less credence to what others had to say. You probably know people who are constantly looking at the bad side of life—the "glass is half empty" crowd. Don't let them discourage you from pursuing your passions.

✦ They read a lot and/or took steps to learn from others. In other words, they balanced their self-confidence with the admission that they couldn't do it all on their own. Even those people who don't have the inclination or time to read can learn a tremendous amount from audio books, lectures, or seminars.

✦ They managed their debt. While debt may have helped them achieve their wealth, many described plans to get debt behind them.

✦ They cultivated the ability to bounce back from failures. They didn't let tough times influence them to give up.

Other studies of millionaires have revealed these characteristics as well:

- Being born with a silver spoon is unnecessary: The majority of millionaires received no inheritance at all.

- Education is essential: More than three-quarters have college degrees and more than a third have advanced degrees.

- Millionaires don't show their wealth: From homes to cars to clothing, the well-to-do tend not to display their wealth. They're perfectly happy to drive older cars and live in modest homes.

- Wealth doesn't require a high income: Most millionaires don't have million-dollar incomes. They accumulated their wealth the old-fashioned way—by living beneath their means and giving their money time to grow.

For every one of those people who loves to display their wealth, there are numerous millionaires who are living modestly. In fact, many people who live as if they're millionaires aren't millionaires at all, unless you count their debt.

There are no deep secrets or luck associated with becoming a millionaire, but the common-sense characteristics they share are well worth implementing in your financial life.

■

A millionaire is the only person who receives letters
from second cousins.
—ANONYMOUS

LIFE IS UPSIDE-DOWN

I grew up in a suburb of Washington, D.C., and one of my earliest financial lessons came from a family friend—a very amiable fellow who could identify as well with children as he could with adults. He enjoyed teaching youngsters about life just as much as he enjoyed debating with my parents and other adults about political affairs. One Friday evening, he came to the door to take my sister, along with his young daughter, to a party. I answered the door, but my sister wasn't quite ready. While he was standing at the door, he said (I can remember it as if it happened last night, although I must have been only seven or eight at the time): "Jonathan, life is upside-down. I'm busy with my career, but I have no money and have to spend Friday night driving my kids to parties. When I'm older, I'm going to have more money, and I'll even have a chauffeur to drive me around. But you know what? I won't need the money or the chauffeur then. I could sure use them now, though. Life is upside-down. When you're young and could use some money, you're poor. When you're older and don't need as much money, that's when you've got it." You won't be surprised that I have remembered that message when I tell you who the messenger was. He was Hubert Humphrey, then a young member of Congress, later called "the Happy Warrior." He did what he said he was going to do: earn more money and have a chauffeur. And he also spent a lifetime in public service dispensing his wisdom to young and old alike.

Timeless wisdom. His remarks to me decades ago are just as accurate today as they were then. Our financial lives are, in many ways, upside-down. There's not a lot we can do about it, but it doesn't prevent us from being able to achieve our financial dreams. If you're in your twenties or thirties, you've got time on your side. Simply take positive steps toward achieving your financial goals. You can't do everything at once, but you can do some things now and more things later.

If you're a late starter or have suffered financial reversals, take some comfort in knowing that it's never too late to start preparing for a better financial future. Don't bemoan your fate. Instead, do something tomorrow that will improve your financial outlook, even if it's a small step like putting a few dollars into a savings account.

■

Where I was brought up we never talked about money
because there was never enough to furnish a topic
of conversation.
—MARK TWAIN

IDEA 5

Go Forth and Let Your Money Multiply

The one thing we all share in common is our desire to achieve financial security. For most people, financial security means financial independence—the ability to meet all foreseeable financial needs out of their own resources. In other words, financial security means being able to afford to retire, whether one wants to retire or not. Everyone wants to be financially independent by the time they retire, but many fall short. Along the way, during our working years, we all want the financial security of being able to cope with whatever financial demands might be placed on us—buying a home, educating the children, and surviving disability, unemployment, or the death of a breadwinner.

You don't have to be lucky to achieve financial security. But you do have to work at it—and the earlier you begin, the easier financial security will be to achieve. As the following shows, achieving financial security entails many different tasks. All of them are important, and each merits your attention.

The Keys to Achieving Financial Security

F FORMULATING OBJECTIVES. You can't get there from here unless you establish some important personal financial-planning objectives (see Idea 1, on page 2).

I ENSURING THAT YOU HAVE ADEQUATE INSURANCE. Always maintain continuous and comprehensive insurance coverage (see chapter 11).

N NEVER GIVING UP CONTROL OVER YOUR MONEY. Don't let other people tell you what to do with your money. You are your own best financial planner (see Idea 82, on page 258).

A ALLOCATING YOUR INVESTMENTS APPROPRIATELY. Deciding how to apportion your investments among stocks, interest-earning securities, and real estate is crucial to your investment success (see Idea 33, on page 102).

N CREATING A NEST EGG. There's nothing like money in the bank to give you financial peace of mind. Kick the spending habit, and get hooked on saving regularly (see Idea 13, on page 46).

C COPING WITH MAJOR LIFE EVENTS. Life deals each of us a variety of cards—some are good, and some are not. Preparing for the unexpected helps minimize financial disruptions (see chapter 11).

I **INVESTING WISELY.** Learning about how to invest, plus putting your knowledge to work, is one of the most important ingredients to your achieving financial security (see chapter 6).

A **ASSURING THAT YOU MINIMIZE INCOME TAXES.** Income taxes take a large chunk out of your income, and there is no reason to pay any more than the minimum that the law obligates you to pay (see chapter 10).

L **LEARNING TO LIVE BENEATH YOUR MEANS.** The only way to accumulate the investments necessary to achieve financial security is to spend less than you earn, and the only way to spend less than you earn is to live beneath your means (see chapter 3).

S **SETTING YOUR RECORDS STRAIGHT.** Organize your records and prepare personal financial statements to get a better handle on your finances (see Idea 97, on page 317).

E **PLANNING YOUR ESTATE.** You'll not only be doing your heirs a big favor by preparing the necessary estate-planning documents, you will benefit during your own lifetime (see Idea 79, on page 247).

C **MEETING COLLEGE EDUCATION COSTS.** The best way to meet college education costs is to undertake a realistic savings plan when the kids are young, then become familiar with the financial aid process as they near college age (see chapter 9).

U **USING CREDIT WISELY.** Credit can be useful to achieving financial security, or it can destroy your financial security. It all depends on how you use it (see chapter 4).

R **PARTICIPATING IN RETIREMENT PLANS.** Maximize your participation in tax-advantaged retirement plans to help assure a comfortable retirement (see chapter 5).

I **INVESTING IN YOUR CAREER.** Devote the time necessary to improve your skills and advance in your career. Your career is your most important income-producing investment (see chapter 2).

T TAKING THE TIME TO ATTEND TO YOUR FINANCES. The time you spend to work on your personal finances is always time well spent (see Idea 98, on page 323).

Y YOU'RE RESPONSIBLE FOR ACHIEVING FINANCIAL SECURITY. It's up to you to take the actions necessary to achieve financial independence. *Grow your money!*

■

The secret of getting ahead is getting started.

—MARK TWAIN

CHAPTER 2

Profiting From a Fabulous Career

Your career is your single best investment. Keeping up-to-date in your field and striving to be a dedicated and hardworking employee will translate into a higher income, more satisfying work life, and better job security. When you decide to change careers, the skills you possess will make the transition into a new career a lot smoother. As a skilled and valued employee, you will also have more opportunity for meaningful work later in life and will be able to retire on your timetable, rather than your employer's.

In short, if you have a choice between spending an hour a day studying the stock market or spending that hour becoming a more skilled employee, the latter will be your more lucrative investment by a long shot. Anyway, later in this book you'll learn how to become an excellent stock investor by spending less than an hour a month.

> *Choose a job you love, and you'll never have to work*
> *a day in your life.*
> —CONFUCIUS

IDEA 6

The Ingredients of Career Success

It's not that difficult to be a success in your career, since most of your competition probably isn't as highly motivated as you are. No matter where you are on the employment ladder, you have the wherewithal to advance in your job and advance your income at the same time. It just takes an investment, primarily an investment in time. The following suggestions will help you on the road to a richer and more satisfying career, even if you find yourself mired in a boring, low-pay job:

✓ **Prepare a plan.** Heaven knows your employer is probably constantly on your back about planning, but do you have a plan of your own? Write a plan that describes what you want to accomplish over the next year. Then prepare a timetable that lists where you want to be in your job over each of the next several years.

✓ **Do your professional reading.** One of the best ways to improve your skills, particularly if you're in a business that requires technical knowledge, is to keep up-to-date with the latest thinking and innovations in your field. In addition to books and professional journals, the Internet offers a treasure trove of useful (and sometimes not so useful and not so accurate) information and training in your career area. If you're interested in a career change, the Internet is also a good place to find out about different careers (see Idea 8, on page 26).

✓ **Take classes.** By attending professional seminars on your employer's dime, taking local continuing education classes, or taking an Internet course, you can hone your professional knowledge and skills. Attending seminars and classes has the added advantage of enabling you to interact with leaders in your field as well as network with your peers.

✓ **Do more than is expected.** You probably know a lot of people inside and outside your workplace who do only what is expected of them and no more. They're clock-watchers, and someday they'll be working for you, if they aren't already. Show your boss and coworkers that you're a "can do" person who always does more than what is expected. It doesn't usually take a lot of effort to show that you are someone on the rise.

✓ **Welcome additional tasks.** There's nothing wrong with asking for additional work or committee assignments, perhaps something that no one else wants to tackle. Whether it's just drudge work or something that your colleagues think is too challenging, jump in with enthusiasm.

✓ **Find a mentor.** If possible, find a higher-up in the organization who can help direct your career, someone who is happy to provide some counsel and direction. Don't be afraid to ask. After all, your good efforts have already shown that you are someone who is adding a lot of value to the company or institution, so your prospective mentor will be flattered by your request.

✓ **Be a mentor.** If you're a people person, by all means utilize that attribute to motivate and help your coworkers achieve great things with you. Your boss will appreciate that you're a team player, indeed a team leader. If this threatens your boss, ask your mentor to help you find a new boss.

✓ **When the time is right, cultivate a specialization.** Ideally, you should use the early years in your career to develop a broad range of job skills. This will enable you to see "the big picture," which will be invaluable as you move up the career ladder. But there will come a time when you will need to begin specializing in a certain area or areas, taking advantage of your talents so that you can add demonstrable value to your organization.

✓ **Focus and follow through.** In this day and age of multitasking and incredible demands placed on workers (and the better you are, the more that's demanded of you), it's easy to lose sight of the need to stay focused on the task at hand. Organize your workspace so that distractions are kept to a minimum. Another victim of modern work life is a lack of follow through. If you find yourself avoiding some of the more perplexing tasks in favor of ones that are easier to accomplish, create a to-do list to ensure you follow through on necessary tasks on a timely basis.

✓ **Develop strong speaking and writing skills.** You will be speaking with your boss on a regular basis. The first time your boss's boss will be aware of you may be through a written report—or, horror of horrors, through an oral presentation. Strong speaking and writing skills are essential to career success and advancement. That's doubly so if your work puts you into contact with customers or clients. If either your speaking or your writing could use some improvement, there are courses and meetings (Toastmasters, for example) that can help.

✓ **Don't be afraid to take risks.** Your career will likely go nowhere unless you're willing if not eager to take risks. That's the primary way advances are made in the workplace, and if you want to be a mover and shaker, you need to embrace risky tasks and projects. Learn to accept failure and learn from failure.

The objective of being the best you can in your career, from a financial standpoint at least, is simple: to maximize your lifetime income potential by making informed career and employment choices and continuously striving to be the best at what you do. Earning more money is fundamental to the plans you have for your life. If you earn a low income, don't equate that with what you are worth. Instead, make choices throughout your career that will enhance your ability to earn more money.

The *Grow Your Money!* reader Web site has additional helpful resources on ways to advance in your career. **w w w**

> ■
>
> *Talent hits a target no one else can hit; genius hits a*
> *target no one else can see.*
> —ARTHUR SCHOPENHAUER

IDEA 7

Advice for Those Who Have Taken a Career Sabbatical

If you have taken time off from your career, or are contemplating such a move, don't become despondent over the prospect of ever being able to gain meaningful employment again. This is a prevalent malaise, but the facts point to a much brighter outlook. Having taken time off, particularly to raise children or to care for other family members, is less and less seen as an impediment to resuming a career. In fact, given the looming shortage of skilled employees, some companies are actively seeking out talented people who have been temporarily out of the workforce. Nonetheless, it is a challenge. But don't shortchange your abilities or feel that you've been so out of it professionally that no one will want you back. Be positive.

Your résumé. Your first concern is probably how to explain your absence from the workforce. If you leave it blank, the prospective employer will probably conclude that you've been in prison. Of course, if you were raising children, that may not be far from the truth. How you explain your absence partly depends on how long you've been away.

✦ **Less than five years.** If the reason for the absence has been staying at home with young children, the employer will probably be concerned with your ability to work effectively while having still-young children. Your résumé and cover letter should emphasize your high energy and ability to cope. Nowhere along the process should you express any misgivings about returning to work.

✦ **Five years or longer.** The longer your absence from the workforce, the more concern the employer will have that your knowledge and skills have fallen behind. (If you're still on sabbatical, pay particular attention to the following.) You need to demonstrate what you have done to stay current and also show any activities you undertook during the hiatus that are relevant. Some examples include attending professional association meetings, taking continuing education courses, maintaining contacts with your colleagues, even keeping up with your professional reading. If you served on any committees or volunteered in the community, all the better. In the final analysis, though, concentrate on selling yourself and the great things you can do for a prospective employer rather than dwelling on the past.

Your job-finding to-do list. Once you have a résumé in hand and confidence in your ability to be a valued employee, here are some to-do items:

❑ **Dust off the Rolodex.** Your best source of information on available jobs and just plain good advice are your former contacts. So rejuvenate your lists. (If they're on a Rolodex, you have indeed been out of the workforce for quite a while.) Tell everyone you know that you're back in the game.

❑ **If you have youngsters, identify family-friendly employers.** The list of companies that are accommodating parents of young families or those who may have older relatives in need of their care is growing by the day. It doesn't contain just giant companies, either. Most communities have locally based employers who are known to be family friendly and who have exceptional workers as a result. Job-sharing arrangements are also becoming more commonplace.

❑ **Be realistic and be flexible.** Finally, don't get discouraged if your search doesn't bear immediate fruit. The whole hiring process can take anywhere from a month to six months anyway. You may have to settle initially for a job that's a peg below the one you left. But your main objective is probably to get back into the workforce so that you can once again strut your stuff. From there, anything is possible.

> ■
>
> *Improvement of one's economic position is helped more by cool persistence than by hot enthusiasm.*
> —WILLIAM FEATHER

MONEY TIP

*Continuing Your Education—
For Consumption or Investment?*

Obtaining more education is usually a good thing, but it does have financial implications, or else I wouldn't bring it up. Narrow-minded financial people like me (I was trained as an accountant, after all) tend to bifurcate courses of study according to their potential to benefit you financially. Sad, isn't it?

Education, particularly adult continuing education but also degree programs, can be acquired for either "consumption" or "investment." Taking an art criticism course would be classified as "consumption," unless you're in the art business. Consumption makes you a better rounded and perhaps more interesting person, but probably not a more economically valuable person. On the other hand, additional coursework in your chosen field of study is (hopefully) an investment in a more lucrative financial future.

If you're thinking of a career change that is going to require a considerable amount of formal education, you need to also consider the economic potential of leaving your current career in favor of a new one. It's fine if you move into a less lucrative career if you understand that in advance. For example, perhaps you're tired of the drudgery and stress in your job as an engineer earning six figures. You dream of getting into psychology or teaching, either of which would require a lot of full-time college work. You certainly need to factor in the income hit you'll be taking in the future on top of the financial sacrifice of returning to school. You also need to be realistic about the job prospects when you complete your schooling. In the above example, psychology jobs may be scarce, while teaching jobs are likely to be plentiful, with attractive fringe benefits in addition.

> ■
> *There is much pleasure*
> *to be gained from*
> *useless knowledge.*
> —BERTRAND RUSSELL

IDEA 8

Considering a Career Change?

Changing careers is becoming the rule rather than the exception. If you're a middle-aged work veteran, how many careers have you had thus far? If you're new to the workforce, ask your parents how many careers they've had. Rare is the individual who is a lifer with one career anymore.

Why do you want to change? If you're thinking of a change, what's the reason? Is it to earn more money or to have a more satisfying work life? The best of all worlds would be to have a more stimulating job that pays more money. That may be a tough combination to achieve. It's certainly within the reach of a business owner, but starting a business is a risky undertaking. See Idea 9, on page 30.

Before changing careers, weigh the pros and cons of your current occupation. Take inventory of what you like or dislike about your job. Are you unhappy with the type of work you do? Or, are you dissatisfied with the culture of the company? If you don't like the way your company does business, you can search for a better employer. But if you're unhappy with your occupation, you may need to make a bigger change. Perhaps you're a worm taster (yes, there is such an occupation), but you'd like to change your career and yet still exploit your sensory skills by becoming a wine taster.

If you've decided that changing careers is in the cards, evaluate your interests and skills. Ask yourself:

✦ What have I done in the past that I really like doing?

✦ What would I really love to do for a living?

✦ Can I use my current skills in my new career?

✦ Do I need more education or training in another field?

Here are a few examples along with possible solutions.

Example 1: During your high school and college years, you loved to write. You always worked on the school newspaper. Now you're working in medical sales, but feel trapped. You might consider changing careers, and becoming an editor or writer of medical publications.

Example 2: You're working as a management and information specialist, but you're tired of the long hours. Your company might offer in-house training for you to become a project manager. This might be an enticing alternative.

Example 3: You fight fires for a living, but have a passion for computers. In this case, you may need to go back to school.

Here are some suggestions if you're considering a career change:

❑ Conduct online research to find possible careers that interest you. Read as much as you can about those fields and the demand for jobs in those areas. Determine what additional training you might need. Today it's a lot easier to get the education necessary to move into many careers because you can enroll in accredited online universities.

❑ Consider doing some part-time or volunteer work to get your feet wet and make personal contacts in your potential new profession.

❑ Weigh the pros and cons of entering a completely new career from scratch versus going into a career where much of your skills and experience is transferable. The former is a much-higher-risk undertaking than the latter.

❑ Determine whether you can learn some new skills at your existing job. Perhaps you've been working in corporate accounting, but want to become a human resources professional. Visit the human resources department at work to get your foot in the door. Simultaneously, you might take night or weekend courses to get some training in counseling and human resource management.

❑ Finally, consider the financial ramifications of a career change. If you do indeed change careers, how will your finances be affected? Here are some questions to consider:

 ? What will additional education or training cost?

 ? Will you need to leave your current job in order to obtain the education and training necessary to embark on your new career? If so, will you have enough money to tide you over, or will you need to take out loans?

? What is the employment outlook in your new occupation? Will jobs be easy to come by?

? How does the expected income from your new career compare with the income you're now earning? If you're certain it's more, that's wonderful. If it will be less, that's okay so long as you factor that into your future spending.

For more guidance for career changers, click on the reader Web site. **w w w**

The test of success is not what you do when you are on top. Success is how high you bounce when you hit bottom.
—GENERAL GEORGE S. PATTON

MONEY TIP

Leave Your Job on Good Terms

The notion of working an entire career for the same employer is a quaint artifact of the past, something our grandfathers might have done. Even if you're one of those rare people who devotes all of their working years to a single career, you're still likely to toil for several different employers.

When you leave a job, whether of your own volition or involuntarily, you might be sorely tempted to tell your boss, in the words of a once-popular song, to "take this job and shove it." But you might live to regret it. Even if you have another job lined up, you may need a good reference from your former employer(s) when you seek other positions later on. Or you may find that, despite the warm fuzzies you feel for your next employer, the devil you now know is better than the devil you don't know, and so you might someday want to go back to your former job. In short, there's nothing to be gained by doing anything that would cause a former employer to return the disfavor in kind. So no matter how acrimonious your leave-taking may be, no matter how much you hate your job, thank your employer for the opportunity he has given you, and periodically check in with your former boss and coworkers to let them know what you're doing.

As you rise in your career, employers are more likely to seek references going way back. I was recently asked to provide a reference for a student I employed for a summer over twenty years ago. He was a candidate for a lofty position in the government that required thorough reference checks from every job he had ever held.

> ■
> *To think twice in every matter and follow the lead of*
> *others is no way to make money.*
> —IHARA SAIKAKU

IDEA 9

Buck the Odds by Starting and Succeeding in Your Own Business

If you decide to start your own business, be sure your expectations are realistic. Don't expect to open a store, put a business online, or hang out a shingle and have people immediately knock down the doors. Statistics have shown that it takes an average of seven years for a new business to become profitable.

As any successful business owner will tell you—and it certainly would help to speak with a few of them—take one small step at a time. Small steps lead to big steps. And don't be discouraged by a failure—keep plugging. Here are the steps you want to take to get from "concept" to "cash flow":

✓ The first step is to find a business you'd love to run in a field where there is a strong demand. Check with similar businesses in your area. Ask people how they got started. Pay particular attention to their pricing and costs. Concentrate on a business where your career experience gives you an advantage. Getting into something entirely new increases the odds of failure. For example, just because you like Japanese food doesn't mean you're qualified to open a sushi restaurant. If you're concerned about not possessing the necessary experience in a business that interests you, consider franchise opportunities.

✓ Determine how much money, or "capital," you need to get your business up and running. Estimate your likely revenue from the operation. What are the business expenses—including rent, utilities, supplies, wages, accounting, taxes, insurance, and the cost of goods? Do you have enough assets to finance it yourself without emptying out all of your savings? If you need loans or business partners, start to investigate possible sources of money.

✓ Whatever figure you come up with for necessary start-up capital, increase it by about one-third. Start-up businesses often run into unforeseen problems. You'll want a little extra for a cushion.

✓ If you're starting a home-based business, you may be the only employee. So you need to check on your tax situation. An accountant or lawyer can advise you on how to organize your company—sole proprietorship, corporation, or partnership.

✓ It's far preferable to start out small with modest overhead. That way, you can work the bugs out of your operation. That old adage "Don't quit your day job" is very sensible, if you can get away with it. But don't expect instant success. You have to build good relationships with suppliers and customers. This takes time.

✓ You need a solid business plan, a document that lists information about every aspect of the business you're starting. It's important to explain why your business and services are needed. The business plan should include realistic financial projections. This is particularly important if you want to get a small-business loan.

✓ You need a marketing strategy, augmented by first-class marketing materials and a Web site. Good sales skills are essential. No matter how good your service or product may be, if you can't effectively thrust it into the public eye, your business may as well not even exist. If you don't have good sales skills, you'll need to develop some quickly. The technical and managerial skills you bring to your business will all go for naught should you be unable to promote and sell your product and yourself.

✓ Don't underestimate the many and varied skills that are necessary to operate and successfully grow a business. It has long been said that a new business owner with strong business skills but a mediocre idea has a better chance of success than an owner with a fabulous idea but mediocre skills.

✓ Once you have your business up and running, work on turning it into a success. There's no substitute for hard work. You must also develop tough skin. Everything doesn't always go your way.

✓ Last but not least, periodically analyze and review your business operations, including costs and profitability. As with your personal finances, regularly evaluate ways you can save money and boost your revenues. Periodically compare your actual results against your business plan, and revise your plan if necessary. Prepare to make changes based on your results, competition, expenses, and the market.

An opportunity of a lifetime. Yes, the odds are against succeeding in your own business, but that doesn't mean you can't buck those odds. Successful small business owners have an opportunity to earn an income that would be the envy of most executives in large businesses. A thriving small business may also be able to be sold for a large sum, enough to put the owner, his or her family, and later generations on Easy Street.

Resources for those considering starting their own business can be found in the special reader Web site. **w w w**

> ■
>
> *Money never starts an idea; it's the idea that starts the money.*
> —WILLIAM J. CAMERON

MONEY TIP

Pension-Plan Advisory

Unfortunately, pension plans—aka "defined-benefit plans" that pay a lifetime income when you retire—are an endangered species. Many private-sector plans are being terminated altogether, and others are having their benefits curtailed. Even public-sector plans may suffer the same fate as federal, state, and local government budgets strain under the weight of promised benefits. Despite these conditions, however, working for an employer with a pension plan may offer substantial benefits in retirement that are tough to duplicate by saving on your own. Here are three pointers:

- **Be realistic about the future of your employer's pension plan.** Whether you currently work for an employer with a pension plan or are considering taking a job that offers a plan, be realistic about how much you can rely on the promised pension when you retire. Thousands of employers have terminated their defined-benefit plans in favor of defined-contribution plans like 401(k)s and 403(b)s. The major difference between the two? The employer kicks in all or most of the money to a defined-benefit plan, but it's up to you to fund most, if not all of your defined-contribution plan. Even mighty IBM, long considered one of the most benevolent employers, has all but abandoned its pension plan.

If it's likely that your employer is going to abandon or curtail your pension plan:

A. You may need to bolster your own annual contributions to retirement savings plans.

B. Your current pension plan may be less of a factor in deciding whether to move to an employer that doesn't offer a plan or that has a plan that is more likely to be continued until you retire.

- **Sacrificing income now may be well worth it to enjoy a nice pension when you retire.** Despite the threats to many pension plans, some employers are committed to maintaining them, particularly public-sector and many nonprofit institutions. The "price" you usually pay is a lower income during your working years. But this may be a price worth paying. For example, to replicate a $50,000 pension with a 3 percent inflation kicker, you would have to amass over $750,000 of retirement savings on your own. A lot of people who work in the public sector gripe about the lower pay, but if they stick it out, they become the envy of their higher-earning counterparts who often end up with considerably lower income from their defined-contribution-plan savings.

- **Think really hard before quitting a job with a pension plan.** If you currently work for an employer who provides a pension plan, consider carefully the financial implications of a job change. This is doubly important if you have many years of service under your belt, because pension plan payouts are heavily skewed to length of service. It's not unusual to see benefits curtailed by 40 percent or more for those who changed jobs or retired just a few years earlier than standard retirement age. So before bailing, find out just how much pension income you'll be sacrificing. If you're being wooed by a company that doesn't offer a pension plan, they may be willing to adjust your pay or benefits to offset the pension income you'll be sacrificing.

See the special reader Web site for up-to-date news and information on pension plan regulations and trends. **w w w**

> *Success usually comes to those who are too busy*
> *to be looking for it.*
> —HENRY DAVID THOREAU

IDEA 10

Your Career Doesn't Have to End When You Reach Retirement Age

One of the best things about having great career skills and an enthusiastic work attitude is that you'll always be in demand, even after you reach retirement age. Surveys indicate that almost two-thirds of the baby boom generation (those born between 1946 and 1964) want to work after age sixty-five. Finances are not the primary reason they want to continue to work, although delaying retirement can boost retirement income a lot, as noted below. The reason most often sited for wanting to continue working is simply that they enjoy working and can't imagine not working. Here are the three ways you can postpone retirement if that's your desire:

1. **Continue working at your job.** Employers fear the loss of talented employees and an increasing number are implementing programs that support those who want to work beyond normal retirement age. So if you are thinking about continuing to work after most of your colleagues have retired, the wind is at your back.

2. **Find a new full-time job.** Perhaps you've tired of your current employment situation or don't like the stress, but don't want to leave the workforce. Depending on your interests and experience, there may be an opportunity to find a better fit with another employer—either in your chosen field or in another field that could benefit from your experience.

3. **Work part-time.** Working part-time rather than retiring cold turkey has a lot of appeal for both lifestyle and financial reasons. You can consider working a reduced number of hours either at your current place of employment or in a new work environment, perhaps an entirely different work environment. Perhaps "phased retirement" is your cup of tea, where you gradually reduce, over a period of a few years, the number of hours you work each week.

Working in retirement will hike your retirement income, perhaps by a very large percentage. For example, if you retire and earn enough working part-time to support yourself, but not enough to add anything to your retirement savings, here's what happens: working for just one year will generate 10 percent extra income from your nest egg when you do retire; three years, 20 percent; and five years, 40 percent! There are two reasons why delaying retirement produces so much more retirement income: First, your retirement savings have more time to grow before you begin tapping into them. Second, each year you continue working is one less year your money will be needed to fund your retirement. Also, by delaying the date you begin collecting Social Security retirement benefits, that income will increase as well, as is explained in Idea 93, on page 297.

I'm a great believer in luck, and I find the harder I work
the more I have of it.
—THOMAS JEFFERSON

CHAPTER 3

Accumulating Real Wealth

A massing considerable wealth isn't very complicated, even for people of modest means. Most multimillionaires started with nothing. Financial security is not a function of how much you earn. It's a function of how much you save, so that's the first step in any wealth-building program. A lot of people with fat salaries are one paycheck away from financial trouble, while many with average incomes are building real wealth. You can put the odds in your favor by taking some easy steps to help you join the wine-and-brie crowd, including:

- Take advantage of tax rules that encourage certain kinds of investments

- Contribute to tax-deferred retirement plans and strive to increase your contributions

- Figure out ways to eliminate unneeded or wasteful expenditures, particularly if you're having trouble saving

- Take advantage of financial opportunities—a raise or a windfall— to better your financial future

> ■
>
> *Nothing is more admirable than the fortitude*
> *with which millionaires tolerate the disadvantages*
> *of their wealth.*
> —REX STOUT

IDEA 11

How Great Wealth Is Created

Perhaps you aspire to exceed the goal of achieving lifetime financial security. Perhaps you want to create wealth that will benefit future generations, be they heirs or charities. Or, perhaps you just want to be rich, stinking rich. If so, here's a short lesson on how wealth has been created in the past and how it will undoubtedly be created in the future. If you truly want to amass riches, you need to have a partner in your financial endeavors. As opposed to those get-rich-quick infomercial gurus who only make promises but don't deliver, your partner will provide you with the financial backing that has been utilized by generations of multimillionaires. You'll be surprised to learn that your partner is Uncle Sam. The tax laws provide big breaks to certain kinds of investments—I'm not talking about oil wells or luxury hotels. These breaks are bestowed on the garden-variety investments you already understand. All of these investments can take advantage of either of the following pair of tax incentives:

1. **The ability to have investment profits taxed as capital gains.** The tax rates on long-term capital gains—gains on investments held for more than a year—are at least 40 percent lower, and can be as much as over 50 percent lower, than the rate at which many other types of investment income are taxed.

2. **The ability to permanently postpone capital gains taxes.**
   There are ways for assets to be transferred at death to heirs (or
   to charity) with no capital gains taxes due.

Keeping your generous Uncle's tax incentives in mind, here are the
ways that wealth is created:

Owning individual stocks. Most rich families got that way by buying individual stocks and holding on to them for the rest of their lives.
So long as they hold on to the stock, they never pay capital gains taxes,
even though the stock probably rises considerably in value over the decades. Then, when they die, their heirs receive the stock with a
"stepped-up cost basis," which means that they generally inherit the
stock at a tax value computed at the date of the dearly departed's death.
So, for example, Granddaddy Warbucks took a $1,000 flier on a new
company a few months after it first issued stock in 1986. He held on to
the stock, Microsoft, until his demise. Granddaddy's heirs will inherit
the stock, not with a cost basis of the $1,000 he originally paid, but
rather with its value as of the date of his death, $230,000. If the heirs
turn around and sell the Microsoft shares right away, they *won't owe
any capital gains taxes.* If they hold on to the stock and pass it on to the
next generation, they, like Grandaddy, will never pay capital gains tax
on the stock. But you don't have to be lucky enough to pick another Microsoft to be able to accumulate a lot of money that isn't eroded by
taxes along the way. An investment of $10,000 in a stock that grows in
value an average of 10 percent per year—that's how much the average
stock price has risen over the past eight decades—will grow to $450,000
in forty years. Investing $10,000 in individual stocks *per year* over
forty years and holding them will amass almost $4,500,000.

But, just as in the pitches for knives in the TV infomercials, "Wait,
there's more." Many dividends are also accorded favorable tax treat-
ment. The dividends paid by *most* corporations—those primarily in
the real estate business are a noteworthy exception—are taxed at a
much lower rate than is the interest paid on government or corporate
bonds. So the best of all tax-avoidance worlds is to buy and hold stocks

of solid companies that regularly increase their dividends. One simple strategy that has been the hallmark of many wealthy families is to buy good dividend-paying stocks that decades hence provide a substantial and rising amount of dividend income to meet retirement needs and, later on, can be passed on to younger-generation family members. Here's an example: Twenty years ago, an investor bought $5,000 of Johnson & Johnson stock that paid a total dividend of $100—a 2 percent dividend yield. Twenty years later, the stock is worth $60,000 and the dividend has risen fourteen times to $1,400. Not only has the price of the stock increased twelve times, the annual dividend payout of $1,400 is now 28 percent of the original investment.

Owning investment real estate. Investment real estate—such as apartments and small office or industrial buildings—works a lot like stock. You enjoy rising income through increased rents and don't pay any capital gains taxes as long as you hold on to the property. If you eventually pay off the mortgage, you could end up with a lot of income from the property. Investment real estate is without doubt one of the best ways for average people to create a lot of wealth. For a game plan for creating your own real estate empire, check out Idea 49, on page 156.

Starting a business. This is the long shot, but being your own boss is the American dream. If you're successful, you can earn a lot of money along the way (while putting whopping amounts into a self-employed retirement plan as explained in Idea 30, on page 93). If you're lucky as well as successful, you'll be able to sell the business for a lot of money. Like individual stocks and real estate, your business can grow in value free of tax on that value until you sell it. Idea 9, on page 30, offers some suggestions for starting your own business.

Another advantage of stocks, real estate, and a family business—if you do sell, the capital gains taxes are usually taxed at a not-too-onerous 15 percent federal tax rate compared to regular income tax rates that range between 25 percent and 35 percent for most taxpayers. The reader Web site provides more guidance on these investment strategies, as well as the current tax regulations for these types of investments. **w w w**

> Great wealth can be created by taking advantage of tax regulations that bestow great benefits on real estate investors, small business owners, and those who buy and hold individual stocks.
>
> ■
>
> *I've been rich and I've been poor. Rich is better.*
> —SOPHIE TUCKER

Are You a Spender or a Saver?
Take the Quiz

If you're in a quandary as to whether you're a saver or a spender, ask your spouse, partner, or a close acquaintance, who will no doubt offer a firm, some might say insensitive, opinion. (For more help on coping with your loved one's annoying financial habits, see Idea 83 on page 263.) Alternatively, you can take the following quiz. There are no right or wrong answers, but they should help you better understand your financial inclinations.

1. The first thing that you think of when you hear the word "bond" is

    ❑ 007

    ❑ An investment that pays interest

2. When you're handed a restaurant check, you

    ❑ Double-check the addition

    ❑ Wonder if you've got enough credit left on the credit card to pay it

3. If you go shopping with ten items on your shopping list, you're more likely to come home with

   ❑ Five items

   ❑ Fifteen items

4. A car has 60,000 miles on it. You think it should be

   ❑ Sold

   ❑ Bought

5. You've just received a raise at work. The first thing that comes to mind is

   ❑ Tiffany's

   ❑ Tiffany stock

6. Which of these expressions brings you more joy?

   ❑ "Dow up 3 percent last week"

   ❑ "Blue Light Special in aisle 3"

7. Which of these statements do you agree with?

   ❑ It costs only a nickel more to go first class.

   ❑ Anything that's first class is a colossal waste of money.

8. At the first anniversary of your first home purchase, you said,

   ❑ I'm very happy here.

   ❑ I'd sure be happier with a bigger house.

9. Whenever you buy something on sale, you conclude that you have

   ❑ Saved money

   ❑ Spent money

10. You define "CD" as

    ❏ A compact disc

    ❏ A certificate of deposit

■

*To acquire wealth is difficult, to preserve it more
difficult, but to spend it wisely most difficult of all.*
—EDWARD DAY

IDEA 12

The Miracle of Tax Deferral

Idea 11, on page 38, shows how the rich get richer by taking advantage of the tax rules. Buying stocks, investing in real estate, or starting a business may not necessarily be what you want (or can afford) to do right now, but that doesn't mean you have to resign yourself to signing big checks to the U.S. Treasury while the fat cats are feasting on their tax shelters. There are other ways to avoid taxes at least until you retire, and you don't need much money to do so. If you and/or your spouse have income from a job, there are opportunities to contribute to tax-deferred retirement savings plans. You probably know what they are (and if not, they are explained and illustrated in chapter 5), but you may not know how financially beneficial they can be. Consider the following:

EXAMPLE. Here is a comparison that shows how much an investor would be able to accumulate and later withdraw in retirement by saving $5,000 per year in each of these plans:

1. A tax-advantaged retirement plan (pre-tax plan, a 401(k) plan, for example)

2. A non-tax-deductible (after-tax) but tax-deferred retirement plan (a nondeductible traditional IRA, for example)

3. A nonretirement (neither tax-deductible nor tax-deferrable) investment account

The $5,000 savings is invested in each of the next twenty years and then withdrawn during retirement in equal amounts over twenty years. The following table shows that tax deferral pays. Even though retirement account withdrawals are usually subject to higher taxes than nonretirement account withdrawals, the greater amount accumulated in the retirement accounts results in higher retirement income even after the loftier taxes have been deducted. Even with the higher taxes paid from retirement account withdrawals, it's what's left over after taxes that counts, and tax deferral wins. For some guidance on how the various retirement plans are taxed, see Idea 26 on page 83.

TAX DEFERRAL PAYS

Contribute $5,000 per Year for Twenty Years Into . . .

	PRE-TAX (DEDUCTIBLE) RETIREMENT PLAN	NONDEDUCTIBLE RETIREMENT PLAN	NONRETIREMENT ACCOUNT
Amount accumulated after 20 years	$205,000	$155,000	$140,000
Annual after-tax withdrawals over following 20 years	$17,000	$14,000	$12,000

You can't have too much—or too little—invested in tax-deferred accounts. The most important things to keep in mind as you begin or continue the delightful task of accumulating great wealth are:

1. If you're just starting out, you can contribute even small amounts to these plans.

2. As your ability to take advantage of these tax-avoidance strategies grows over the years, you'll be able to contribute quite a bit of money—upward of $20,000 or more per year if you contribute to both a retirement plan at work and an IRA. Of course, the more money you can stuff into retirement plans, the more money you'll have when you retire. In fact, under current tax regulations, it's almost always advantageous to accumulate as much of your retirement-earmarked money as possible in tax-deferred accounts.

See the special reader Web site for more illustrations of the miracle of tax deferral as well as a tax update. **w w w**

Contributing as much as you can to tax-favored retirement plans will considerably increase the amount of income you'll enjoy when you retire.

SELF-TEST

THE DIRTY DOZEN—THE BIGGEST WASTES OF MONEY

Imagine you are in court and Judge Pond asks how you plead—guilty or not guilty—to each of the following money wasters. Summarize your pleading below.

	GUILTY	NOT GUILTY
1. Playing the lottery	❑	❑
2. Buying a course that shows you how to get rich quick with no money	❑	❑

3. Buying a car that you can't pay off within three years ❑ ❑

4. Investing in something you don't understand ❑ ❑

5. Designer-label clothing ❑ ❑

6. Holding on to investments for sentimental reasons ❑ ❑

7. Buying anything to keep up with the Joneses ❑ ❑

8. Expensive restaurants ❑ ❑

9. Buying something on sale that you don't need ❑ ❑

10. Narrowly defined insurance, like cancer insurance or life insurance that will pay off your credit cards ❑ ❑

11. Big-ticket items that are seldom used, like a second home, boat, or snowmobile ❑ ❑

12. Extending the maturity date of a mortgage when you refinance ❑ ❑

Tote up your transgressions to prepare your pleading.

HOW DO YOU PLEAD?

❑ **Very guilty** (more than six)

❑ **Somewhat guilty** (three to six)

❑ **Not guilty** (fewer than three)

IDEA 13

Devising a Plan to Reconcile Your Gross Habits with Your Net Income

Errol Flynn once noted: *"My problem lies in reconciling my gross habits with my net income."* It's a very common problem. At the risk of belaboring the obvious: living beneath your means is the fundamental underpinning of creating financial security for you and your family. It's hard to argue otherwise unless you can be assured of receiving a whopping inheritance, winning the lottery, or finding a mate who is loaded with dough. Otherwise, you're consigned to a life of spending less than you earn. Cutting expenses is never as difficult as one thinks. Like dieting, it's the thought of having to cut back that keeps us hungering for more—even when we aren't hungry. But just a cursory look at where your money goes will probably reveal several items that can be eliminated or reduced. If you're not saving enough, do you really have any other choice? Find a few simple and painless ways to cut back, and be sure to reward yourself by putting the savings somewhere where you can watch them grow.

To get you thinking about unearthing ways to save a few bucks in your day-to-day spending, here are some ideas that are small potatoes—but put enough of them together over enough time and you'll accumulate some serious money. There's also some space for you to enter your own estimates.

	Typical Weekly Savings Amount	Your Own Weekly Estimate
Take muffin and coffee to work rather than buy en route.	$ 15–20	$ _____
Bring lunch to work rather than go to a restaurant or deli	15–30	_____
Reduce lottery ticket purchases.	5–15	_____
Patronize less expensive restaurants.	10–25	_____
Take public transit to work or carpool.	20–50	_____

	Typical Weekly Savings Amount	Your Own Weekly Estimate
Buy generic items at the drugstore and supermarket rather than brand-name products.	10–20	_____

Other ideas that you have:

_____	$_____	$_____
_____	_____	_____
_____	_____	_____
_____	_____	_____
_____	_____	_____

Expected weekly savings	$ 75–160	$_____
Expected annual savings	$ 3,900–$8,320	

How about $75 a week? If you start to monitor where you spend your daily money, you're almost certain to come up with some ideas. If you can find $75 a week of avoidable costs, here's how much that amounts to over the years at an annual investment return of 7 percent:

A Small Amount of Money Saved Regularly Adds Up

5 Years	$ 23,000
10 Years	$ 56,000
20 Years	$ 170,000
30 Years	$400,000
40 Years	$860,000

It gets better. The above example shows how much money you can amass by regularly (it has to be regularly to work) saving small amounts of money, $75 a week in the example. If you put the money in a tax-deductible plan at the office and also add in an amount equal to the taxes you save, you will amass even more wealth. For example, if you put $75 into your 401(k) or 403(b) plan and you're in the 25 percent income tax bracket, you'll save about $19 in income taxes, which you could add to the $75 without being any worse off financially. Here's how this strategy will fill your coffers.

A Small Amount of Money Added to Your Workplace Savings Plan Adds Up to Even More

5 Years	$ 29,000
10 Years	71,000
20 Years	215,000
30 Years	500,000
40 Years	1,075,000

Of course, once you get into the savings habit, like any addiction, you'll want to do more. So if it's $75 this year, why not $100 next year after you find some more ways to cut costs or the next time you get a raise. (See page 54 for some help on making the most of a raise.) The reader Web site has some up-to-date cost-cutting suggestions and resources and a place for you to share your own and see what other readers have done. w w w

---

Getting into the habit of saving regularly, even small amounts, can amass a sizable nest egg over the years and decades.

■

Beware of little expenses. A small leak will sink a great ship.
—BEN FRANKLIN

MONEY TIP

Help Yourself and the Economy by Practicing "Reverse Keeping Up With the Joneses"

Keeping up with the Joneses is as American as credit-card loans and interest-only mortgages, and just as financially deleterious. For whatever reason, we, as well as every member of our household, feel compelled to live up to the standards of our neighbors, coworkers, nursery school classmates, anyone who has more things than we have. Instead of trying to keep up with the Joneses, I'm enthusiastically recommending that all my readers practice the reverse. In other words, while it's important for society at large to spend lavishly—remember that consumer spending fuels two-thirds of our economy—you shouldn't get caught up in a profligate lifestyle. So my advice is to do whatever you can to cajole your friends and neighbors to buy things. It shouldn't take much effort to persuade someone else to consume. Simply talking about how great the grand life is will impel many to try to live the grand life out of fear that you'll do it first. But—and here's where the "reverse" comes into play—you should quietly restrain your spending. Reverse keeping up with the Joneses enables us to have the best of both worlds—continued high consumer spending to keep the economy growing, while you and I are saving for the future.

> ■
>
> *Budgeting:*
> *Nobody was ever meant*
> *To remember or invent*
> *What he did with every cent.*
> —ROBERT FROST

IDEA 14

Out, Out, Damned Budget

If you enjoy preparing, maintaining, and reviewing a family budget, that's wonderful. Read no further. There are plenty of Web sites that ease the chore of budgeting. On the other hand, if you don't like to budget, or if you've tried to budget in the past to no good effect, here's an idea that will help you reach your current and future goals without the hassle.

Getting down to basics. The purpose of a budget is very simple: to find out where you spend (or, perhaps, squander) your money in order to find places to cut back so that you can begin to save or increase your savings. The rub is that in order to monitor your spending you have to account for everything you spend, which is about as exciting as watching your neighbor's home movies.

So let's stick with the basics: ***The objective of a personal budget is to achieve a desired level of saving.*** For example, you may be saving 5 percent now, but would like to move that up to a higher percentage. Or, you may not be saving, but would like to start putting some money into a savings account. Conventional thinking says that in order to increase your savings, you should find out where your money goes in order to identify ways to cut back. That's all well and good if you want to take the time to account for everything you spend. Most of us are busy enough already without finding time to budget. If you're time constrained or just budget phobic, here are three ways to shortcut the process:

✦ **Platinum strategy—It's not your spending that matters.** If you're saving already, but want to save more, just go for it. If the higher savings level starts to strain your checkbook, you'll probably adjust your spending automatically because you'll suddenly become cognizant of ways to cut back on your spending, if for no other reason than to avoid bouncing checks. In other words, let nature take its course. The key here is to ***gradually*** boost the amount you save. Unless you know you can manage it, suddenly doubling or tripling the amount you save is bound to lead to disappointment.

✦ **Gold strategy—If you're starting from scratch, start small.** Similar to the "platinum strategy," rather than preparing a budget, start saving a small amount, 1 percent of your salary or perhaps $20 a week. You probably won't even notice it, but if it pinches you, refer to the "silver strategy," below. Once you get used to your initial savings level, boost it a bit. Over time, you could well become a world-class saver. Idea 23, on page 76, will show you the good news (and the goodly amount of wealth) awaiting those who start saving a small amount of money and gradually increase their savings from there.

✦ **Silver strategy—If you can't save at all, pay with cash.** I'll bet you dollars to doughnuts that if you have found it impossible to save, the problem involves your day-to-day spending, things like lattes, lunch at work, dry cleaning, and restaurants. If you put a lot of daily expenditures on a credit card, it simply exacerbates the problem. There's nothing like forking over cash to better understand the impact of a purchase. Get into the habit of paying cash for the stuff you buy and pretty soon you'll start to identify stuff you're buying that you don't really need. Avoiding them will work wonders on your checking account balance, which will in turn allow you to move up to the "gold strategy."

You don't need to be tethered to a budget to accomplish your money goals. Financial success is dependent on how much you save. If you get your savings in line, a spending budget is unnecessary.

■

To spend is human, but to save is divine.
—JONATHAN POND

MONEY TIP

Chump No More: Using Online Coupon Codes

Whenever you order something online, you probably notice a section on the checkout page that invites you to enter a coupon or promotion code. If you're like me, you feel like a chump, because you know that someone else who has the code is going to pay less than you. But you have a fair chance of being able to locate the sacred code thanks to a gaggle of Web sites that allow you to search for them. Offers run the gamut from free shipping to a discount—sometimes a fat discount—on the item you're purchasing.

There are a couple of ways to take advantage of online coupon codes. First, if you intend to shop at a particular site, use a search engine to search for a specific coupon you desire. For example, if you're interested in buying something from Sears, search for "Sears coupon code." You'll find a variety of sites that provide coupon codes. Just make sure they'll work for the item you want to buy and they are up-to-date. Alternatively, if you want to cast a wide net to find out what coupons are available for online shoppers, simply enter "coupon code" in your search engine.

When you find a coupon you want to use, it's just a matter of visiting the retailer's Web site and entering the coupon code when you check out. The discount will be automatically deducted. Then you can have the good feeling that comes from knowing that you're saving money on your purchase, leaving it to others to pay full price. The special reader Web site contains a list of the best coupon code Web sites. **w w w**

■

There is no dignity quite so impressive, and no independence quite so important, as living within your means.
—CALVIN COOLIDGE

IDEA 15

Save Your Raise

Saving part of each raise is a quaint notion—one that your parents probably utilized, much to their financial betterment. The next time you get a raise, rather than thinking about ways to spend it (or worse, spending it before you get it), put at least a portion away for a more prosperous future. Here are my recommendations, depending on your own situation:

✦ **If you have a retirement savings plan at work . . .**
   If you can't afford to save the entire raise (after all, inflation takes a toll on your living expenses), put as much as you can into your retirement savings plan at the shop. Not only do you add to your tax-deferred retirement account, but you also save income taxes. For example, if you contribute an additional $200 a month to the plan and you're in the 25 percent federal income tax bracket, you'll also reduce your tax bill by $50 ($200 deductible contribution times 25 percent). So toting this up, putting $200 of your raise into the plan actually makes you $250 better off, since Uncle Sam is rewarding you with a $50 monthly tax saving. If part or all of the contribution is matched by your employer, all the better. Had you simply spent, rather than saved the money, $50 of taxes would have been taken out of the raise, leaving $150 to spend. So the choice is yours: spend $150 or save $250.

✦ **If you don't have a workplace retirement savings plan . . .**
   Your employer may be able to transfer electronically all or part of your raise to a retirement account held at a brokerage or mutual fund company. If not, ask the company that handles your investments to withdraw said amount from your paycheck (if permitted) or your checking account. Either way, instead of you getting your hands on the money with all the associated tempta-

tions, it is automatically relocated to a more fruitful pasture. Finally, if you don't yet have a retirement account, it's easy to set up. After all, the investment companies would love to have your business.

✦ **If you want to set money aside to acquire something before retirement . . .**

The most important thing is to view your raise as an opportunity to benefit you in the future. If you're contributing to your retirement plans in good measure, but other worthwhile expenditures loom, like a first home down payment, home improvements, or college, then simply have the money moved from your paycheck or checking account into an investment account (or, in the case of college, perhaps a 529 plan account) that will provide a decent return without risking your principal. See Idea 24, on page 80, for some tips on where to invest short-term money.

Don't let a financial opportunity pass you by. Plan now to use a good slice of your next raise to improve your financial future.

■

Oh money, money, money! I often stop to wonder how thou canst go out so fast when thou comest in so slowly.
—OGDEN NASH

IDEA 16

Deciding What to Do with a Financial Windfall

Windfalls can come in many forms—an inheritance, a bonus at work, a legal settlement, or lottery winnings, for example. Such an event can be an emotionally charged time, so it's best to take some time before making any major decisions. While you may eventually need professional advice, be very wary of those who call you offering to help. It's far better to choose your own advisers in your own time.

Psychological issues aside, most people who receive a windfall are in a real quandary about what to do with it. So here is a checklist, in order of priority, that will help you decide how best to utilize your newfound wealth:

❑ **First, pay off credit-card loans and other high-interest debt.** Rather than viewing the loan payoff as a reason to add to your credit card balances once again, consider this an opportunity to avoid running up costly balances in the future.

❑ **Second, if the windfall is received in cash, temporarily put the rest in safe short-term investments.** Don't feel compelled— or let anyone convince you—to invest the money immediately. You can always wait a few months, and large amounts of cash should usually be invested gradually anyway. (See Idea 24, on page 80, for advice on selecting short-term investments.)

❑ **Third, if you've been unable to maximize your retirement plan contributions in the past, set aside enough money to be able to fund your retirement savings plans, including IRAs, for the next several years.** Think of this as an escrow account that will allow you to reap the tax savings and tax deferral from retirement plan contributions.

❑ **Fourth, splurge with some of the money to do something you and your loved ones have long desired, but haven't been able to afford—a trip or new car, for example.** By all means use a portion of your windfall to indulge yourself. But exercise some self-restraint, keeping in mind the legions of people who have squandered a fortune in a matter of months.

❑ **Fifth, consider setting aside a portion to make extra payments against your mortgage or to make a single, lump-sum payment to reduce the time it takes to pay off the mortgage.** Paying down housing debt, starting with the home equity loan, is often a smart way to deploy your windfall. As described in Idea 52, on page 165, paying off the mortgage will dramatically improve your retirement prospects, and this could be a great opportunity to work toward that goal.

❑ **Sixth, use a portion to make worthwhile home improvements.** Sensible home improvements are every bit as worthwhile an investment as putting money into a mutual fund. For tips on making home improvements and surviving the ordeal, see Idea 55, on page 176.

❑ **Finally, invest the rest for a more secure financial future.** Last but not least, if anything is left over after doing all the good things noted above, put the money away to improve your financial future. If there's enough to allow you to increase your living expenses, great, but don't fall victim to lavishing yourself into a worse financial plight than the one that preceded the windfall.

Will you need professional help? While you might wait awhile before seeking investment counsel, if the windfall is a whopper, you should speak with a tax professional (a CPA or lawyer who specializes in taxes, not a storefront tax preparer) to determine whether your new financial status requires utilizing strategies to reduce your future tax bite. You should also retain the services of an experienced estate-planning attorney to see if your will needs to be changed or if there are certain strategies you may need to employ to avoid or reduce estate taxes later on. Idea 82, on page 258, will help you go about the chore of selecting competent and trustworthy advisers.

More than anything, though, consider any financial windfall an opportunity to achieve a better financial future—not just for the next year or few years—but for the rest of your life.

> A financial windfall can be an opportunity for you not only to improve your current financial status but also achieve financial security sooner rather than later.
>
> ■
>
> *When people suddenly become prosperous, they also become preposterous.*
> —LAURENCE J. PETER

CHAPTER 4

Using Debt to Your Advantage

Borrowing is the ultimate conundrum in our financial lives. Used wisely for the right reasons, it can open your life to more abundance than you could achieve without it. But unwise use of debt can impede financial progress for many years. The tips in this chapter will help you take advantage of debt so you can achieve a brighter financial future. Few of us escape this world without experiencing occasional financial challenges that may make it difficult to handle our debt obligations. If you find yourself in this situation, read on for ideas for working through your problems and improving your future credit record.

> ■
>
> *It saves a lot of trouble if, instead of having to earn money and save it, you can just go and borrow it.*
> —WINSTON CHURCHILL

IDEA 17

Borrow for Things That Will Appreciate in Value

Despite the media's constant harping about the evils of debt, borrowing (using other people's money) is an essential tool for achieving financial security. In our society, you can borrow to acquire just about anything, but there are very few things that are worth going into debt for. Here's the caveat in seven words: Never borrow to buy a depreciating asset. In other words, don't borrow for something that isn't going to provide you with lasting and ever-increasing benefits in the future. That pretty much leaves out most things that people borrow money for. Most people borrow to finance either current spending or to buy something that loses value over the years, like, dare I say, a car.

Three and a half worthwhile reasons to go into hock. I can think of only three and a half things that qualify as appreciating assets and are therefore candidates for using your good credit:

1. **A home.** While the majority of homes in this country are owned free and clear, most of them didn't start out that way. A home is the perfect example of why borrowing can benefit you in the future. You borrow to buy a home, work assiduously to pay off the mortgage, and forever after enjoy owning a mortgage-free domicile. All the while (well, at least most of the time), the value of your home is appreciating. Anyway, this scenario works so long as you resist the temptation to use your home as a personal piggy bank to borrow for stuff that depreciates in value. See chapter 8 for more ideas on buying a home.

2. **Education.** Education for your kids or yourself is an expensive proposition—one beyond the immediate resources of most families. Despite your best efforts to secure scholarships, grants, or gifts from wealthy aunts, you may have to borrow to pay bur-

geoning college costs. Education is a great reason to borrow, because your return on investment not only is high, but should last for decades, long after you've paid off those annoying student loans. For more suggestions on financing college or graduate school, see chapter 9.

3. **Sensible home improvements.** Home improvements fall into two categories: the sensible and the preposterous. The acid test is not how good the improvement makes you feel; rather, it's how good the improvement will make the future buyer of your home feel. Worthwhile improvements add substantial value to your home and, therefore, are worth borrowing for, particularly if the alternative is to move into a more expensive manse (see Idea 54 on page 171, for more on that).

4. **Investment real estate.** Real estate is so costly that it's the rare person indeed who can afford to pay cash for it. Borrowing to invest in real estate can work very well, so long as you avoid overpaying for the property (see Idea 48 on 153). But even if you acquire a property at a good price, investing in real estate is still a risky proposition. That's why I consider this a "half" worthwhile reason to borrow.

High-risk borrowing. There are two other areas where borrowing may reap substantial rewards, but these are riskier still, compared with borrowing for a house, an education, and home improvements. This duo is (1) borrowing to invest in stocks and bonds and (2) borrowing to start or sustain a business. While you (or your investment adviser) may think you have the Midas touch in selecting winning investments, investing in stocks, bonds, and mutual funds with borrowed money (called investing on "margin") can result in very large investment losses if the investment markets go against you. Borrowing to start a business or to sustain a business that may be suffering is even riskier.

> Borrowing gets a bad rap, but there are some very worth-while reasons to go into hock, notably to acquire things that will provide lifelong benefits to you and your family.
>
> ■
>
> Live within your means, even if you have to borrow to do so.
> —JOSH BILLINGS

MONEY TIP

Establishing Your Good Credit for the First Time

Contrary to popular opinion, earning a fat income or loading up on credit cards is not the best way to establish your credit. The most important item in computing your credit score is your payment history—no matter how much or how little credit you have. Late payments will harm your credit rating. The next most important matter is the amount you owe. If you come close to maxing out on your credit card limit, your score will be dinged even if you always make on-time payments. If you can't pay off the entire balance every month, try your darnedest to keep the outstanding balance below 50 percent of your credit limit. It also helps a bit if you have a variety of credit accounts, not just credit cards, since the rating agencies will conclude that you can handle several different kinds of credit. So, department store cards, student loans, and yes, even car loans (for more on those, see Idea 66, on page 205) will help you establish your good credit. Finally, if you find that your credit balances are creeping up, keep in mind that there's no rule against paying cash for the stuff you need.

> *If you would like to know the value of money, go and*
> *try to borrow some.*
> —BENJAMIN FRANKLIN

IDEA 18

Getting Richer With Borrowed Money

Perhaps there is nothing better than being debt-free, and achieving that happy position by the time you retire will almost assure a financially comfortable retirement. But during your working years, using borrowed money can help you build up your wealth. Here are a couple of examples of the ways borrowed money can make the difference between simply achieving an okay retirement and achieving a wealthy retirement.

EXAMPLE: Harrison Homeowner buys a $250,000 home, paying $25,000 down and taking out a thirty-year 6 percent mortgage. Roger Renter prefers to rent, so he invests his $25,000, earning an average annual return of 7 percent, and pays $1,200 a month in rent. Let's assume that Harrison's property taxes and maintenance costs rise by 5 percent a year and Roger's rent also rises by 5 percent per annum. Who has spent the most on housing over thirty years? While Harrison has enjoyed some tax savings from his mortgage payments and property taxes, after taking those savings into consideration, he has still paid about $200,000 more than Roger. But before concluding that renting is cheaper than owning, two other important items need to be considered:

    A. **Value of Roger's investments compared with equity in Harrison's house.** If the appreciation in Harrison's house averaged 5 percent per year, it will be worth almost $900,000 more than the value of Roger's investment account. That's the advantage of leverage—the use of borrowed money to acquire a higher-priced appreciating asset. Roger didn't use leverage, so his original investment of $25,000 was only 10 percent of the value of Harrison's home investment.

B. **Future housing costs.** The second important consideration is how much our two protagonists will have to pay for housing in the future. Since Harrison is now mortgage free, his housing expenses will consist almost entirely of property taxes and home maintenance and repairs. On the other hand, Roger will continue paying rent and be subject to the whims of his landlord.

But home ownership can't be taken lightly. It's no wonder that most new homeowners lie awake at night worrying about their enormous debt obligations. But over the years they—and you—can benefit mightily from the use of borrowed money.

EXAMPLE: Laney Landlady bought a multifamily rental property that generates sufficient rental income to pay all mortgage and operating costs. Laney plans to retire in twenty years, so she took out a twenty-year mortgage on the property. She expects the apartment building to appreciate by 5 percent a year and plans to raise rents 3 percent per year. If she achieves her expectations, Laney will have a very valuable retirement asset. The property will have appreciated by 150 percent, so she could sell it at a very substantial gain. If she continues to hold the property, she will receive a steadily rising rental income (which will have already risen 80 percent since she purchased the property)—an ideal source of retirement income.

The use of borrowed money enables real estate investors to parlay a relatively small investment into considerable wealth. But while long-term home ownership is an almost sure bet, owning and managing income-producing real estate is a riskier proposition. Would-be real estate owners should be prepared—and have the financial wherewithal—to endure the periodic crises that bedevil all rental property owners—major repairs, appalling tenants, weak rental markets, etc. If you are intrigued by the possibility of buying rental property, first take a cold shower and then peruse Idea 48, on page 153.

> One of the best ways to create a lot of wealth is the use of borrowed money to acquire real estate, including a home and/or income-producing properties.
>
> ■
>
> *If you think nobody cares if you're alive, try missing a couple of car payments.*
> —EARL WILSON

IDEA 19

Manage Your Home Equity Loan Like a Business

If you've tapped into your home equity credit line, do you have a plan for repaying the loan over an appropriate period of time? It must be human nature, but whenever a homeowner obtains a home equity credit line, previously unrecognized opportunities to spend large sums of money become immediately apparent. Before you take money out of your credit line, you should have a timetable for paying it back. Take a cue from well-run businesses that borrow for short- and long-term purposes and pay off those loans accordingly. If you've used your credit line to buy a car, for example, you should pay off the loan within two or three years. (Incidentally, if you must borrow to acquire a car, using a home equity loan [HEL] is often preferable, since, contrary to a garden-variety car loan, the interest on your home equity loan is probably tax-deductible.) Home equity lines that are accessed for longer-term purposes, like home improvements or college tuition, can be paid off over a longer period of time, say a decade or so. What you want to avoid under any circumstances is a situation where you are simply increasing your borrowing with no end in sight. In short, don't let your HEL turn into a financial hell.

> Pay off your home equity loan over a reasonable period of time, just like a well-run business.

IDEA 20

Pay Off Your Credit Cards Later Rather Than Sooner

Conventional wisdom suggests that paying off high-interest credit cards should be your number one priority before putting any money away for the future in savings accounts, retirement savings plans at work, or anywhere else. The reasoning for this guideline is financially sound. Why put money into an account that will probably earn less than 10 percent when you're paying interest on a credit card that's approaching 20 percent? Financially sound advice, for sure, but I often encourage a somewhat different and controversial approach to the pay-off-the-credit-card versus save dilemma: do some of both.

Here's my reasoning: First, there is no joy forthcoming from making payments against outstanding credit card loans, department store cards, gas company cards, etc. It's usually a monthly reminder of past spending sprees. Depending on the extent of the indebtedness, you might be looking forward to years of paying down the loans without making much if any progress toward a brighter financial future. On the other hand, putting some money, even a little bit of money, away for the future is always good for the soul, particularly for those souls who have little or nothing in the way of savings. So here's my strategy for paying off your credit cards later rather than sooner.

1. Figure out how much you can save each month to pay down credit card and other loans. Don't be overly ambitious in setting

a target. It's better to come up with an amount that you know you can comfortably afford rather than set a target that will be discouragingly difficult to achieve.

2. Depending on how much you owe on the cards, plan to put 50 percent to 75 percent of your monthly savings against the loans. The more debt you have, the more you should be putting toward reducing the loans. One thing you want to avoid is simply making the minimum required payments each month. If you pay just the minimum, you'll probably be in a nursing home before you pay off the cards. By the way, I hope I don't need to remind you that you should make only minimum use of these cards, lest you continue adding to the outstanding balances.

3. Here's the fun part. Your "extra money" should be first put into a savings account at your bank or credit union in order to build up a small cushion for any financial emergency that might arise. At a minimum, this cushion should be enough to pay a couple of months' worth of card payments in the event you run short at some point in the future.

4. Here's the even more fun part. Once you have enough money in your savings account, you should then put your extra money into a retirement savings plan. If one is available at work, by all means participate in that so that you can enjoy some tax savings and possibly a match from your employer. Absent a workplace plan, you can always start making monthly contributions to an IRA account.

5. If you are blessed with more abundant resources in the future, for example a raise or bonus at work or a cash gift from relatives, don't use this happy event as an excuse to increase your spending commensurate with the increase in income. Instead, put one third toward your credit cards, one third into retirement savings, and enjoy the remaining third.

If you conclude that paying off your credit cards later rather than sooner is a crazy idea, you're in good company. After all, this strategy results in higher interest charges and increases the time it takes to pay off your debts, blah, blah, blah. But there's a lot more to creating a wonderful financial future than simply making loan payments month in and month out. Those who have followed my strategy in the past have said that doing so has given them a much more optimistic outlook knowing that they're creating a future in addition to paying for the past. Some have told me that participating in their retirement savings plans for the first time motivated them to save even more each month.

For additional information on better credit card management, click on the reader Web site. **w w w**

> While eliminating credit card debt is an important goal, so is saving for a more secure future. Try to do both, even though it will take longer to pay off your credit card loans.

MONEY TIP

Managing Your Student Loans

If you have student loans, your payment coupon book may be thicker than an unabridged dictionary. No matter how large or small your loan balances might be, you should plan on how long you want to spend paying them off. You can consolidate the loans with a thirty-year repayment period, but who wants to take that long? There's no law against paying off student loans early. While at least some of the interest you pay on student loans may be tax deductible, the longer you take to pay off the loans, the higher the interest you pay.

What to do with extra money? If you're sailing along making timely payments on your student loans, the time may come when you have some extra money available either to make extra payments against the student loans or to contribute to a retirement savings plan at work, like a 401(k) or 403(b) plan. Which to do? If you have high-interest student loans, you may be better off adding the extra money to your regular payments. On the other hand, if your loan interest is not so high—less than 8 percent—you might want to put some or all of the extra money toward your retirement savings plan at work. At a minimum, you'll get a tax break for the money you kick in and if the employer offers a match, you'll get some free money to boot.

> ■
>
> *A banker is a fellow who lends his umbrella when the sun is shining and wants it back the minute it begins to rain.*
> —ANONYMOUS

IDEA 21

Getting Out of Debt Problems

There is no easy way out of debt problems, but you should first try to dig out from under your hill of bills yourself before taking more drastic action such as seeing a credit counselor or filing for personal bankruptcy. One way or another, you can and will emerge from your predicament. It's not the end of the world. In fact, many who have trod the well-worn path of overindebtedness emerge with much-improved money habits and a bright financial future. The best and most enduring financial lessons are often those hardest learned, I'm afraid.

First try to solve the problem yourself. Here are six steps you can take to solve your financial problems. There are no quick fixes; expect to endure some psychological and financial pain. But working through these problems yourself is preferable to the alternatives discussed later.

1. **Find out where you stand.** Summarize all of your debts, including the total amount due now, the amount due later, the amount overdue, and the minimum payment requirements.

2. **Prepare a bare-bones budget.** You must prepare a budget that cuts your living expenses to the bone so that you can meet your monthly loan-payment obligations. After housing payments and food, debt payments should be the third item in your emergency budget. If, like most people in your predicament, credit cards caused the problem, take the scissors to all but one or two cards, but don't close the accounts when you eventually pay them off, as that could negatively affect your credit report.

3. **Prioritize.** If you have many debts from different sources and you aren't sure that you'll be able to pay them all on time, prioritize. Work out a plan for paying the most important bills and for avoiding late charges. Missing an important bill might lead to your car being repossessed or to the shutting off of your electricity. Beyond meeting minimum payments for all your bills, pay off the bills with the highest interest rates (like credit cards) first.

4. **Speak with your creditors.** If you're unable to make a loan payment on time, contact the lender (before they contact you) to explain your circumstances and work out a payment plan. They may agree to grant you a temporary reduction or delay in payments, or they may waive your late charges. Don't expect them to work miracles, but if you keep lenders informed of your circumstances, many will be accommodating. Also, don't avoid calls or letters from creditors under any circumstances. Creditors would rather know that you are trying to work things out than fear that you are trying to evade your debt.

5. **Don't be easily seduced by debt consolidation loans.** The idea behind debt consolidation is that you take out one loan to cover all your debts. Paying only one loan in low monthly installments sounds like just what the debt doctor ordered—but this

may well be the kind of thinking that got you into credit trouble in the first place. Lower monthly payments usually extend the loan over a longer period of time. Moreover, consolidating loans often frees up your credit cards, leading to even more debt.

6. **Don't become a debt recidivist.** If you're able to repair your credit yourself, the time will come (it may seem like an eternity) when you will return to a firmer financial footing. Many people, armed with generous credit card limits once again, lapse back into their old free-spending ways. It's the equivalent of successful dieters subsequently regaining all their lost weight. But keeping good financial habits will pay off—and pay off big.

It's a lot easier to save when you know you'll get to keep the money, instead of feeling that it's all going toward paying off last year's binge. (If the cause of your debt problems was something beyond your control, you already know how important it is to save and will welcome the opportunity to resume saving.) It feels good to accumulate some savings, and if your finances catch the flu again, you'll be able to recover a lot faster. Remember, until you get into the habit of spending less than you earn—living beneath your means—you won't save a penny.

If you find that you are over your head in debt—beyond your ability to work out of it with your current income—speak with your creditors again. Contact each creditor and explain why you are overextended. They may be able to arrange an easier repayment plan. Many creditors will go along with a reasonable plan under which they will receive their money slowly if you show that you are trying to pay your debts, not avoiding them. Most creditors prefer doing this to repossessing the goods or taking you to court, which is time consuming and costs them more in the long run.

Next, try credit counseling. If you have financial problems that you can't resolve on your own, the next step is to consult a credit counselor. Various institutions offer such counseling, including many banks and credit unions, family service agencies, and nonprofit consumer-credit-counseling organizations. If you are slightly overextended, the agency will usually help you develop a repayment plan for a nominal monthly fee. The agency may take monthly payments from you and distribute them to your creditors. The agency also talks to the creditors and may get them to agree to a delayed or reduced payment. By the way, make sure that you are dealing with a credit counselor who is affiliated with a *nonprofit* consumer-credit-counseling service. There are a variety of charlatans out there who hold themselves out as credit counselors and have slick advertising campaigns but who will do nothing more than wreak further havoc on your predicament.

One important thing to remember: if you use a consumer-credit-counseling organization, it will be reported to the credit bureaus and noted on your credit record. That fact should not deter you from using a credit counseling service, particularly if your only other alternative is filing for bankruptcy. While you may ultimately have to resort to bankruptcy, give credit counseling a try first.

Personal bankruptcy, when all else fails. If you find that neither your own good efforts nor those of a credit counselor can salvage your situation, personal bankruptcy may be your only alternative. Some attorneys make it sound easy, but you should consider it only as a last resort. Bankruptcy is by no means the end of the world, but it will impede your access to credit for at least a few years.

For up-to-date information on dealing with debt problems and finding a legitimate credit counselor, visit the special reader Web site.

w w w

If you're chockablock with debt, don't avoid the problem. Take an organized approach to the challenge so that you can emerge with a bright financial future.

■

If it isn't the sheriff, it's the finance company; I've got more attachments on me than a vacuum cleaner.
—JOHN BARRYMORE

IDEA 22

Buffing Up Your Credit

If your credit rating could stand some burnishing, here's a to-do list that will help you do so. Don't expect a quick fix, but taking action now to improve you credit record will help make it easier to borrow in the future under more favorable terms.

First, check your credit reports for errors. You are entitled to request and receive a gratis (free) credit report once a year from each of the three credit bureaus—Equifax, TransUnion, and Experian. You may do so by visiting *www.annualcreditreport.com* or by calling (877) 322–8228 to request your three reports. Chances are you will have an error on at least one of the credit reports. Review each report carefully and follow the instructions for correcting any erroneous information on the dispute form that accompanies your report. The credit bureaus are required to investigate any items you dispute and correct any erroneous information on your report.

Second, pay your current obligations on time. Chances are that any besmirchments on your credit record are due to falling behind on making payments. While this information can remain on your credit report for many years, credit card companies and other lenders tend to forgive such sins if they happened sporadically in the past and your more recent record shows a nice string of on-time payments. So your most important assignment is to make on-time payments every month—early payments are even better, even if it's only minimum payments. If this is too much of a strain, review Idea 21, on page 69, for guidance working with your creditors or a credit counseling organization to devise a plan to help you better manage your debt repayments.

Third, take action to enhance your creditworthiness. The objective here is to be able to show the credit grantors that you are making steady progress at managing your financial obligations. Make sure that at least some of the companies that extend you credit report to the credit bureaus. Many may not, including banks and credit unions and gasoline card companies. Be particularly careful about managing the loan balances on those that do report. Keep the outstanding balances as low as possible, ideally under 50 percent of the maximum allowable loan. Eventually, though, you'll want to get into the habit of paying off the entire balance each month. While the credit grantors may not appreciate that habit—the scalawags—the credit bureaus will.

If you've had trouble paying off credit cards in the past, you may be tempted to return your card to the credit card company along with a few not-too-well-chosen words. But closing out accounts may negatively affect your credit, since the credit agencies consider the ratio of total debts to total available credit. So keep the paid-off card while remembering that there's no law that says you have to use it. In fact, the best way to retaliate against the credit card company is to not use the card. They don't collect any fees from the establishments that accept your card, and they don't collect any interest off you. If you eventually want to close out some charge accounts, do it slowly, starting with the most recently acquired accounts. You should keep your older accounts open because they show that you have a longer credit history.

Special note to those with a particularly checkered credit history. If you have had some severe problems in the past, perhaps including loan charge-offs or bankruptcy, don't despair. (If you had to file for personal bankruptcy, you're not alone. In the past decade, more than one out of every ten U.S. households went bankrupt.) You can reestablish your credit faster than you probably think. If you can't qualify for a traditional credit card, obtain a secured credit card. A secured credit card works just like a regular credit card except that any balances you run are secured by a deposit you have made with the credit card company. Also, open a savings account at your bank or credit union to demonstrate that you're working toward a better financial future and to show potential lenders that you've got some money set aside to pay off future obligations.

Most important, don't give up. Stories abound of people who have turned around an awful credit record in just a few years. Some have even qualified for a mortgage a mere three years after filing for bankruptcy!

The special reader Web site contains additional information and suggestions for improving your creditworthiness. **w w w**

Taking action to improve your credit standing will make it easier to achieve important financial goals in the future.

■

Nowadays people can be divided into three classes—
the Haves, the Have-Nots, and the
Have-Not-Paid-For-What-They-Haves.
—EARL WILSON

MONEY TIP

Need a Short-Term Loan? Borrow From Your IRA

If you need some extra money quickly, perhaps to pay income taxes or for an unexpected home or car repair, you can borrow from your IRA account once each year per account. As long as you redeposit the money in your IRA account within sixty days, no penalties or taxes are assessed. This once-per-year privilege applies to each IRA account if you have more than one. So if you have multiple IRA accounts, you could make a withdrawal more than once a year. But be careful. If you don't replenish your IRA within the sixty-day limit, you'll pay taxes on the distribution and, unless you're over age 59½, the withdrawal will also probably fall victim to a 10 percent penalty.

CHAPTER 5

Putting Money Away for a Prosperous Future

While successful financial planning requires attention to several important areas, including getting your debt under control and maintaining sufficient insurance coverage, none is more important than saving regularly and investing those savings wisely. It's easy to get discouraged because you don't think you're saving enough and are confused by the many available retirement accounts. This chapter will illustrate why even saving at a modest level can amass a considerable retirement nest egg. You'll also learn the best ways to invest your money to take maximum advantage of the tax breaks bestowed upon retirement savers.

IDEA 23

The Tortoise Beats the Hare: Getting Rich Slowly

How many times have you heard someone say that the most important thing you can do with your money is to contribute to all your available retirement plans **to the max?** Let's tote up how much that will set you back. The typical employee can contribute about $15,000 to a 401(k) or 403(b) retirement savings plan at work (more if age fifty or older), plus another $5,000 or $6,000 into an IRA. That comes to about $20,000 for a single person (or $40,000 for a dual-career couple). Well, that's just fine if you can spare a few hundred dollars a week that you know you won't need until after you retire. It's entirely understandable for people to say, "I can't spare the $385 a week that they say I need to save, so why even bother getting serious about saving for the future? I guess I'm consigned to spending my golden years working under the Golden Arches."

Hold on. Before envisioning a retirement spent working in the company of teenagers whose hormones are on overdrive, remember that nothing in your financial life involves an "either/or" decision. It's not a question of "either I save an amount that I can't afford to save or I'm destined for deprivation, so why save at all?" Instead, start saving an amount you can afford and build up from there as your income increases and you manage to get your living expenses under control. In fact, you may not need to save $385 a week to accumulate a big retirement stash.

Here's an illustration of how much you can amass if you start saving $100 a week, increasing that level by 5 percent each subsequent year, and invest the money smartly so that it grows an average of 8 percent per year.

THE $100 ROAD TO RICHES

Savings Period		Amount in the Kitty
15 years	=	$ 200,000
20 years	=	400,000
25 years	=	700,000
30 years	=	1,200,000
35 years	=	2,200,000
40 years	=	3,800,000

If you can spare a C note a week now, you may still be less sure about increasing that level of savings year in and year out. But it shouldn't be much of a challenge. After the first year, you need to increase your savings by a paltry five dollars a week—equivalent to a single designer latte a week. After the second year, at a 5 percent annual increase, you'll have to add another $5.25; after the third year, $5.75. That should be affordable. In fact, once you get the good feeling that comes from the savings habit, you'll probably want—and be able to afford—to add more than the small 5 percent annual increments.

If $100 a week is a bit (or a lot) more than you can part with now, start with less. The important thing is to make saving habitual. It's a good habit, and one that you're likely to want to continue and improve upon.

> Gradually increasing your savings can generate great wealth, even if you start small.

MONEY TIP

Both a Saver and an Investor Be

There's a whopping difference between "saving" and "investing." Saving regularly and investing those savings wisely are two important ingredients to achieving the financial security that all of us desire. It's important to recognize that these are two separate matters. Unless money mysteriously appears on your doorstep or you have the good fortune to have relatives who just give you money, you have to save (i.e., spend less money than you take in) in order to be able to invest. But some people who are pretty adept at saving aren't very good at investing or may think saving money and sticking it in some safe savings account is sufficient. Of course, saving and simply letting those savings sit in low-yield savings accounts is better than not saving at all. However, it's unlikely that you'll be able to achieve your financial dreams if your money doesn't grow at a rate that outpaces inflation—which it probably won't with savings accounts or CDs. If you're a bit queasy about investing your savings or you don't know anything about investing, chapter 6 will help you become a savvy investor and chapter 7 will show you how to be a very successful investor.

> ■
>
> *Remember that money is of a prolific generating nature. Money can beget money, and its offspring can beget more.*
> —BENJAMIN FRANKLIN

MONEY TIP

Advice for Those for Whom the Lottery Is Their Primary Retirement Plan

In some states the average annual lottery spending per capita (that includes children and infants) tops $700. That means a family of four would be spending $2,800 per year on the lottery to be average. Since many people see the lottery for what it really is, a government money grab primarily from those who can least afford it, they don't participate. That means a lot of families in our example are spending far more than $2,800. What a pity. If you want to spend a couple of bucks a week, that's fine. But too many people are sacrificing their future financial security on the slim hope that they'll somehow win the lottery, and they're usually in front of me in the convenience store checkout line carefully deliberating on the number they want to play or the scratch ticket they want to buy. Worse, whenever they cash in on a scratch ticket, do they pocket their winnings for future investment? Not a chance. They go back on line to buy more tickets.

IDEA 24

Making the Most of Money You're Going to Need Within a Few Years

While you clearly benefit from taking a long-term view when selecting and managing your investments, there are times when you need to be assured you can tap into some money in just a few months or in a year or two without risking a large loss in principal. Such situations may arise when, for example, college tuitions need to be paid, you're planning to buy a first or second home, you're planning home improvements, or another big-ticket item is on the horizon. (See chapter 9 for help in coping with big-ticket items.) The investment industry offers a couple of alternatives under the umbrella of "short-term investments" or, in Wall Street lexicon, "cash-equivalent investments," which usually pay decent interest with little or no risk that you'll lose principal. Both money market mutual funds and short-term-bond mutual funds offer okay, albeit unspectacular, returns with virtually no risk in the case of money funds, and with low risk of principal loss in the case of short-term-bond funds. CDs and U.S. Treasury bills are another possibility. They have a maturity date, but cashing them in before maturity if you have to shouldn't whack your principal very badly. By carefully comparing the yields offered by various short-term investment securities, you can make the most of your money. After all, why settle for a 2 percent return in a savings account when you may be able to get twice that or more in other safe, short-term investments? In fact, with many short-term investments you can change from one to another quickly and without concern about capital gains taxes or fees.

Finding the best returns. As opposed to stocks and bonds, short-term investments are pretty straightforward. With a little bit of effort, however, you can make the most of these otherwise mundane investments. Here are some suggestions to help you make the most of your short-term investments:

✓ **Shop for a CD.** If you're in the market for a CD, a little shopping around—even outside your hometown—could reap some rewards. First compare rates among banks in town; banks are in hot competition with each other these days. If you have a broker, check with him or her about CD offerings that the brokerage firm may have. Finally, several Web sites list the highest-yielding CDs in the country. Check the special reader Web site for a list. Remember, as long as the issuing bank is FDIC insured (or, if offered by a credit union, is backed by credit union insurance), you really shouldn't care where your CD comes from. You just want the best yield.

✓ **Compare money-market-fund yields.** If you have an account with a mutual fund or a broker offering several different kinds of money market funds, be sure to compare yields to make sure the one you select offers the best *after-tax* return. This may require you to periodically compare the returns among various money market funds, but, hey, if you can improve your return by periodically switching among money market funds, it's more money in your pocket.

✓ **Save on Treasury bill purchases.** If you regularly buy T-bills, consider buying them directly from the U.S. Treasury at no cost. Simply visit *www.savingsbonds.gov* for information and applications for buying Treasury securities online. If you don't want to go through the effort of buying T-bills online directly from the U.S. Treasury, compare the fees of your bank with those of your brokerage firm.

You may be able to afford to ignore the above. It's kind of a shame to have to consign some of your money to low-risk investments, because you do sacrifice some investment returns in exchange for safety. This begs the question, Can you afford to take more risk with the money? Say, for example, that you have a $25,000 tuition bill due next year. Ask yourself how badly you would be hurt if, say, a lousy stock market lopped 20 percent off the $25,000. If you have abundant other resources such that losing $5,000 or so of the tuition-earmarked money wouldn't be a big deal, rather than opting for a lower-yield short-term investment, as enumerated above, invest the money so that it has a chance to grow. True, you could lose some money, but since the stock market rises far more frequently than it falls, the odds of beating the returns of short-term-investments are with you

The *Grow Your Money!* reader Web site provides updated guidance on making the most of short-term money. **w w w**

> Unless you can afford to lose some principal, money that is going to be needed soon should be put into low-risk savings. But rather than consigning the money to low-interest savings accounts, shop for the best rates on safe investments that pay higher interest, including:
> ✦ Money market funds
> ✦ CDs
> ✦ Treasury bills
> ✦ Short-term-bond mutual funds
>
> ■
>
> *Life is tons of discipline.*
> —ROBERT FROST

IDEA 25

Preparing for a Financial Emergency Can Cost You Thousands

Your parents or other well-meaning individuals may have told you about the importance of maintaining an "emergency savings fund" of readily accessible money in case you need some cash fast. But keeping money in low- or no-interest accounts in order to have money available for a financial emergency that may never arise is both expensive and unnecessary.

Here's how much investment income you'll sacrifice by letting $5,000 languish in your checking account to pay for a potential financial emergency rather earning a 7 percent return by investing it:

Years	Investment Income Sacrificed
5	$ 2,000
10	10,000
20	14,000
30	33,000
40	70,000

What a waste of money! If you have an emergency savings fund, stop the madness! Invest the money in a mutual fund or other security that has a decent opportunity to grow over the years. At a minimum, put it in a money market fund or CD. Then if a true financial emergency arises (something you desperately want to buy that goes on sale does not constitute a financial emergency), you can get your hands on the money in a day or two without having to pay much, if anything, in penalties or taxes.

> Don't sacrifice investment income by putting money into a checking or low-yield account to prepare for a financial emergency.

IDEA 26

The Best Ways to Invest for Retirement

Choosing the best retirement plan accounts can be confusing. You may have several choices—perhaps more than you think. Depending on your circumstances, some retirement plan investments are superior to others. In general, any that permit you to contribute tax-deductible dollars are where your money should go first. If, on top of the tax deductibility, your employer offers matching dollars, all the better. But after you've contributed to all tax-deductible retirement plans for which you qualify, you'll still probably want to contribute to other tax-advantaged investments. The following priority list and notes should help you identify those tax-advantaged investment accounts and investments that are best for you:

Retirement Plan Priority List

1. Best — Employer plan with a match

2. Next best Unmatched employer plan or Roth IRA (tie)

3. Next — Self-employed plan (see Idea 30, on page 93, for the best self-employed plans)

4. Next — Deductible traditional IRA

5. Next — Nondeductible traditional IRA

6. Next — Buying and holding individual stocks and real estate

7. Next — Tax-deferred annuities

Notes

✦ **Employer plan with a match.** "Free money." That's what you get when your employer matches a portion of your 401(k) or 403(b) contribution. Indeed, if you eschew the employer match, you're one sandwich short of a picnic. If you're just starting out saving for retirement and your employer offers a match, this is a great way to jump-start your investing.

✦ **Unmatched employer plan.** If your employer doesn't offer a match, contributing to an unmatched plan will still garner you some income tax savings. If your employer does offer a match, you're well advised to still participate beyond the level where the match ends.

✦ **Roth IRA.** The Roth IRA is listed as a "tie" with an unmatched employer plan in the Retirement Plan Priority List. Debate rages among those who worry about such things as to which is preferable. Here's my take: At a minimum, contribute to any workplace plan up to the match level. After that, make unmatched contributions if you can use the tax break. Otherwise, and if you qualify, consider making a Roth IRA contribution, which doesn't entitle you to an immediate tax break but offers substantial benefits later on, since all withdrawals from the Roth will likely be tax-free. Ideally, and hopefully you can work your way up to this, you should do both— make unmatched employer-plan contributions and, if you qualify, make Roth IRA contributions as well. (If you're one of the many who are befuddled by Roth IRA **contributions** versus Roth IRA **conversions,** see Idea 28, on page 88.

✦ **Self-employed plan.** Whether you work for yourself full-time or earn even a smidgen of part-time self-employment income, the tax gods bestow great benefits on those who contribute to self-employed retirement plans. Idea 30, on page 93, will help you select the best self-employed retirement plan.

✦ **Deductible traditional IRA.** If you qualify for a deductible traditional IRA, making a contribution will save taxes now and avoid taxes later on until you begin making withdrawals. While a Roth IRA contribution is a better choice if you also qualify for one, opt instead for the deductible IRA if you need the immediate tax savings.

✦ **Nondeductible traditional IRA.** Just about everyone who earns income from a job or who has a spouse who is in the workforce can make a nondeductible IRA contribution (see Idea 29, on page 92). While you don't get an immediate tax break, the ability to defer taxes on income and capital gains earned in the IRA account more than justifies making a contribution. By the way, if you are over age seventy and still in the workforce, you can't contribute to a traditional IRA, but, if you qualify, you can still contribute to a Roth IRA.

✦ **Buying and holding individual stocks and real estate.** While not often considered in the context of tax-advantaged retirement savings plans, buying and holding individual stocks and real estate provide the same tax-deferral benefits as the garden-variety retirement plans. Why, you might ask? Because the tax regulations permit capital gains from stocks (not stock mutual funds) and investment real estate to be deferred until the investment is sold. In fact, these investments offer an advantage over retirement plans in that they are not subject to often-onerous regulations. For example, you can liquidate any individually held stock and real estate holdings before age 59½ without incurring early withdrawal penalties, and you don't have to begin making minimum required distributions when you turn 70½.

✦ **Tax-deferred annuities.** Tax-deferred annuities are last on the list. While you may benefit from a tax-deferred annuity as part of your retirement savings arsenal, these should generally be considered only after the aforementioned retirement plans have been and will continue to be fully funded.

Be sure to check out the special reader Web site for the latest information on qualification rules and contribution limits for the various retirement savings plans and investments. **w w w**

Chances are you qualify to contribute to a variety of retirement savings plans. Some plans offer more advantages than others, and choosing the more advantageous plans can add considerably to your retirement nest egg.

Earn a little, spend a little—less.
—JOHN STEVENSON

IDEA 27

Saddled with a Lousy 401(k) Plan?
Roll Your 401(k) Plan Into an IRA After You Turn 59½

If you're stuck with a mediocre 401(k) plan, and heaven knows a lot of employees are, there may be a glimmer of hope. Many plans allow workers who are at least age 59½ to roll their 401(k) plan investments into an IRA of the employee's choosing while continuing to participate in their company's 401(k) plan. So if you're over age 59½, you're unhappy with your plan choices, and you're comfortable with the greater investment choice offered by an IRA, ask your plan administrator if you can do an IRA rollover with the money you have accumulated in the plan. Of course, you should continue to participate in the plan thereafter, but at least you will have moved a good chunk of the money away from the clunkers into more productive investments.

> If you have poor retirement plan investment choices at work and are over age 59½, you may be able to sow that money in greener pastures.

MONEY TIP

Investing in Your Employer's Stock?
Stock Purchase Plan, Okay; 401(k) Plan, Not

If you work for a company whose stock is publicly traded, it's way too risky to put more than a dollop of company stock in your 401(k) plan, and if you have done so or are forced to do so, federal regulations enable you to lighten up either immediately or after a couple of years, at most. The financial fortunes of some loyal employees have and will continue to be decimated by a plunging stock, à la Worldcom and Enron. Not only did many employees of failed companies lose most of their retirement savings, but they lost their jobs to boot. If you want to own the stock (after all, you're an insider), do so through the company's stock-purchase plan. Many plans offer the stock at a discount that is too good to pass up even if you sell the stock shortly thereafter. Unless you have a tremendous amount of money, though, try to limit your holdings of a single stock—your employer's stock or any single stock, for that matter—to 10 percent to 20 percent of your total investment holdings. Then if the bottom falls out of the share price, you won't have to work an extra couple of decades to make up for the loss.

IDEA 28

Should You Make a Roth IRA Conversion?

Roth IRA conversions were the rage when they were introduced in 1998, but since then they have fallen off the radar screen. That's too bad, because many people who stand to benefit from Roth conversions fail to take advantage of them. True, they cost money, and the penurious will naturally need some strong convincing to take the plunge, so get ready for some persuading. But first, definitions may be in order. There are really two species of Roth IRA:

Roth IRA contributions. A Roth IRA contribution is similar to an old-fashioned nondeductible traditional IRA contribution, with one big difference. While both are made with after-tax dollars (in English, that means you don't get a tax deduction for the contribution), withdrawals from Roth IRAs are generally entirely tax free, including any growth in value of the investments. In contrast, that growth would be taxed when withdrawals are made from a nondeductible traditional IRA. Another advantage of a Roth IRA is that you don't have to begin making minimum required distributions beginning at age 70½. Therefore, if you can afford it, you could let all that Roth money grow for the rest of your life and pass on an obscene amount of money to your heirs. That's the good news. The bad news is that there are income limitations that preclude a lot of people from making Roth IRA contributions. For more information on where Roth IRAs may fit in your retirement savings arsenal, see Idea 26, on page 83.

Roth IRA conversions. In addition to making annual contributions to a Roth IRA account, the tax rules also permit many people who already have traditional IRAs to convert them into Roth IRAs and enjoy all of the subsequent bennies noted above for Roth IRA contributions. That's the good news. The bad news is that you'll have to pay taxes on everything you convert except the original value of any nondeductible IRA contributions you made along the way. But that's not such bad news, since you'll be able to withdraw the Roth money later totally free of federal income taxes. Even if you don't have a traditional IRA now, you may in the future when you roll over your company retirement savings plans when you change jobs or retire. You're never too old to consider a Roth conversion, and many retirees stand to reap substantial benefits from doing so.

Should you consider a Roth IRA conversion? While everyone's situation is different, the following guidelines will help you make the right decision on a Roth IRA conversion, if you qualify under the stringent income restrictions. But don't be discouraged if you don't qualify for a Roth conversion now. Hope is on the horizon (2010, see the end of this Idea).

The younger you are when you convert to a Roth IRA (as well as make annual contributions to a Roth), the better. But it's probably never too late to consider a conversion, even if you're already retired. Here are three important matters to consider:

1. **How long will it be before you expect to make withdrawals from a Roth?** A Roth conversion will probably work if you don't need to tap into the money for at least ten years, but the longer you can wait, the more tax-deferred, tax-free growth you'll be able to enjoy. This means that even retirees may benefit

from a Roth conversion, because a sizable portion of the money you have in traditional IRAs when you retire won't be accessed for at least ten years, since you're planning for a retirement of thirty years or more, aren't you? (If all of your IRA money is likely to be needed within a decade, you may be in trouble.) By converting this traditional IRA money to a Roth IRA now, you'll enjoy a higher after-tax income in your later retirement years.

2. **Do you expect to be in the same or higher tax bracket when you're retired?** If so, the Roth should be beneficial. If you expect to be in a lower tax bracket (most retirees won't be), then a Roth conversion (or Roth contribution, for that matter) may not be worthwhile.

3. **Can you afford to pay the taxes due from the Roth conversion with money that is outside your retirement accounts?** It doesn't make sense to take money out of retirement accounts (which will be subject to taxes and, perhaps, penalties) to pay the taxes due from a Roth conversion. You'll need to have enough nonretirement-account money to be able to pay the taxes.

All in all, you have a lot to gain by considering a Roth IRA conversion, but you need to do some homework first. If you have a tax adviser, make an appointment. Most financial services firms, including banks, brokerage firms, and mutual fund companies offer worksheets and software on their Internet sites. By using these resources, you can figure out how much you stand to benefit from a Roth IRA conversion. Chances are, you'll find that a Roth IRA conversion will reward you with a higher retirement income. Though the younger you are, the more time you'll have to allow the Roth IRA to work its magic, Roth IRA conversions can work even for people in their sixties and seventies. Consider the following examples of what happens when three different people make Roth IRA conversions at differing stages of life:

Examples of the power of a Roth conversion. Here are three examples of how much more income accrues to those who make Roth conversions (when compared with leaving the money in a traditional IRA):

Example	Years Until Commencing Withdrawals	Number of Withdrawal Years	Higher Income From Roth Conversion
1.	30 years	25 years	25%
2.	20 years	10 years	20%
3.	10 years	20 years	15%

Here's an explanation of the first example. Someone who makes a Roth conversion thirty years in advance of beginning withdrawals and who expects to withdraw the Roth money over twenty-five years will enjoy a 25 percent higher after-tax income than she would have had the money been left in the traditional IRA. These examples take into account the effect of the taxes that had to be paid when the Roth conversion took place.

The third example shows that even a retiree can boost his income from a Roth conversion. Someone who has recently retired figures he can get by on other resources, like traditional IRAs and Social Security, without tapping into the Roth IRA for ten years, after which he figures he'll withdraw it over two decades. This later-life Roth IRA conversion will boost his after-tax income by 15 percent compared with his income had he left the money in a traditional IRA.

Roth conversions for all, beginning in 2010. If you earn too much money to qualify for a Roth IRA conversion, be patient. Starting in 2010, Roth conversions can be made without any income limitations. Even Bill Gates will qualify! This could be an opportunity that's simply too good to pass up.

The special reader Web site will keep you up-to-date on the current rules pertaining to Roth IRA conversions. **w w w**

> Converting traditional IRAs into a Roth IRA is often an outstanding way to increase your retirement income, despite the taxes you'll have to pay when you make the conversion. Beginning 2010, Roth IRA conversions will be permitted regardless of your income.

IDEA 29

Yes, Virginia, You Do Qualify for an IRA Contribution

Whether they're given bad advice, just don't understand, or are looking for an excuse not to part with the money, many workers forgo making IRA contributions on the incorrect grounds that they don't qualify for them. The rules state that if you have job income or your spouse has job income, you qualify for an IRA. Even people over age 70½ who are still working may qualify to make a Roth IRA contribution. So, if you or your spouse has a job or earns income from self-employment, repeat the following three times: "I can make an IRA contribution." No matter how many other retirement plans you have or how lofty your income may be, you can do an IRA. If you're fortunate enough to have a very high income, you may not be able to qualify for a tax-deductible or Roth IRA, but you can still do a nondeductible IRA. IRA contributions can and should be an important part of your retirement savings, particularly if your workplace plan choices are limited or your employer doesn't offer a plan. (See Idea 26, on page 83, for guidance on deciding which plans are best for you.)

Find the latest IRA qualification rules on the special reader Web site. **w w w**

> Almost anyone who is still breathing can contribute to an IRA.
>
> ■
>
> *He who will not economize will have to agonize.*
> —CONFUCIUS

IDEA 30

Retirement Plans for the Self-Employed Simplified

You don't need to have your own full-time business to take advantage of self-employed retirement plans. If you moonlight or just work part-time, self-employed retirement plans offer great tax benefits. In fact, if you can spare the money, you may be able to put **100 percent** of your net profit from self-employment into a plan and deduct it to boot. There are several plans from which to choose, but three are at the head of the class and work especially well if you have no other employees. If you're in the market for a self-employed plan, chances are one of them is just right for you.

1. **SEP Plan.** A SEP plan, that's an abbreviation for "Simplified Employee Pension" plan, is often the best choice, particularly if you are newly self-employed or your income from self-employment is pretty modest. Think of a SEP as a self-employed retirement plan with training wheels. You can always move on to two-wheeler (self-employed 401(k)) or a rocket (defined-benefit plan) later on. The main attraction of a SEP is, as the name implies, simplicity. There is very little paperwork involved and there are no annual tax reporting requirements. That's because a SEP is considered an IRA by our friends at the Internal Revenue Service (hence, the common moniker "SEP-IRA"). Special benefit for procrastinators: Most self-employed retirement plans need to be set up by December 31, although contributions can be made

up to the time of filing the return. But a SEP can be set up (and funded) after the end of the tax year. Another clear advantage of a SEP is that annual contributions are discretionary. If you run short in a particular year and have no money to contribute or have to cut back on the amount you contribute to your SEP, no problem. SEP contribution limits are very generous, capping out at over $40,000, which is a lot for most of us. On the other hand, if you can afford to put away even more, consider the other two self-employed plans described below.

2. **Self-employed 401(k).** The self-employed 401(k), also called a solo 401(k), requires a bit more paperwork (your brokerage firm or mutual fund company may have gratis prototype plans) and must be set up by December 31, but it allows you to put more money into the plan than a SEP. In fact, up to certain limits you can put as much as 100 percent of your net income from self-employment into the plan, which could be particularly appropriate for those who moonlight and can afford to put away all or a substantial portion of their self-employment income. Finally, the level of annual contributions is discretionary and you can generally borrow (if you must) from your self-employed 401(k) plan.

3. **Defined-benefit plan.** While the annual contribution limits for SEP-IRAs and self-employed 401(k) plans are generous, they're chump change compared with what you can put away and deduct in a defined-benefit (DB) plan. But the ability to shelter literally hundreds of thousands of dollars from Uncle Sam each year comes at a price. A DB plan has to be set up by an actuary (the joke goes that actuaries are people who are too boring to be accountants) no later than December 31 and require lots of annual paperwork and tax filings, all of which require annual fees. What's more, contributions are not discretionary, so, depending on how the plan is structured, you may have to make contribu-

tions in years when you have no or much-reduced self-employment income. So, despite the potential for gargantuan tax deductions, opting for a defined-benefit plan requires some careful forethought. DB plans work especially well for those who have high income from self-employment (six figures at least) and can expect to maintain a high income level. These high-octane plans are particularly appropriate for persons in their fifties or older who want—and can afford—to create a substantial retirement purse in a short period of time.

Your special reader Web site contains guidance on other retirement plans for those who have income from full- or part-time self-employment, as well as up-to-date information on the features, regulations, and contribution limits of self-employed plans. **w w w**

Which Self-Employed Retirement Plan Is Best for You?

❑ **SEP.** Easy to set up and maintain; flexible; best first-time plan.

❑ **Self-employed 401(k).** Easy to maintain and flexible; higher deductions than a SEP.

❑ **Defined benefit.** Very high deductions, but can cost thousands to set up and maintain; best for those with high self-employment income that is likely to continue indefinitely.

> If you ever have income from full- or part-time self-employment, be sure to take advantage of the very generous tax breaks available to those who contribute to self-employed retirement plans.

IDEA 31

Smart (and Painless) Ways to Add to Your Investments

Human nature often gets in the way of the dual tasks of saving and investing. Saving is difficult enough, and once you've saved, it takes yet more effort to put those savings to work for you. But there are a pair of ways to easily accomplish both tasks without having to lift a finger. Both of them involve electronic transfers of money to an investment account. Ah, better living through electronics:

1. **Automatic withdrawal.** If you participate in a retirement savings plan at work, you're already benefiting from automatic withdrawal, since the money is taken out of your paycheck and invested on your behalf. It's also easy to request an increase in the amount of money that's going into the plan. Go for it! If and when you begin to build up your investments outside your employer's plan, keep in mind that most mutual fund companies and brokerage firms also allow you to invest automatically. You specify a fixed amount to be withdrawn at regular intervals from your bank or credit union account, and voilà, the money is moved into your investment account. Your employer may also permit money to be withdrawn from your paycheck and automatically transferred to an IRA or brokerage account. It's a great way to begin and stick with a regular investing program. For example, a lot of people who have the best of intentions about contributing to an IRA every year have trouble coming up with the cash to make a contribution. The cash is just, well, gone. Solve that problem by having money withdrawn each month and automatically put into the IRA account.

2. **Automatic reinvestment.** You can also take a page from your workplace retirement plan—which automatically reinvests interest, dividends, and capital gains—by arranging to have the same done for money held outside your 401(k), 403(b), tax-sheltered an-

nuity, or other retirement savings plan at work. This can work for any mutual funds, exchange-traded fund, or dividend-paying stocks that you own. Just make sure you don't have to pay a fee for the privilege. One other caveat: if you're reinvesting investment income in a brokerage account (as opposed to a retirement account), you'll have to pay income taxes on that income, even though you didn't receive it in cash. However, that's a very small impediment to doing the right thing by automatically reinvesting.

It's a good thing. Investing regularly and painlessly through automatic withdrawal and/or automatic reinvestment is easy to do. It's also a very smart thing to do. While you may not realize it, you're actually dollar-cost averaging, which has been hailed since before your parents were born as one of the best ways to add to your investments. Dollar-cost averaging involves investing a fixed amount in a particular investment—a mutual fund or stock—on a regular basis. The trick is to stick with your plan regardless of whether the investment value rises or falls. Because you're investing a fixed amount at fixed intervals, your dollars buy fewer shares when the stock or mutual fund price is high and more when it is low. The typical investor does the opposite, preferring to buy more when the price is high and getting rid of an investment that has declined in value. That's why the average investor barely makes money, while you, the disciplined automatic investor, will do very well.

For more information on automatic investment, including helpful Internet resources, visit the reader Web site. **w w w**

The best way to get rich by saving regularly is to have your retirement and other savings contributions electronically moved to your investment accounts.

■

The greatest things ever done on earth have been done little by little.
—THOMAS GUTHRIE

IDEA 32

Free at Last: Deciding What to Do with Your
Retirement Savings Plan When You Change Jobs

The days of spending an entire career working for the same employer
are pretty much over. In the old days, a nice pension plan was ample
reason to stick with a single employer. But employers by the thousands
are terminating their defined-benefit plans and substituting them (or
even where defined-benefit plans are still provided, augmenting them)
with defined-contribution plans like 401(k)s and 403(b)s, which are
also the staple of employers who never offered a pension plan.

The advantage of defined-contribution plans is that they're portable—
you can take the money with you when you change jobs. Easy enough,
but what's the best way to transfer those valuable resources? It's not all
that complicated, but some pitfalls await the uninformed.

❏ If you want to impair your future financial security . . .

Some people, actually many people, simply cash out their 401(k),
403(b), or other workplace plan when they change jobs. This is
hugely shortsighted (unless you're facing foreclosure, personal bankruptcy, or some other financial calamity), and I don't want to sully
these pages with any discussion of this alternative. Rather, I'll provide an example of how cashing out—even a relatively small amount
of money—can mess up your financial future. A thirty-five-year-old
has accumulated $25,000 in a company 401(k) plan. To reward him-
self for the job change, he decides to cash out the plan investments
to buy a $25,000 car. That's too bad. First, after paying income taxes
and a 10 percent early withdrawal penalty, he nets only about
$16,000. But that's nothing compared with the income he'll sacrifice
in retirement. Had he left the money in the 401(k) plan or rolled it
over into an IRA and never added another cent, in thirty years this
paltry $25,000 alone would have amassed enough money to pay him
$12,000 ($5,500 in current dollars) a year for the rest of his life.

❏ **If you like your former employer's plan . . .**

When it comes to making financial decisions, sometimes the best thing to do is nothing. If you're comfortable with your former employer's plan, and it offers some decent investment choices, you will probably be allowed to keep it there. Also, leaving it with your former employer buys you some time to weigh other alternatives that will be described next.

❏ **If you like your new employer's plan . . .**

If your new employer's plan permits rollovers, you can always move the money into that plan. Since you'll be participating in the new employer's plan anyway, consolidating your former workplace plan with the new one will simplify your investment decision-making.

There may be a couple of other advantages for you to keeping your money in a 401(k), 403(b), or similar non-IRA retirement account:

✓ These plans offer the highest level of protection from creditors. (The protection accorded to IRA plan holdings depends on state law.)

✓ Depending on the rules of a particular plan, loans may be available. (Loans of greater than sixty days are not permitted from IRAs [see page 75.])

❏ **If you prefer to manage the money on your own or want more choice . . .**

Rolling the money in your former employer's plan into a traditional IRA is a popular choice, particularly among those who prefer to manage the money on their own or who have an investment adviser who is up to the task. (Unfortunately, you cannot transfer the money directly into a Roth IRA.) You might also opt for a rollover into an IRA if the breadth and quality of both your former and current employers' plans are wanting. Unfortunately, far too many workplace retirement plans offer just a handful of choices, many of which range from mediocre to awful, whereas an IRA account may offer literally thousands of choices. Depending upon how comfortable you are with investing, having that many choices may be either a blessing or a curse. If having so many choices is daunting, you can always invest the money in a "life cycle" fund that does all the selection and diversification and rebalancing work for you. (See Idea 39, on page 125.)

Here are a pair of additional advantages of rolling over your plan to an IRA:

✓ An IRA offers easier access to your retirement money once you begin making withdrawals compared with a workplace plan.

✓ Once money is in a traditional IRA, it can be converted to a Roth IRA if you qualify. If you are contemplating a Roth IRA conversion (see Idea 28, on page 88), avoid transferring the money to your new employer's plan, since you probably won't be able to move the money into an IRA before you leave your new job.

Logistics. Whatever choice you make, if you're moving the money, be sure it qualifies as a "direct rollover." A direct rollover involves either a transfer directly from the plan administrator to the new plan or IRA account or a check sent to you but made out to the new plan or IRA account (which you should forward to the new plan or account within 60 days). Ask the firms that manage your old (and new) plan for help if you're unsure how to do this.

Finally, your choice may be tempered by any redemption fees that may be assessed by making a particular transfer. Chances are there will be no redemption fees, but you should check, particularly if you work in a nonprofit organization, where, shamefully, some of the plans assess redemption fees to keep you tethered to what is likely to be a pretty dismal plan in the first instance.

Opportunity awaits job changers who make wise decisions about the disposition of any workplace retirement savings plans, like 401(k) or 403(b) plans.

MONEY TIP

What's Your Number?

Do you know your "number"? Americans love a shortcut, and when it comes to putting money away for the future, we become fixated on our "number." That is the amount of money you will supposedly need to amass in order to be able to afford to retire. The media and many investment companies like to use numbers to scare the daylights out of you. They suggest that people who are about to retire need at least $1 million in the kitty in order to have any hope of averting starvation later on. Of course, $5 million is better; it will allow you to be, in the words of one publication, "beer and pretzels rich." Talk about sleep depriving.

First, if you don't achieve the mythical number don't conclude that you'll be condemned to a retirement replete with deprivation. Most people, including the vast majority of current retirees, can retire quite nicely on far less than what some news article or TV talking head says they'll need. Second, rather than obsessing over what you need to do to achieve some number, focus instead on the basics of sound financial planning as presented throughout *Grow Your Money!*

■

Annual income twenty pounds, annual expenditure nineteen ninety-six, result happiness. Annual income twenty pounds, annual expenditure twenty pounds ought and six, result misery.
—CHARLES DICKENS

CHAPTER 6

Becoming a Savvy Investor

Investing wisely and well is essential to achieving your financial dreams. In this chapter and the chapter that follows, you will find a plethora of ideas and tips that help you become a better investor, whether you're a neophyte or fancy yourself an investment pro. Of all the important financial matters that must be attended to—from paying off debt to securing insurance, from meeting college costs to planning for retirement—investing is the one area that requires regular attention. But don't think that investing is too complicated, however. You'll find in the pages that follow that it isn't. In fact, this is a great time to be an investor, because there are so many great ways to invest even a small amount of money.

IDEA 33

Create a World-Class Investment Portfolio with Just Six Investments

Diversification, which means spreading your money around among a number of different investments in order to reduce the risk of big losses, is arguably the most important element of successful investing, but too many investors (and their advisers) don't pay enough attention to it. That's a shame, because it's not that complicated. In fact, you can assemble a world-class well-diversified investment portfolio with just six mutual funds:

1. **Large-company stock fund.**

2. **Mid-sized-company stock fund.**

3. **Small-company stock fund.**

4. **International stock fund.**

5. **Corporate bond fund.**

6. **U.S. government bond fund.**

If you need some help understanding the nomenclature, some information on each of these categories follows:

✦ **Large-company stock.** *Large-company* (or *large-cap*) mutual funds invest in stocks of the large, well-established companies, generally those with a value on the stock exchange (*market capitalization* or *market cap*) greater than $10 billion. Because of their large size, large-cap stocks are not expected to grow in value as rapidly as mid-sized and smaller companies. But because of their relative stability compared with other stock categories, investors are well-advised to include large-company stocks in their investment portfolios. When stock prices decline, large-company stocks, which often pay dividends, tend to decline less than other stock categories.

✦ **Mid-sized-company stock.** *Mid-cap* stocks are stocks of medium-sized companies with market caps ranging from $2 billion to $10 billion. Like *small-cap* stocks, they offer growth potential, but they also offer some of the stability of larger companies. They tend to grow well over the long term.

✦ **Small-company stock.** Investors own *small-company* (or *small-cap*) stocks (companies valued at under $2 billion) for their growth potential. Many of these companies are relatively new. How they will do in the market is often difficult to predict. Because of their small size, changes in company fortunes can affect stock prices dramatically—both upward and downward. If successful, these investments can generate significant gains.

✦ **International stock.** *International stocks* are stocks of foreign companies. Some trade on U.S. stock exchanges as "American Depository Receipts" (ADRs), but the majority must be purchased on overseas stock exchanges. Adding international stocks to an investment portfolio enhances diversification, since there many excellent overseas companies that are benefiting from a booming world economy. And since the world doesn't move in lockstep, these companies can do well even when the U.S. economy is in the doldrums.

✦ **Corporate bonds.** As the name so clearly suggests, these are bonds issued by corporations. Based on the financial strength of the issuing corporation, there are two categories of corporate bonds and the mutual funds that invest in them: *investment-grade corporate bonds,* which are higher-quality corporate bonds and provide interest income with limited risk, and *high-yield corporate bonds,* which are issued by weaker companies. The latter (called "junk bonds" in less polite company) pay higher interest, but the risk of default—in other words, possibly losing your original investment— is also higher.

✦ **U.S. government bonds.** Backed by the full faith and credit of the U.S. government, these offer total protection from bond default, although the value of government bonds will fluctuate with interest rates, like all bonds and bond funds. There are a couple of types of U.S. government bonds: U.S. Treasury bonds (most issues are actually called treasury "notes" rather than "bonds") are the best known. A second category of U.S. government bond is mortgage-backed securities, such as those issued by the Government National Mortgage Association (GNMA or, phonetically, "Ginnie Mae"). There are also agency bonds issued by various government agencies.

✦ **Municipal bonds.** While municipal bonds were left out of the "gang of six" investments, they may be appropriate if you're in a high tax bracket and you want to invest in a nonretirement brokerage account. The primary attraction of municipal bonds is that the interest they pay is generally not subject to federal income tax. Since municipal-bond-fund prices do not appear in the daily papers and the bonds are inconvenient for the individual investor to buy and manage, municipal-bond mutual funds are a useful way to invest in municipal bonds while avoiding these problems. Interest earned from bonds issued in the investor's own state, including from so-called "single-state municipal-bond funds," is generally free of both federal and state income taxes.

Now that you understand the various investment categories, let's turn our attention to how your investment might be divided among those six categories. The following table shows how it might be allocated to achieve a nicely balanced and diversified portfolio of 60 percent in stocks and 40 percent in bonds. Incidentally, an allocation of 60 percent in stocks (spread out among various types of stocks) and 40 percent in bonds (spread out among various types of bonds) has long been considered an excellent starting point for those—and that includes you—who need to decide how they will diversify their investments.

INVESTMENT DIVERSIFICATION ILLUSTRATION

Large-company stock fund	25%
Mid-sized-company stock fund	10
Small-company stock fund	10
International stock fund	<u>10</u>
Subtotal stock funds	<u>60</u>
Corporate bond fund	20
U.S. government bond fund	<u>20</u>
Subtotal bond funds	<u>40</u>
Total	<u>100</u>%

There are several ways to put together a well-diversified portfolio using

+ actively managed mutual funds (see Idea 34, on page 107),

+ index funds or exchange-traded funds (see Idea 38, on page 121),

+ lifestyle or target funds (see Idea 39, on page 125),

+ individual stocks and bonds (see Idea 43, on page 139),

. . . or a combination of the above.

You can do very well diversifying among the six investment categories. If you want to do even better, consider some additional investments described in Idea 45, on page 144.

The *Grow Your Money!* special reader Web site offers up some excellent mutual funds in all six categories. **w w w**

> You can invest like the pros with a diversified portfolio of a mere six investments.
>
> ◼
>
> *Don't gamble! Take all your savings and buy some good stock and hold it 'til it goes up, then sell it. If it don't go up, don't buy it.*
> —WILL ROGERS

IDEA 34

Making the Most of Your Mutual Fund Investments

Mutual funds have long been a great way to invest, whether (a) you or your adviser takes an active role or (b) you prefer to sit back and, in the case of autopilot funds, let others do all the work (see Idea 39, on page 125) or (c) you're quite content earning solid returns with unmanaged index funds and exchange-traded funds (ETFs) (see Idea 38, on page 121).

The garden-variety mutual fund offers a low-cost, professionally managed diversified pool of stocks, bonds, or other investments. But not all mutual funds are alike. Here are some important matters to consider when you go shopping for the best funds:

✦ Always know what types of investments are inside your mutual funds. Do they contain stocks, bonds, or cash investments (like U.S. Treasury bills or large-denomination bank CDs)?

✦ Understand risk. Stocks are riskier than bonds. Bonds are riskier than cash investments (U.S. Treasury bills, bank CDs, and the like).

✦ Evaluate your goals and how long you have to invest. Are you saving for retirement, or are you socking away money for the short term to build up your cash reserves? If you're already retired, you may think you should be investing for the short term. But keep in mind that you should plan, financially at least, to have your money support you until your nineties. So you'll always need some money in stocks. You want your money to grow to keep up with inflation. Bonds and cash investments don't provide much, if any, growth.

✦ The longer the time period you have ahead of you to invest, the more money you can safely keep in riskier investments like stocks. That's because you have more time to make back any losses.

✦ It's hard to go wrong investing in funds that assess low costs and deliver strong returns without taking a lot of risk. The lowest-cost funds are often no-load funds (these are funds that can be purchased without a sales or redemption charge). You can buy no-load funds directly through a mutual fund company's toll-free number or on the Internet. But whether you buy funds on your own or through an investment adviser or through your retirement savings plan at work, be sure you don't neglect the "expense ratio" (annual fees as a percentage of fund investments). Higher fund expenses can be a drag on investment profits.

✦ Compare fund returns year by year, as well as the average annual return over three-year, five-year, and ten-year periods. Identify funds that show consistent returns.

✦ Compare how the fund has performed versus the performance of its peers and that of a comparable market index. One of the most popular stock market indexes is the Standard & Poor's 500, affectionately known as the S&P 500. Aim for the lowest-cost fund with the most consistent performance that has stood up well against both similar funds and their benchmark indexes. There are lots of funds that meet those criteria, but it does take a bit of digging to find them.

✦ Avoid investing in several mutual funds that own the same stocks or bonds.

✦ Mutual funds that invest in stocks in a single industry or a single country should not comprise a major portion of your holdings. Opt instead for funds that cast a wide net. Avoid putting too much of your money in funds that invest in a narrow market sector.

✦ Invest in different types of funds with different levels of risk to create a less risky batch of investments overall. This is known as "diversification." (See Idea 33, on page 102.) Diversification is the key to boosting performance while insulating your overall investment performance from suffering big losses in a down market.

✦ Consider automatic dollar-cost averaging or having money taken out of your checking or savings account periodically to invest in mutual funds. This way, you're buying more shares when prices are low as explained in Idea 31, on page 96. You may already be doing this with your retirement savings plan at work.

✦ Keep tabs on the performance of your mutual funds in relation to other similar funds, at least annually. Also, make sure you're well diversified. Once you've achieved this admirable goal, you needn't panic when any of the markets fall out of bed. You'll have plenty of other investments to cushion the blow.

✦ The Internet is a great source for information on mutual funds, including the fund screens that can help you pick funds based on the type of fund, its fees, and its performance.

Visit the special reader Web site at your convenience for Internet sites and information of interest to mutual fund investors. **w w w**

> The more you understand about mutual funds, the sooner
> you will be able to achieve your investment goals.
>
> ■
>
> *Anyone who thinks there's safety in numbers hasn't*
> *looked at the stock market pages.*
> —IRENE PETER

IDEA 35

Idle Cash Need Not Earn Paltry Returns

Check out how much interest you're earning on any idle cash you have sitting in a bank or brokerage account. If you don't like what you see, you can probably earn a better return without switching to another institution.

✦ **If you've got money in a bank or credit union.** Most, but not all, banks and credit unions pay a laughable rate of interest on cash residing in checking or savings accounts. For example, I recently received an e-mail from someone who had $75,000 in a savings account earning just one-half percent interest. My recommendation to this poor soul is the same as it is to you: move the money into a six-month or one-year CD unless you are absolutely certain you're going to need it within a short period of time.

✦ **If you've got money in a brokerage or mutual fund account.** Hopefully, any idle cash in your brokerage or mutual fund account is automatically "swept" into a money-market mutual fund that pays good interest. Unfortunately, and this applies particularly to smaller accounts, some institutions park the cash in a much-lower-yielding deposit account. If you find yourself in this situation, find out if your cache can be swept into a higher-paying money-market mutual fund. If that's not possible, perhaps you can invest it in a CD.

For sources of current information on the kinds of returns you should be able to earn on your cash stash, refer to the *Grow Your Money!* reader Web site. **w w w**

There's no reason to let idle money languish in accounts that pay little or no interest when there are so many available alternatives.

◾

If only God would give me some clear sign! Like making a deposit in my name in a Swiss bank account.
—WOODY ALLEN

IDEA 36

What Kind of Investor Are You? Take the Quiz

The following questions will help you determine how comfortable you are with risk. After answering the questions, follow the instructions at the end of the questionnaire to find out how comfortable you are with investment risk.

1. Indicate which type of investor profile best applies to you. The following explanations may help you identify your investor profile:

   ✦ An **aggressive** investor wants to achieve high long-term investment returns even if that means that the investments will periodically experience major short-term changes in investment values.

✦ A **moderate** investor wants to achieve a balance between earning attractive long-term-investment returns and reducing fluctuations in value.

✦ A **conservative** investor seeks stable growth in his or her investments over time even if it means somewhat lower returns over time. A conservative investor is not as comfortable as other investors with the ups and downs of the stock market.

(Please check only one box.)

❑ Very conservative (1)

❑ Conservative (2)

❑ Moderate (3)

❑ Aggressive (4)

❑ Very aggressive (5)

2. If a stock you bought doubled in price in a year, you would

❑ Sell all your shares (1)

❑ Sell half your shares (2)

❑ Not sell any shares (3)

❑ Buy more shares (2)

3. An investment loses 15 percent of its value in a market correction one month after you buy it, and assuming nothing fundamental has changed in the company you invested in, its just that the stock market has experienced a broad decline, you would

❑ Sit tight and wait for it to move back up in price (4)

❑ Sell it and rid yourself of worry if it continues to decline (1)

❑ Sell half of it and invest the money elsewhere (3)

❑ Wait for the stock market to rebound and then sell it (2)

❑ Buy more shares since the stock is even more attractively priced now (5)

4. The investment performance over two years (eight quarters) of three investments is summarized below. Which would you prefer to invest in?

❑ Investment A (5)

❑ Investment B (1)

❑ Investment C (3)

	Investment		
	A	B	C
1st quarter	+ 8%	+1%	+3%
2nd quarter	− 3	+1	+2
3rd quarter	+11	+1	0
4th quarter	+11	+1	+2
5th quarter	−12	+1	−1
6th quarter	+21	+1	+2
7th quarter	−6	+1	+1
8th quarter	+7	+1	+3

5. How important is it for your investment returns to beat the rate of inflation?

(Please check only one box.)

❑ It's more important to preserve my principal than to beat inflation. (1)

❑ Other investment objectives, like receiving interest and dividend income, are more important than beating inflation. (2)

❑ Beating inflation should be balanced with other investment objectives like receiving dividends and interest. (3)

❑ Beating inflation is important, but it must be balanced
with taking prudent risk. (4)

❑ Beating inflation is essential to meeting my investment
goals. (5)

Your scorecard. Once you've checked off the boxes, summarize
your score below by putting the number in parentheses after each response that you checked. Then add up the total.

1. ____
2. ____
3. ____
4. ____
5. ____

Total ____

If your total score is 10 or less, consider yourself a **conservative**
investor.
If your total score is between 11 and 19, you're a **moderate**
investor.
If your total score is 20 or higher, you're an **aggressive**
investor.

While hopefully your result was the same as you indicated in the
first question, if it is not, give some credence to the notion that your investment comfort level may be different than you originally thought.

Understanding your comfort—or lack of comfort—with investment risk can be helpful in deciding how to choose and diversify
your investments. On the other hand, don't let an aversion to, or a

love of, investment risk cause you to invest in extremes. In other words, a conservative investor shouldn't eschew stocks and an aggressive investor may not be able to afford the risk of investing entirely in stocks.

The *Grow Your Money!* reader Web site contains examples of how you might want to diversify your investments based on your age and whether you are a conservative, moderate, or aggressive investor.
www

> Determining how comfortable you are with the ups and downs of the investment markets will help you devise a "sleep tight" investment plan.
>
> ■
>
> *Nothing tells in the long run like a good judgment, and no sound judgment can remain with the man whose mind is disturbed by the mercurial changes of the stock exchange. It places him under an influence akin to intoxication. What is not, he sees, and what he sees, is not.*
> —ANDREW CARNEGIE

IDEA 37

Investing When You're Just Starting Out

If you're just starting out as an investor and you're bereft of the amount of money you think you need to be an investor, don't just stick what you have in a savings account. True, many mutual funds require a minimum initial investment of $2,000 or more, but there are many ways to get around that impediment. You can invest like the pros for as little as a dollar and work up from there. If you are indeed starting from scratch, don't be shy about asking your parents or grandparents for some help if they can afford it. At least drop some hints, like: "I'm really anxious to begin investing; all I need to do now is to have some money to start." The following may be even more effective when speaking with your parents: "I'm really anxious to set aside some money for the future, but unless I can find a way to get started, my only hope is to move back home for a few years while I build up my investments." The latter approach has been shown to loosen up even the tightest parental purse strings.

Here's a list of ways to invest smartly even if you're not yet very smart about investing:

1. **Spend some time learning about investing.** The ideas and tips appearing in this and the next chapters will help you learn the jargon and strategies necessary to launch a successful investment program. If you are indeed starting from scratch—you don't know a stock from a bond—be sure to review the investment tutorial at the special reader Web site. You don't need to be an expert to become an effective investor, but you should strive to learn as much as you can about investing. It will be time well and profitably spent.

2. **Investigate the best places to invest a small amount of money.** A little bit of investigation will uncover many opportunities to invest a small—even a lilliputian—amount of money. Depending on your own situation, here are the alternatives to consider:

   ❏ **Retirement savings plan at work.** If your employer offers a retirement savings plan, this is often the best place to start investing. First, you don't need one red cent to begin investing, since you simply instruct your employer to deduct your contribution from your pay. You can certainly afford to contribute at least 1 percent to the plan, can't you? Not only are you putting money away for your future, but you're also reducing your income tax bite. If your employer offers a match, you get some free money to boot. See Idea 26, on page 83, for more help on participating in your retirement savings plan at work.

❑ **Low-minimum mutual funds.** While most mutual funds impose pretty hefty minimum investment requirements, some will let you invest a more modest amount, often starting with a $500 minimum. IRA accounts often have a lower minimum-investment requirement than brokerage accounts, and starting out your investment program with an IRA is a great way to go, particularly if you don't have a retirement savings plan at work.

❑ **Low-risk interest-bearing investments.** If you're a bit skittish about investing your money in retirement plans or mutual funds, or you would like to set aside a bit of money for financial emergencies before taking that plunge, you don't need to consign these savings to your checking account or some bank savings account that pays a barely measurable amount of interest. You might consider putting your money into a six-month or one-year bank CD or opening up a brokerage or mutual fund account and putting the money into a money-market fund for starters. Then if you need to tap into the money, you can do so at no cost or, in the case of the CD, where an interest penalty may be imposed, very low cost.

Finding a good place for your money—one that will welcome your limited resources—is half the battle. The other half is identifying investments that enable you to diversify your money. Common wisdom suggests that you need $20,000 or more in order to spread your money around among various categories of investments like large-company stocks, international stocks, and corporate bonds. (See Idea 33, on page 102.) This is not the case anymore, however. There are a variety of ways to diversify your investments with short money. Read on.

3. **Consider investments that offer "instant" diversification.** Making sure your money is adequately diversified from the get-go is also a challenge for nascent investors. The trouble with investing all your money in a single mutual fund is that you run the risk of losing a good bit of money if the particular market sector favored by your fund takes a shellacking. Of course, since you don't have a lot of money to lose, but it's all the money you've got, why not develop good diversification habits early in your investment career? Fortunately, there are abundant choices that achieve instant diversification in a single fund, including:

   ❏ **Lifestyle funds** that diversify your money across several investment categories according to how comfortable you are with investment risk. (Take the test in Idea 36, on page 111, to find out.)

   ❏ **Target funds** that diversify and gradually adjust your diversification according to the date you plan to retire, even if it's decades away.

   ❏ **Balanced funds** that maintain a fixed allocation of your money, typically 60 percent in large-company stocks and 40 percent in U.S. government and corporate bonds.

Chances are your workplace retirement plan offers these funds; if not, they will be offered through the mutual fund company or stock brokerage firm of your choice. Lifestyle and target-date funds are described in more depth in Idea 39, on page 125.

As your investment money increases . . . As your good efforts at saving and investing start to bear fruit, you will be able to add to your stable of investment holdings, which, if you do it right, will help you improve your diversification and increase your investment returns. Here are some examples:

✦ You can expand your investment horizons beyond stocks and bonds to include real estate by investing in a real estate mutual fund. See Idea 42, on page 135.

✦ You will be able to dabble in "sector funds" if you think a particular market sector, like high tech or health care, is destined for strong gains. Idea 45, on page 144, has some strategies for investing in sector funds.

✦ You will eventually be able to afford individual stocks and bonds in addition to mutual funds. Deciding when to add individual securities is explained in Idea 43, on page 139.

Having the financial wherewithal to expand your investment holdings will help you appreciate why, as the old saying goes, "The rich get richer." Good luck on your journey.

Your *Grow Your Money!* reader Web site contains more information and recommendations, as well as an investment tutorial, for investors who are new to the investment game. **w w w**

Great First-Time Investments

✓ Lifestyle fund

✓ Target-date fund

✓ Balanced fund

Investment beginners are not precluded from investing in a wide range of excellent funds, and the sooner you start learning about investing, the better.

■

There are more important things in life than a little money, and one of them is a lot of money.
—ANONYMOUS

MONEY TIP

Shun Those Who Think They Can Predict the Future of the Investment Markets

There will always be people who think they can predict the future of the investment markets. Those who say they can either have an agenda—they want to sell you something or promote their firm—or, more likely, are delusional and should therefore be encouraged to seek mental health counseling. It's impossible to predict with complete accuracy how the investment markets will fare, particularly over the near term.

Therefore, I urge you to shun those who are convinced they can predict the future of the stock market or interest rates or who talk convincingly about the prospects of a particular stock. One very popular TV stock predictor has a success rate of about 49 percent. In fact, flipping a coin has consistently produced better investment returns. Yet countless people hang on his every word. But, to his great credit, he has sparked an interest in the stock market among many investors, particularly young investors. They should just avoid blindly following his stock tips.

Never invest based upon the opinion of someone who has the audacity to suggest that they can predict the future. But just as bad as following the fantastical and fallacious forecast of a single person is following the crowd. It was the crowd mentality that bid up the dotcom stocks back in the late 1990s. Here is a technique that will almost certainly keep you out of trouble: do the opposite of what the crowd is doing. In other words, sell when the mob is euphoric and buy when they're morose. This is very, very difficult to do, but you'll probably be better off financially if you can muster the courage to do so. This is called "contrarian investing" and is explained in Idea 40, on page 129.

> ■
>
> *Talking to politicians about the economy is like talking*
> *with eight-year-olds about sex. They have heard all the*
> *words, but they haven't a clue.*
> —MICHAEL ARONSTEIN

IDEA 38

When It Comes to Investing, Average Is Pretty Good

A recent study has proved again an overlooked truth of investing: you don't have to be a pro to make money in the markets. *Au contraire,* while most mutual funds lure investors with the prospect of market-beating returns, a growing mountain of evidence shows that the vast majority of funds that handpick stocks just don't deliver above-average returns over time. Actively betting on where stocks are headed can actually hurt performance. *Index funds* and *exchange-traded funds* (ETFs)—mutual funds that passively mirror the performance of a specific index, such as the Dow Jones or S&P 500—often prove to be a better bet. Index funds are sold by mutual fund companies while ETFs are sold on the stock exchange.

Who wants to be below average? The majority of actively managed mutual funds—including many of the ones that are ballyhooed in the financial press and enthusiastically recommended by the investment community—fail to achieve the level of their benchmark index, the measure of average gains or losses in their segment of the market. Oh, the shame. In rising markets, the majority don't make as much money as their peer-group index. That's bad enough. But in declining markets, the majority of them *lose* more money than the average among their peers. Isn't that special?

The aforementioned study of mutual fund performance showed that of mutual funds that choose among large-capitalization stocks—the big companies tracked by the S&P 500—seven in ten had below-average returns during the past five years. Among actively managed funds investing in midsize and small companies, eight in ten were laggards. With international stock funds, almost two thirds fell short of their benchmark. In short, index funds beat them time and time again.

Index funds and ETFs are dull by definition, at best brainless beauties that rise and fall when the market rises and falls. Average returns are what they deliver—no more and no less, and variations among them mostly result from differences in the fees they charge. In a word, they're bland. But bland can be beautiful.

Index funds and ETFs to the rescue. If, on the other hand, you are counting on the healthy returns that buy-and-hold investing offers, to help carry you safely to and through retirement, then indexing deserves a serious look. Here's why:

✦ **Index funds and ETFs are cheap.** Low-cost mutual funds are always a good idea. The more a mutual fund charges, the smaller your return. One reason index funds have grown in popularity is that most don't cost much, as well they shouldn't. Since they're passively managed, with no stocks to research and no strategy to conceive and apply, index funds have few employees or other costs. In short, it's easy to find an index fund or ETF whose annual fees are a fraction of what an actively managed fund charges. There are additional savings if you put index funds in a taxable brokerage account. Since these funds generally don't do a lot of selling of shares they hold, the funds don't have to pass on hefty capital gains to their shareholders who would otherwise have to pony up the taxes. (See Idea 69, on page 214.)

✦ **Index funds and ETFs mean less stress.** Diversifying your money among the various categories of stocks and bonds—and keeping it there—is essential for anyone with savings to build or protect. Typically, stocks and bonds don't fall in value in the same year. No matter how impatient an investor you are, sticking with a diversified portfolio is the best way to grow your money. No matter how cautious or aggressive you are, proper diversification is the way to stop inflation from eating away at it.

The problem with stocks and bonds, though, is that they tempt investors to try to time the market—that is, to jump in and out of investments in a vain attempt to buy low and sell high. These efforts to beat the market tend to hurt returns. Not surprisingly, individual investors are no better at predicting market movements than the professionals. In fact, research has shown, year after year, that the average investor earns far *less* than the market averages.

Index funds and ETFs don't shield you from the market's ups and downs, but when used to build a diversified portfolio, they make it less harrowing to buy and hold your investments. You never have to worry that your funds will suffer losses in excess of the average, because index funds and ETFs *are* the average. When you're tempted to shift money from a lagging sector to a recent winner, try to remember the lesson the market is always teaching: no one knows the future.

✦ **Average return is darn good.** It is possible to beat the market averages, but to do so takes more time and expense—time and expense that you may not be willing to commit. Hundreds of mutual fund managers manage to beat the averages. But most of them do not. Even those managers who have enjoyed past glory don't necessarily produce future success. Every year, many fund managers who previously have had the Midas touch end up crashing.

An average return starts to look pretty good under these circumstances. Rather than relying on stock market geniuses to guide your investments, you can opt for the inherent genius of the market itself: its general tendency is to rise at a pace that outstrips inflation.

✦ **Selection is a snap.** With nearly twenty thousand actively managed mutual funds, sorting them out can be a challenge to those pressed for time. The choice is a lot easier with index funds and ETFs. It comes down to picking those funds that give you instant diversification by tracking the broadest indexes. The biggest, broadest, most useful benchmark indexes are these:

- The Wilshire 5000 Index comprises almost all U.S. stocks traded on major exchanges. Funds based on this index are often called "total stock market" index funds.

- Standard & Poor's 500 Stock Index (the S&P 500) is often cited by newscasters who are explaining how stocks performed for the day. (Another one cited, the Dow Jones Industrial Average, measures only thirty stocks.)

- The Russell 2000 Index selects the smallest 2,000 of the 3,000 largest U.S. companies commonly traded, making it a benchmark for small-company (also known as small-capitalization or small-cap) index funds.

- The MSCI EAFE Index is a mouthful that stands for Morgan Stanley Capital International Europe, Australasia, and Far East Index. This mega-index is comprised of twenty-one country indexes representing most of the developed markets overseas.

- The Lehman Brothers Aggregate Bond Index includes U.S. government, corporate, and mortgage-backed bonds. Most "total bond market" index funds are based on this.

Be wary of index fund and ETF tinkerers. You can further simplify your selection by ruling out classes of funds that are not index funds in the strict sense, but rather tinker with the fund holdings in an attempt to beat the index. These so-called "enhanced" index funds are actually a form of active stock-picking.

Indexing is easy. A simple and well-diversified portfolio can be built with just a handful of index funds and ETFs. Regardless of which funds you choose, first check performance: poor performance relative to the similar index funds usually means fees are higher, eroding returns.

While there are no absolutes when the subject is market performance, when looking at spans of a decade or more, stocks tend to perform quite well on average. Index funds and ETFs take advantage of this historical fact, by doing whatever the market does. In this case, following the crowd may, for you, be the right way to go. For another angle on set-it-and-forget-it investing, see the next Idea.

While the best that index funds and exchange-traded funds can do is generate average investment returns, average is pretty good, particularly if you want to take a hands-off approach to your investing.

■

With enough inside information and a million dollars,
you can go broke in a year.
—WARREN BUFFETT

IDEA 39

Putting Your Investments on Autopilot

So-called "life-cycle funds" are growing like kudzu and for good reason, because you can invest money—even a small amount—in a single fund that

✦ Diversifies across several important investment categories,

✦ Holds either mutual funds with solid performance histories or individual stocks and bonds that are actively managed, and

✦ Regularly rebalances your holdings (see Idea 40, on page 129, for an explanation of rebalancing).

Many mutual fund families have introduced a stable of life-cycle funds. They are becoming particularly popular among those who participate in workplace retirement plans like 401(k) and 403(b) plans and tax-sheltered annuities (TSAs). The main attraction is the simplicity of investing in a single all-purpose fund rather than having to pick from among a long list of retirement savings plan choices. While life-cycle funds do offer simplicity, they also need to be evaluated, just like any other investment. But most life-cycle funds range from pretty good to excellent. If you just don't want to be bothered with investing, they're a wonderful solution. Likewise, even if you're into investing, life-cycle funds deserve a good look.

Life-cycle funds come in two flavors.

✦ **Lifestyle funds.** Lifestyle funds are usually offered as a series of mutual funds under such names as "conservative," "income," "balanced," "growth," and "aggressive." Each individual fund is invested in a particular mix of stocks, bonds, and cash. For example, a "growth" fund would hold a much higher percentage of stocks than a "conservative" fund, which would be heavily invested in bonds. Most lifestyle funds hold individual securities. If you're interested in a lifestyle fund but aren't quite sure which category is right for you, take the quiz in Idea 36, on page 111, to find out what kind of investor you are.

✦ **Target funds.** Target funds, or target-date funds as they're often called, are designed to change the way your money is diversified as you get nearer retirement. Target funds are easy to identify because they have the target dates in their names: 2015, 2030, 2040, for example. All you need to do is guesstimate your retirement date and select a target fund that's nearest that date. The manager of the target fund will gradually change the allocation over the years. These "funds of funds" typically hold several different stock and bond funds within a single fund family in various proportions to suit an investor who is at a specific stage in life, for example, a younger person with decades to invest, a preretiree who desires to invest a bit more conservatively, or a retiree who needs investment income. In essence, the manager of a target fund will gradually reduce stock exposure and increase bond exposure as the years pass.

One potential drawback is that someone who intends to retire at roughly the time the fund "matures" may not be well served by then staying in such a fund if most of the money is in bonds and short-term securities. While the fund will likely have eliminated a good deal of investment risk by its end date—75 percent in bonds and cash equivalents is typical—that may not be the right way to handle your investment allocation. Most new retirees need at least as much of a growth component as an income component in their portfolios, because retirement is not an "end date." Rather, it's the beginning of a time during which the investments must provide not only income but also growth of principal—a period of time that will likely span decades. So make sure you thoroughly understand how the money will be invested as you near retirement. If the fund will be invested too conservatively for your tastes, you can always select a target fund with a date later than your intended retirement. For example, if you're going to retire in 2015, you can have a higher growth component as your retirement date nears if you invest some or all of your money in a 2020 or 2025 fund.

If lifestyle funds and target-date funds are your cup of tea, your *Grow Your Money!* reader Web site has a rundown of some of the best. **w w w**

> Autopilot investments, including lifestyle funds and target funds, provide a diversified portfolio of investments that are regularly rebalanced in a single investment.

CHAPTER 7

Supercharging Your Investments

Most investors can't even keep up with the market averages. Therefore, if they're underperforming, some people have to beat the averages, and you might as well be one of them. The matters covered in the last chapter show you how to become a very competent mutual-fund investor. This chapter covers areas that will help you supercharge your investments. The goal: to transform you from a competent investor to an outstanding investor. Here's a rundown of what follows:

- Becoming a contrarian investor

- Four can't-miss investments for the next decade

- Adding individual stocks and bonds to your portfolio

- Investing in sector funds

- Figuring out when to sell an investment

- Surviving a market decline

- Buying income-producing real estate and undeveloped land

IDEA 40

There's Something Nice About Being a Contrarian

The word "contrarian" has a bad connotation. It implies someone who always takes an opposing stance, someone who likes to argue just for the sake of arguing. But when it comes to investing, being a contrarian can be a very effective investment strategy. Moving opposite the Wall Street herd, contrarian investors prefer to buy stocks in periods of maximum pessimism and to sell stocks when investor enthusiasm drives up stock prices to astronomical levels. Thus, contrarians are perfectly comfortable with unloved stocks. They're also happy to sell stocks that have become Wall Street darlings. Suffice it to say, contrarians themselves are not Wall Street darlings, because they're, well, so contrary. But if you have had some experience investing in both up and down markets, you probably have some appreciation for the wisdom of deviating from the hysteria that inevitably accompanies rising and falling investment markets.

While it's important to maintain a consistent approach to investing, it's equally important to resist the hysteria that often influences the investment markets. That's why so many investors—and investment advisers—fare so poorly over the long term. What follows are illustrations of the reaction of the herd versus that of the contrarian to various conditions in the stock and bond markets.

Reactions to Changing Markets

✦ **Stocks are rising:**
- **The herd:** "I've got to move more money into stocks. I don't care how much they've risen. I don't want to miss out."

- **The contrarian:** "Stocks are awfully expensive, and everyone thinks stocks will just keep rising. I've made some good money, but I'm going to lock in those gains right now by selling some of what I own, because stocks don't rise forever."

✦ **Stocks are falling:**
- **The herd:** "I can't stand losing money, and it looks like there's no end to this bear market. I've got to cut way back on my stocks."

- **The contrarian:** "There's blood on Wall Street, and the speculators are unloading stocks. Stocks are a lot cheaper now than they were a few months ago. I'm going to buy some solid but beaten-down stocks."

✦ **Bond prices are falling (which means interest rates are rising):**
- **The herd:** "It's bad enough losing money on stocks, but now my bonds and bond funds are taking a pasting. It's time to switch out of bonds and put more into stocks."

- **The contrarian:** "Yes, my bonds have been through a rough patch, but that's because interest rates have risen. So I'm going to take advantage of higher interest rates by buying some more bonds."

✦ **Bond prices are rising (which means interest rates are falling):**
- **The herd:** "Bonds have been making money recently, and I want to be where the action is, so I'm buying bonds."

- **The contrarian:** "I've been getting some gains in my bond holdings, but with interest rates falling, this is hardly a time to be buying more bonds. If anything, I'll lighten up a bit."

Becoming a moderate contrarian. Some professional investors are dyed-in-the-wool contrarians. They are as happy to be out of stocks when everyone else is euphoric about stock market prospects as they are to plunge into stocks amid a plunging stock market. But that's too dangerous a strategy, because no one can reliably predict the future of the stock or bond markets. The last thing you want to do is make major shifts in the way you invest, whether you follow the herd or are a contrarian. But taking a contrarian approach to the way you invest will empower you to make smart investment decisions that are not in sync with what everyone else seems to be espousing. Further, you can be a contrarian without deviating from your investment diversification target. Here are two ways to be a moderate contrarian:

1. **Periodically rebalancing your investments.** If you have paid close attention to how you diversify your investments and you select good investments, it's hard not to be a successful investor. But periodically rebalancing your investments is icing on the cake, because it forces you to make contrarian investment decisions while sticking to your long-term investment strategy. Rebalancing is a mild but very smart form of contrary investing. Here's how rebalancing works. Before you can rebalance, you need to establish a diversification target for your investments, for example, 60 percent stocks and 40 percent in bonds. Over time the investments you own will change in value. After one year, let's assume your allocation has changed from 60/40 to 65 percent stocks and 35 percent bonds, because the stock market rose more than bonds did (as is usual over the long term). The task at hand is to sell enough stocks and buy a like amount of bonds to get back to the 60/40 target allocation. Now, you may ask, why is rebalancing a contrarian investment strategy? As is done in our recent example, rebalancing forces you to sell stocks after they've risen in value. Rebalancing also forces you to buy

stocks on the cheap—after they've fallen in value—at a time when the Wall Street herd is abandoning stocks. Rebalancing also forces you to buy stocks after they've fallen in value, as was done in our example. The other thing that rebalancing does is it forces you to buy bonds after interest rates have risen, which is exactly what you want to do—lock in higher interest rates. But rebalancing usually involves only small shifts in your overall investment holdings, so you're not making a major move. This is good.

2. **Identifying out-of-favor securities to invest new money.** Occasionally you'll have some money that needs to be invested. A maturing CD, a gift from Granny, an IRA contribution, or you just have a small brokerage account for speculation. In these instances, you can exercise your contrarian proclivities by following your instincts rather than the herd. If everyone in the office is plowing money into stocks, buy bonds. If a stock you like has taken a drubbing lately but still has good prospects, buy that stock. It's on sale. If a couple of experts on the financial news shows predict the imminent demise of small-company stocks, buy a small-cap stock fund. It's fun being a contrarian, and the odds of success are in your favor.

The reader Web site includes sources of information on and investments favored by contrarians, as well as an illustration of portfolio rebalancing. **w w w**

Contrarian investors don't win any popularity contests, but avoiding the herd mentality can help you avoid ill-timed investments.

◼

The time to buy is when blood is running in the streets.
—BARON ROTHSCHILD

IDEA 41

Investment Returns Make a Big Difference

As noted elsewhere in these pages, and it bears repeating, the two most important ingredients to achieving your financial dreams are, first, to save regularly, and second, to invest those savings wisely. It's not sufficient to be proficient in just one area. You can be a diligent saver, but it won't amount to very much if your investment returns are lackluster. You could also be a whopping good investor, but it's impossible to rely solely on investment gains to turn a small amount of principal into a large assemblage of money, so you must keep adding consistently to your savings.

Investment returns do matter, as the following table will attest. It answers a question that you may one day ask: "I'd really be in good financial shape if I could only have an additional $100,000 saved by the time I retire. How much extra will I need to save?" The answer depends on how much you can expect your money to make.

HOW MUCH MONTHLY SAVINGS IS REQUIRED TO ACCUMULATE $100,000?

YEARS UNTIL RETIREMENT	AVERAGE ANNUAL INVESTMENT RETURN		
	4%	6%	8%
10	$680	$620	$540
20	280	220	170
30	140	100	70
40	80	50	30

What a difference investment returns make. For example, if you're twenty years from retirement and want to add an extra $100,000 to the kitty, you must save an extra $280 a month if you expect to earn an uninspiring 4 percent average return (sad to say, that's about what the typical investor makes). If you can earn a decent and reasonably achievable 6 percent return, your required savings declines by $60 per month to $220. An 8 percent return is within your reach if you devote some time to your investments and avoid following the crowd (they're the ones that make 4 percent); then your required savings drops another $50 per month to $170—40 percent less than what is needed with the 4 percent return of the average investor.

More good news. Investment returns also make a big difference when you begin withdrawing money when you're retired. See the next table that shows how much you can withdraw from a $100,000 nest egg over 25 years.

HOW MUCH YOU CAN WITHDRAW PER MONTH FROM $100,000 OF INVESTMENT HOLDINGS OVER A 25-YEAR RETIREMENT

AVERAGE ANNUAL INVESTMENT RETURN		
4%	6%	8%
$530	$640	$770

Note: This example assumes that the investment principal will be used up after 25 years.

If you can manage to earn a 6 percent return, you'll be able to withdraw 20 percent more from your $100,000 than the 4 percent investor before using up your principal 25 years hence. The 8 percent investor's income will be over 40 percent higher than that of the 4 percent investor.

One more matter before pressing forward: Don't let the possibility of high investment returns cause you to moderate your savings. Investment returns are far from certain. Savings, on the other hand, are the surest way to build up your wealth. The most financially successful people are both good and consistent savers and successful investors.

Achieving better investment returns during your working years and after you're retired can result in a much higher retirement income.

■

One of the funny things about the stock market is that every time one man buys, another sells, and both think they are astute.
—WILLIAM FEATHER

IDEA 42

Four Can't-Miss Investments

You can do quite well, thank you, by investing in the garden-variety large-company, mid-sized company, small-company, and international stocks, with a generous helping of government and corporate bond funds (as explained in Idea 33, on page 102), but if you want to juice up your returns, consider in addition the following four investments that will amply reward you over the next decade. In fact, while some of these investments may seem risky, they add more diversification to your investments. The beauty of enhancing diversification, even with risky types of investments, is that it actually decreases overall investment risk because you're better diversified. And adding new types of investments has also been shown to increase returns. Decrease risk while increasing returns. You can't beat that. Here are the fab four:

1. **Emerging-markets stock funds.** Most investors realize the importance of investing in foreign stocks, but they don't do a very good job of it for a couple of reasons. First, they invest too little in this important category, not realizing how important it is. At least 10 to 15 percent of your money should be devoted to foreign securities, and many investment professionals recommend a considerably higher percentage. Second, investors tend

to invest too narrowly in foreign stock funds. Some are content with a large-cap international fund that invests primarily in stocks traded on the major foreign stock exchanges. But their money would be better diversified if they also owned an emerging-markets stock fund that invests in stocks of companies in developing countries like China and India. The economic prospects of emerging markets over the next decade are nothing short of spectacular. Unless you have a lot of money to invest, buy an emerging markets fund that invests in multiple countries instead of one that targets a specific country. Since political and business conditions in emerging markets can be turbulent, a general fund protects your investment better.

2. **Real estate funds.** Real estate is an important investment category. While the only way to get rich in real estate is to own it yourself (see Idea 48, on page 153, for thoughts on that), you can still put some jingle in your pocket simply by owning real estate mutual funds, and you won't have to repair a tenant's leaky faucet over the weekend. While real estate goes through feast or famine cycles, it's still a very solid long-term performer, worthy of around 5 to 10 percent of your total stock holdings and perhaps a bit more.

3. **Commodity funds.** Commodity investments are a crapshoot. Make a mistake and you could have twenty tons of pork bellies dumped in your front yard. The commodity markets are dominated by oil, but they also includes such necessities as metals, timber, corn, uranium, and, a commodity that is becoming increasing scarce, water. This is an interesting and increasingly necessary component of a fully diversified portfolio. The investment industry, always striving to please (so long as it can make a few bucks) is offering a variety of commodity funds, including natural resources funds, mining funds, and funds that invest in commodity futures. One attraction to commodities beyond their intrinsic value is that they usually move in a different cycle from

those of stocks and bonds. In investment jargon, that means that commodities can reduce investment fluctuations. But commodities are still risky, so limit them to 5 to 10 percent of the stock side of your portfolio.

4. **Multisector bond funds.** While stocks add the sizzle to an investment portfolio, bonds are also essential because they add value and stability to your holdings in the event of a flat or declining stock market. But it's a challenge identifying the best bond categories: corporate, U.S. government, foreign, high-yield—the list goes on. This is where multisector bond funds (also called diversified bond funds) can resolve the dilemma. One of the advantages of mutual funds in general is that you pay someone a relatively small amount of money (1 percent or so) to lie awake at night worrying about your money. Fund managers also have a lot more experience and access to research and information that we mere mortals lack. For the perplexed bond investor, multisector bond funds may be the answer. A multisector bond fund invests in a variety of bonds, including corporate bonds, high-yield (also called "junk" bonds), government bonds, and international bonds. One attraction is that the manager of a multisector bond fund has a much longer leash than, say, a corporate-bond-fund manager or a government-bond-fund manager. So, depending on current market conditions and the outlook for various bond sectors, the manager of a multisector fund decides which sectors are the most attractive. If you don't mind or, indeed, would prefer that a bond-fund manager casts a wide net in search of income and capital gains, consider a multisector bond fund for a portion of your bond holdings.

Incorporating these categories in your portfolio. A diversification illustration incorporating the six major investment categories appears on page 106. Here is an expanded illustration that incorporates the four additional investment categories just enumerated.

EXPANDED INVESTMENT
DIVERSIFICATION ILLUSTRATION

Large-company stock fund	20%
Mid-sized company stock fund	8
Small-company stock fund	7
International stock fund	5
Emerging-markets stock fund	5
Real estate stock fund	10
Commodities fund	5
Subtotal stock funds	60
Multisector bond fund	10
Corporate bond fund	15
U.S. government bond fund	15
Subtotal bond funds	40
Total	100%

If you will kindly visit the *Grow Your Money!* Web site, you will find some top-drawer mutual funds in each of the four categories.

This quartet of investments will add some sizzle to your investment returns over the next decade.

■

With globalization, the big [countries] don't eat the small, the fast eat the slow.

—THOMAS FRIEDMAN

IDEA 43

A Rich Recipe: Adding Individual Securities to Your Mutual Fund Portfolio

Aren't mutual funds enough? Mutual funds (including index funds and exchange-traded funds) offer a lot of advantages, and you can do very well earning excellent investment returns exclusively with funds. Funds are also about the only way you can invest in certain investment categories like small-cap stocks and international stocks, unless you have a very large pot of money to invest. But mutual funds also have some disadvantages, in particular the lack of control over the income taxes that the mutual fund passes on (which is perhaps an important consideration for investments you have in taxable brokerage accounts, as opposed to retirement accounts, where dividends, interest, and capital gains aren't taxed until you begin making withdrawals after you retire), and with respect to bond mutual funds, there is the possibility that your fund could lose value if interest rates rise.

More important, rather than cede the management of one's investments to an anonymous manager, many investors prefer to invest in individual stocks and bonds on their own. If that describes you, wonderful. If not, that's okay as well. Buying individual securities definitely allows you more control over your investments. And as long as you hold on to a stock or bond, you owe no taxes on its appreciation in value. Also, buying individual bonds and holding on to them until they mature avoids the risk inherent in bond mutual funds that rising interest rates will cause a loss in the value of the bond fund. True, your individual bonds will also lose value if interest rates rise, but that is of little importance if you hold on to your bonds until they mature.

Investments in individual stocks and bonds also have some disadvantages, including the time and expense necessary to manage them effectively. It can be expensive to achieve adequate diversification with a portfolio of individual stocks and bonds, although commissions are pretty low at many brokerages.

It takes two to tango. By combining both methods of investing—mutual funds and individual stocks and bonds—you can take advantage of the opportunities that both ownership methods offer. Once the money you have available to invest reaches a level where you can afford individual investments—that could be as little as $50,000—you should consider striking a balance between both methods to take advantage of the desirable features of each. Most successful long-term investors will invest in—and benefit from—both individual securities and mutual funds.

How to fit individual stocks and bonds into your investment portfolio. The extent to which you include individual stocks and bonds in your portfolio will largely depend on two matters: your personal preference and the amount of money you have to invest.

1. **Personal preference.** You may be perfectly content with mutual funds, or you may prefer individual investments. Either view is fine, so long as you keep an open mind. I think that investors are best served by a combination of both of these investment methods, and I hope you won't reject individual bonds and particularly individual stocks because you think they're too complicated or too risky. They're not. At the other extreme, I trust you won't reject mutual funds altogether, because mutual funds are the only way for most investors to play some important market segments.

    The amount of time you have available to monitor your investments will also influence your preference for mutual funds or individual securities. If you have neither the time nor the interest to choose individual securities, then you may opt for mutual funds exclusively (or use an investment adviser to help you with individual securities). But choosing and keeping up-to-date on a handful of individual securities need not be time-consuming, and the more interest you take in your investments, the better all of your investments will fare.

2. **How much you have to invest.** Unlike mutual funds, where you can begin investing with $3,000 or less, buying individual stocks and bonds requires considerably more money to achieve adequate diversification. A pair of illustrations follows.

Sample Portfolios That Incorporate Both Mutual Funds and Individual Securities

A $50,000 Portfolio. If you have $50,000 available to invest, there is enough to begin investing in some individual stocks, although not yet enough to buy individual bonds. In the following table, which assumes an investment allocation of 70 percent stocks and 30 percent bonds, $15,000 is devoted to individual stocks. This should be enough to own three or four different stocks in different industries. While this may not be enough to achieve the level of diversification you would like in the individual stocks, you also have $20,000 of stock mutual funds, which are, of course, well diversified. So considering the entirety of your stock investments, you certainly should have sufficient diversification.

A $50,000 PORTFOLIO

Investment allocation: 70% stocks and 30% bonds

	STOCKS	BONDS
Mutual Funds	Total Stock funds: $20,000	Total bond funds: $15,000
Individual Securities	Total individual stocks: $15,000 (in 3–5 stocks)	Total individual bonds: $0
	Total Stock and Stock Funds: $35,000	Total Bond and Bond Funds: $15,000

A $100,000 Portfolio. When a portfolio approaches six figures, investors who are interested in buying individual stocks and bonds should have enough money to be able to do so. In the following illustration, which assumes a 50 percent stock and 50 percent bond investment allocation, I've split the total stock money in half so that it is equally divided between stock funds and individual stocks. On the bond side, I've skewed the weighting a bit toward individual bonds, since you will probably need around $10,000 to buy an individual bond issue. Here, then, an investor might be able to buy one U.S. Treasury note, one municipal bond, and one corporate bond. Be cautious, however, if you adopt a similar approach toward buying individual bonds with a portfolio of this size. Be sure to limit your individual municipal and corporate bond purchases to highly rated issuers. (You don't need to worry about quality with Treasuries, since they are the safest of all bonds.)

A $100,000 PORTFOLIO

Investment allocation: 50% stocks and 50% bonds

	STOCKS	BONDS
Mutual Funds	Total Stock funds: $25,000	Total bond funds: $20,000
Individual Securities	Total individual stocks: $25,000 (5–8 stocks)	Total individual bonds: $30,000
	Total Stock and Stock Funds: $50,000	Total Bond and Bond Funds: $50,000

Be sure to check out this special reader Web site for more recommendations on adding individual securities to your investments.
w w w

You don't have to have a well-lined purse to be able to afford individual stocks and bonds, which are usually an excellent complement to mutual funds.

■

Gentlemen prefer bonds.
—ANDREW MELLON

IDEA 44

The Truth and Nothing but the Truth

If I ever need somebody to explain something in a way that no one will ever be able to understand, I'll hire a financial firm. While some strive to do a good job of showing their clients how their investments have fared, many investment statements are still paragons of obfuscation. Actually, it's quite easy to provide a statement that tells you precisely what happened to your investments over the past quarter, or six months, or year. (Avoid reviewing investment performance more frequently. Doing so will drive you nuts.)

The following Investment Performance Summary contains a format that you can take straight to whoever oversees your investments. In just six lines, you can receive an informative summary of just how your investment account performed. Then you don't have to lie awake counting sheep and wondering how your investments really did. If you manage some or all of your money on your own, you should fill out the following summary yourself.

INVESTMENT PERFORMANCE SUMMARY

Name: _____

Period measured: From: ___/___/___ To: ___/___/___

　　　　　　　　Mo/day/year　　Mo/day/year

		EXAMPLE
1. Beginning balance in investment account	$_____	$100,000
2. Plus: money added to account	$_____	6,000
3. Subtract: money withdrawn from account	(_____)	(2,000)
4. Subtract: commissions and fees	(_____)	(1,200)
5. Add or (subtract) investment gain or (loss) for the period	_____	5,500
6. Equals ending balance in investment account	$_____	$108,300

Be sure you understand exactly how your investments fared, whether you use an adviser or invest on your own.

■

Don't speculate unless you can make it a full-time job. Beware of barbers, beauticians, waiters—or anyone— bringing gifts of "inside" information or "tips." Don't try to buy at the bottom or sell at the top. This can't be done—except by liars.

—BERNARD BARUCH

IDEA 45

Investing Profitably in Sector Funds

Sector funds (also known as *specialized funds*) are not mutual funds in the pure sense, although many investors seem to think they are, given the popularity of many sector funds, including the many exchange-traded funds (ETFs) that invest in particular market sectors. While a sector fund is diversified in so far as it invests in stocks of many companies, a sector fund restricts those investments to a single industry, such as banks or high-tech companies or health care. So while a garden-variety mutual fund or an ETF that is diversified across several different industries won't suffer too much if a particular industry falls on hard times, a sector fund in that hapless industry could suffer big-time. But many investors are attracted to sector funds because they almost always dominate the list of best-performing mutual funds over a past quarter or past year. That shouldn't come as a surprise, because if a particular sector is flying high, chances are that the sector funds will be beating the daylights out of more diversified funds. I hate to bring up a bad memory, but think back to the late 1990s when investor money poured into high-tech funds and dot-com funds that dominated the financial news.

Sector fund don'ts and dos. If, in spite of my admonitions, you become tempted to put some money in sector funds, please don't bet the ranch on them. Put no more than 10 to 15 percent of your money into sector funds. Also, please don't buy a sector fund solely because it was a recent high performer. Instead, pick a sector fund because you are excited by the prospects for stocks of a particular sector, in other words, a particular industry. And this leads me to my strategy.

Sector investment strategy. Here is one way to invest wisely in sector funds without getting caught up in the hysteria surrounding those that have recently posted whopping gains.

❑ **First, identify promising sectors.** There are a couple of ways of identifying industries that are considered to have excellent prospects over the next year or few years. If you have a stockbroker or an investment adviser, he or she may be able to provide you with some recommendations. Or, you could go to the library and check out the *Value Line Investment Survey,* which ranks over ninety different industries for probable performance over the next year.

❏ **Second, identify top-notch sector funds.** After identifying a promising industry, you should then go about the task of identifying a good sector fund in that industry. This process is no different from the process of locating any good mutual fund. Be forewarned, however, that in spite of the popularity of sector funds, funds are not available for many industry categories. Here are some industries that have a sufficient number of sector funds to allow you to identify a good one among them:

✦ Communications

✦ Energy/natural resources

✦ Financial services

✦ Health care

✦ Leisure

✦ Precious metals

✦ Real estate

✦ Retailing

✦ Technology

✦ Utilities

For some up-to-date tips on sectors and sector funds worthy of your consideration, check the *Grow Your Money!* reader Web site.
w w w

> While riskier than diversified mutual funds, sector funds are an appealing way to invest some money in a particular industry that interests you.
>
> ■
>
> *The meek shall inherit the earth, but not the mineral rights.*
> —J. PAUL GETTY

IDEA 46

Sayonara: Deciding When to Sell an Investment

You may agonize whenever you purchase an investment. Deciding when to *sell* an investment is often an even tougher decision. Perhaps that's why most investors don't do a very good job of it. One of the biggest drags on investment performance is holding on to a sullied investment too long. It's true that every investor has occasionally sold out a good investment too soon or failed to get out of a lousy investment soon enough. That's life. But you don't want to make a habit of it. Here, then, are some suggestions for deciding when to sell a mutual fund, stock, or bond.

Figuring out when to sell a mutual fund. The first rule of mutual fund selling: don't be too quick. Consider the following unfortunate but surprisingly common scenario. An investor chooses a stock mutual fund based solely on its strong past performance. Over the next few quarters, however, the fund's performance begins to lag compared to that of its peers. Disappointed, the investor sells in favor of another fund that has recently been going gangbusters. Alas, shortly thereafter, the fund that was sold once again posts solid results, while the recently purchased replacement fund begins to produce sordid results. The investor must conclude that he or she can do nothing right. In this case the problem was not with the funds but with the investor. And the problem is knowing when to sell.

There are several factors that would make selling a fund appropriate.

If a fund's performance deteriorates, as in the case described above, it is of critical importance to assess the cause of the poor performance. Investors who buy a fund on the basis of its investment category (large-cap, small-cap, short-term corporate bond, etc.) and/or its investment style (growth, value, or a combination of the two) must judge the fund according to how well it's performing compared with the averaged performance of similar funds.

Worse is an investor who sells off a fund that is doing well in its category, but its category happens to be going through a rough patch. If large-cap stock funds made 8 percent on average so far this year and government bond funds lost 4 percent, you may think your government bond fund that lost 2 percent should be jettisoned from your portfolio and that your large-cap stock fund that made 3 percent is a comparative winner. But allocating your investments appropriately— and this includes bond funds as well as stock funds—is far more important to your investment success than trying to chase what seems to be the hottest fund category. In the example cited, if one of those funds deserves to be sold, it is the large-cap stock fund that is lagging its peers.

In particular, a fund that seems to be consistently underperforming its peers clearly becomes a sell candidate. Here's the rule I've used successfully for many years:

Never sell a mutual fund on the basis of underperformance unless and until it has underperformed its peer group average for two consecutive years.

If you are diligent in selecting really good funds, chances are that you will rarely have to sell a fund on the basis of this rule. But it will happen from time to time.

You may have to sell a fund simply to raise cash in order to rebalance your portfolio (see Idea 40, on page 129). In these instances, there will obviously be some funds that you may like more than others. Compare their performance against that of their peers and, depending on how much you need to rebalance, sell some or all of the fund that is least attractive to you at that time.

Figuring out when to sell a stock. Knowing which stocks in your portfolio to sell, and when to sell them, are at least as important as knowing when to buy a stock. One rule that is elusive to most investors is that any stock you now hold that you don't currently consider to be an attractive "buy" candidate should be a candidate for sale. Of course, potential capital gains and losses must be taken into consideration if the stock is held in a brokerage account. (In a retirement account, capital gains aren't subject to taxes if you sell a stock held within a retirement account. Taxes are due only after you begin making withdrawals from a retirement account, with the exception of a Roth IRA.) But you don't want to hold on to a stock if it doesn't have attractive future prospects. So if you ever find yourself saying: "That stock has served me well in the past, but I certainly wouldn't buy any more of it today," why should you continue to hold on to that stock? Also, don't hold on to a stock for sentimental reasons. If you feel obligated to honor the memory of some long-gone relative who bequeathed you some stock that doesn't look too hot right now, you can prudently honor their memory by holding onto just *one* share.

Deciding to sell a stock is not necessarily an either/or decision: either to sell all of the position or hold on to all of it. That's not what the professional investors do unless they are absolutely certain that this stock is going to fall out of bed. Instead, the pros will sell a portion of the position—say half—and then defer making a decision on the other half. That way, if the stock rebounds, they're still players. On the other hand, if their fears are realized and the stock price drops, their exposure to that stock is less than if they had done nothing.

Figuring out when to sell a bond. Selling a bond before it matures is a decision that should not be taken lightly. First, you shouldn't buy a bond unless you intend to hold it until it matures. Nevertheless, there may be situations where you have to sell bonds to raise cash or to rebalance your investments or because it just makes good financial sense to sell the bonds. One major and compelling reason why you might want to sell a bond is if the financial condition of the issuer—a corporation or a municipality—is deteriorating. Hopefully you don't get into that position. That's why buying only highly rated bonds, or better yet, U.S. Treasury securities, is always a preferable way to go. That way, it's unlikely you'll ever have to sell a deteriorating bond at a loss. But if you do have to liquidate a bond before maturity, there's nothing better than having a reliable broker who will endeavor to get you a good price. In addition, an experienced broker will keep you apprised of any changes in the credit status of your bonds. Another important role of your broker is to advise you about which of the bonds you own are the best candidates for sale. All that said, the best route to go if you anticipate having to sell the bonds before maturity is to buy U.S. Treasuries, since they are far easier to sell than corporate or municipal bonds.

You may not have a lot of time to devote to monitoring your individual investments, but following the these guidelines shouldn't be that time-consuming. If you use an investment adviser, be sure to communicate your ideas about when you think an investment should be sold. But it's your money, and the more *discipline* you can place on sell decisions, the better your investments will fare over the years and decades.

Discipline in selling an investment is at least as important as discipline in buying. Investors tend not to pay enough attention to selling, although the sell decision is actually not very complicated.

■

Bull markets are born on pessimism, grow on skepticism, mature on optimism and die on euphoria.
—MICHAEL B. STEELE

IDEA 47

Surviving a Market Decline

What would you do if the Dow Jones Industrial Average dropped 800 points next Monday? What would you do if Dr. Bear arrived at your doorstep, draining 25 percent from the value of your stocks slowly, ever so slowly, over the next two years? Or what would you do if interest rates skyrocketed, leaving your bonds and bond funds seriously wounded? These events happen all the time. Stocks slumped badly for a period beginning in 2000. In fact, the stock market has suffered corrections of 10 percent or more 109 times since 1900—over once a year on average. "Correction" is a polite word for "calamity." That is, if someone else is losing money in a declining market, that's a correction. If it's your or my money, though, it's a calamity.

How you react to these miserable investment experiences will play an important role in your long-term investment success. Just as in all other areas of investing, *discipline* is key. Many investors overreact to unexpected market downturns. Of course, market downturns are always unexpected. Here are some guidelines that will help you to continue to invest successfully even when the financial world seems to be in the midst of collapse:

✦ **When in doubt, doing nothing is often best.** Many investors react too suddenly to adverse market conditions, and they almost always do the wrong thing. In fact, selling when one should be holding, or even buying, is an almost surefire way to lose money. As uncomfortable as it may seem at the time, doing nothing may be the best way to react during a crisis. A long-revered Wall Street maxim is to "never sell into the market weakness." Wait until things settle down. Also, be very wary of the immediate opinions of experts in the midst of and right after the crisis. Ask yourself, "If they are such experts, why didn't they predict this mess in the first place?" For the unvarnished truth on those who style themselves market forecasters, see page 120.

✦ **Diversification is your best defense.** Spreading your money among various categories of stock investments, interest-earning investments, and real estate investments has always been and will continue to be the best way to cope with unfriendly markets. That's because when some categories are diving, other categories are likely to be thriving or at least maintaining their value. The better diversified you are, the better position you will be in to emerge from the scary market relatively unscathed.

✦ **Always remember that you are investing for the long term.** Declining stock, bond, and real estate markets aren't that uncommon. But, unless you recently got a terrible prognosis from your doctor or you're going to need a chunk of money to acquire something in the near future, you're investing for the long term, and all of the declines we have experienced in the past have been more than offset by even larger subsequent gains. No matter how badly the markets are faring, no matter how dismal the prognoses of the pundits, a decade from now the market travails will be a faint memory.

If you must do something . . . It may be too much for you to simply sit by idly when the market is in the process of declining, particularly if you're a conservative investor (as evidenced by the results of the quiz you took in Idea 36, on page 111). So if market conditions are particularly bad or if you really fear that the stock market is headed for disaster, you could make some **minor** modifications to your investment diversification. I emphasize **minor** changes, because if you start to make major shifts in investments, you are, in effect, timing the market. Market timing doesn't work, and disastrous investment markets are a relatively rare occurrence anyway.

Here's an example of a minor modification: If your current investment allocation is 60 percent stocks and 40 percent interest-earning securities, you might reduce your stock exposure to 50 percent if that will help you sleep better at night. But again, the risk is you may sell your stocks just before they recover. Another problem with making even minor changes in your investment strategy is, how do you decide when to go back to your original investment-allocation approach? It may be easy to lighten up on stocks when you are scared, but it's really tough deciding when to get back in. This is how bad it can get: I had a caller on a radio talk show who said he had become frightened of stocks and got out of the market entirely. He was in a quandary about when to get back in and wanted my opinion as to whether it was a good time to do so. I asked him when he had got out of stocks. It had been many years prior, and stock prices on average had more than **tripled** since this poor chap abandoned his good senses. Don't let fear get in the way of sensible investing.

> Taking a long-term perspective amid declining markets will help you avoid making unwise changes in your investments.
>
> ■
>
> *A speculative stock is one that a whole lot of people own, but they have no idea why they own it.*
> —ANONYMOUS

IDEA 48

Quick Ways to Evaluate a Real Estate Investment

It's too bad more people don't invest in income-producing real estate, because it's one of the best ways for people of average financial means to create wealth. True, being a landlord is no picnic, but a lot of people don't seem to mind it. If the real estate bug ever catches you, please, please, please avoid the biggest sin inexperienced (and even a few experienced) real estate investors commit: overpaying. If you pay too much, the property is almost a sure loser from the outset. At best, it will take many years of pouring more money into the property until it reaches the point where its income equals your outgo.

Rules of thumb. If you're ever in the market for real estate, there are a couple of easy calculations that you can make to decide if the property is reasonably priced:

1. **Rent multiplier.** The simplest way to evaluate a property is to compare the price you'd have to pay for it with its current gross yearly rental income—called the "rent multiplier." Any property selling for much more than seven times total annual rental is likely to yield a negative cash flow; in other words, your rental income won't be sufficient to cover your mortgage and operating expenses, let alone make a profit. To determine the rent multiplier, which compares the total selling price with the current gross annual rental, use the following formula:

   Rent multiplier = Selling price ÷ Total annual rental income

   For example, the asking price of a duplex is $300,000, and it generates $25,000 in annual rent. The rent multiplier is calculated as follows:

   Rent multiplier = $300,000 ÷ $25,000 = 12 times rental income

   The property is selling for twelve times annual rental. As I just mentioned, any property that is selling for much more than seven times the gross annual rental is probably not going to be a particularly good investment. Also remember that if you put a sizable cash down payment into the property to assure a positive cash flow, you're only fooling yourself; there's an opportunity cost associated with tying up a lot of cash that could otherwise be earning income in lower-risk securities. Incidentally, professional real estate investors generally won't pay more than five to six times gross annual rental.

2. **Capitalization rate.** Calculating the capitalization rate—or "cap rate," as the veteran real estate investors call it—is a more detailed method of evaluating a property. The cap rate is determined as follows:

Capitalization rate = Net operating income ÷ Total amount invested

For example, an investor is considering investing in an apartment building requiring a total investment of $500,000. It has a net operating income over the most recent year of $42,000. The capitalization rate is calculated as follows:

Capitalization rate = $42,000 ÷ $500,000 = 8.4%

A cap rate of 8 percent or higher is considered desirable, so this property may be worth investigating further.

Some words to the wise: make sure the amounts to go into the cap rate formula are realistic. *Total amount invested* should include both the down payment and the borrowed money necessary to buy the property, while the *net operating income* is the total rental income (allowing for vacancies) less all the expenses except mortgage interest and principal repayments.

When calculating either the rent multiplier or the capitalization rate, beware of a favorite trick called "bumping to market," which is used by real estate agents and owners to make a deal look more attractive. Bumping to market is raising rent projections from what they actually are to what they "ought to be," according to a so-called market level. Don't believe these pie-in-the-sky projections.

Where will you get the down payment? Lenders will probably want a much higher percentage down payment for an investment property compared with what they'd ask for if you were buying a home that you're going to live in. Don't let your zeal to buy income-producing real estate get in the way of your otherwise good judgment. In other words, avoid borrowing against your home or, worse, cashing in retirement accounts to scrounge up the down payment. Despite what you may have heard, it's very difficult to buy real estate through an IRA account. For starters, since you can't borrow within an IRA, you'll have to pay for 100 percent of the property out of the IRA. Even if you have that much money in your retirement accounts, it's not very prudent to tie up so much retirement money in a piece of real estate. Other pitfalls await such strategies, but I think you get the point.

Be patient. Don't let the above rules of thumb discourage you from seeking out properties that pass muster. They're tough to find in strong real estate markets. Also, forget about buying single-family homes and condos for rental purposes. The numbers just won't work. Opt instead for multifamily dwellings, small apartment buildings, and, perhaps, small commercial or industrial properties. If you can find the right property at the right price, the opportunities to build a lot of wealth are sumptuous, because once you get bitten by the real estate bug, you'll likely end up owning a small real estate empire.

The *Grow Your Money!* special reader Web site offers other guidance and rules of thumb for investing in income-producing real estate, including tips on being a landlord or landlady. **w w w**

> Investing in income-producing real estate is an excellent way to accumulate a lot of wealth so long as you avoid overpaying for a property.

IDEA 49

Why Not Be Lord or Lady of the Land?

Are you not cut out to be a landlord or landlady? Why not be lord or lady of the land, instead? Buying *undeveloped land*—also called *raw land*—can have tremendous potential for price appreciation, but it also carries high risks.

The downsides. Raw land purchases often end up being raw deals unless you plan to commercially develop the property later on, or perhaps build a retirement residence on it. Successful investors in undeveloped land need deep pockets. Since undeveloped land doesn't generate any income, your money will probably be tied up for a long time. It's difficult to finance undeveloped land for more than a few years. In addition, finding the right kind of property takes some real expertise. Another cautionary note: large parcels of land that sell for peanuts usually spell trouble, not *bargain*. The price is cheap for a number of good reasons—lousy location, difficult access, bad drainage. So if the land you want to purchase has more moose per square mile than people, don't expect to make any money on it. Land in particularly desirable areas, on the other hand, is always very expensive to purchase. In other words (with no offense intended to the good people of Kansas), a quarter acre in Manhattan, New York, is a lot more valuable than four hundred acres in the suburbs of Manhattan, Kansas.

Go for it. Unless you are totally turned off by the caveats noted above, why not look around for some undeveloped land? There's no rush, but if you keep your eyes open, you might eventually find an attractive property. Avoid situations where land developers are trying to sell small tracts of land for supposed future development. Rather, local real estate brokers who are familiar with the market can be invaluable advisers. Here are some things that would-be land barons should keep in mind when evaluating a property:

✦ **Physical condition.** The size, shape, and topography of the property are critical, as are drainage and subsoil conditions.

✦ **Economic factors.** State and local economic conditions are particularly important considerations. Appreciation may depend on local employment, how diversified the economic base of the area is, as well as the income growth of its inhabitants.

✦ **Governmental factors.** Zoning regulations and building codes can critically affect future development possibilities. Local tax and environmental regulations may have significant implications for development as well.

✦ **Demographics.** Growing populations and shrinking household sizes are favorable demographic trends, because they indicate the need for more residential housing.

The key to success is to buy land that is relatively close to rapidly developing areas and is in the path of the direction of the development. If not you, your parents probably comment on how highly developed areas in nearby communities were just woods a couple of decades earlier. "Oh, if only I had bought a piece of that land back then" is the common lament. Well, there's still time to find those tracts a bit farther out of town. A lot of people have and will continue to make a ton of money investing in undeveloped land. One of them might as well be you. Go for it!

Owning undeveloped land is expensive, but can be enormously rewarding, so consider becoming a land baron or baroness.

■

The best investment on earth is earth.
—LOUIS GLICKMAN

CHAPTER 8

Buying and Maintaining a Home

If you're not yet a homeowner, you probably yearn to be one. If you already own a home, in spite of occasionally questioning why you ever bought the albatross in the first place, you probably have some questions about paying down the mortgage, moving versus remodeling, and reducing your costs. If you haven't sufficiently indulged your edifice complex, you may be thinking about a vacation home. Whatever your situation may be, this chapter will help you make smart domiciliary decisions.

IDEA 50

Tricks of the Home-Buying Trade

A home will probably be the second-best investment you'll ever make (your career is first, as discussed in chapter 2). It will certainly be the most expensive investment you'll ever make. I'm not talking about the mere $439,000 that the house originally cost (or the $43,900 your parents originally paid when they bought their first house). I'm talking about what it costs to maintain it. But that's beside the point. Aside from the quality-of-life advantages of owning a home, there are two very significant financial benefits (beyond the obvious tax deductions for mortgage interest and property taxes):

+ You have the opportunity to be mortgage-free by the time you retire or shortly thereafter. See Idea 52, on page 165.

+ The home can be a source of additional income during retirement for downsizers.

Buying a home is no simple task, particularly for first-timers, who tend to let emotions get in the way and who are simply uninformed about the many nuances of the real estate market. I can't help you if your emotions get the better of you, but the following information will help both new and experienced homebuyers to be better-informed purchasers:

How much house can you afford? Before getting tied up in the theatrics of finding a home, take a dispassionate look at how much you can afford to pay. Figure out how much more it will cost you to own a home compared with renting. After you factor in the tax savings from mortgage interest and property tax deductions, you may be pleasantly surprised to find that the cost of owning won't be much more than what you are paying in rent.

Keep in mind that when you start looking for houses, you'll always find "better" houses that are beyond your price range. That's understandable, and it happens to all home buyers. Someone who is looking at $2 million homes would dearly love to buy a $3 million home, because it's a "better" home. Set a reasonable target price (although you'll probably end up spending more than your target).

You should also find out if you qualify for assistance for lower-income homebuyers. Check with state and federal housing agencies, because they may have a program for you even though your income isn't all that low.

Are you financially prepared to look for a house? Three matters need to be attended to:

1. Is your credit rating okay?

2. Have you cleaned up your debts?

3. Do you have enough money for the down payment?

Rather than addressing these issues after you begin your house search, why not go to a lender and get a preapproved loan? This will also put you in a much better negotiating position.

The amount a lender may lend you is *not* necessarily the amount you can comfortably borrow. Ask yourself if buying a house that costs the maximum you can afford will leave you so short that you won't be able to furnish it, much less take a vacation for the next decade.

Begin your search. Almost 80 percent of all home searches begin on the Internet. You can search through literally hundreds of online listings, take virtual tours, and view photographs of neighborhoods and homes. The Internet can be a valuable resource to help you narrow your search. Be realistic in your search. While location is important, so is affordability. First-time home buyers often have to settle on housing that isn't quite as nice as the home they grew up in. But that's okay. The goal is getting into a home. You can always trade up later on if you must.

Negotiation. When it's time for negotiations, it's the time to hold your emotions in check. You obviously want the home, but until you have purchased it, it's just a house. If this is the first time you've purchased a home, be sure to enlist the assistance of family members or friends who have purchased houses in the past. Otherwise, you can rest assured that you'll pay too much.

Negotiation need not be an unpleasant experience. Stressful, yes; unpleasant, not necessarily. Understanding the reason the seller is selling can be helpful and give you some perspective. If the seller is

particularly anxious to sell, for example, that puts you in a better negotiating position.

Purchase-and-sale agreement. A purchase-and-sale agreement
(P&S) is a contract between a buyer and a seller that specifies the
terms and price of the sale. Prior to signing the P&S and forking over
the deposit, you should ask an attorney to review it. You will want to
include some contingencies in the agreement, typically including
obtaining the financing (which will require the lender to appraise the
property), a satisfactory home inspection, and a clear title. A contin-
gency will let you back out of the P&S if a stipulated event arises, for
example if the home inspection finds that the house is built over a
nuclear waste dump.

Inspection. The real estate agent who is working for the seller may—
or may not—have a conflict of interest in recommending an inspector, so you may want to retain one on your own. You should receive
a written report from whomever you use. It also is very helpful to ac-
company the inspector during the inspection to discuss any problems
the inspector may uncover. It's actually kind of fun, and a good inspector can be very helpful in advising you about making repairs and
minor improvements later on.

Mortgages. Stick with garden-variety mortgages. Your parents probably survived quite nicely on an old-fashioned fixed-rate mortgage,
and these are still the best mortgages for many first-time home buyers if interest rates are relatively low at the time the mortgage is taken
out and you expect to stay in the house indefinitely. Adjustable-rate
mortgages with reasonable caps on future rate increases are also fine.
Avoid unusual financing arrangements, notably interest-only mortgages where you never pay down principal and adjustable-rate mortgages (ARMs) with substantial future hikes in the interest rate. These
latter mortgages were the cause of the recent subprime-lending deba-
cle. Homeowners had been induced into taking low-interest ARMs
whose interest rates rose dramatically in future years.

Good luck on your home search. You'll do fine.

For more information and a detailed home-buyer's checklist, see the *Grow Your Money!* reader Web site. **w w w**

> Understanding the nuances of the home-buying process can minimize the stress for first-time home buyers.
>
> ■
>
> *House, n. A hollow edifice erected for the habitation of man, rat, mouse, beetle, cockroach, fly, mosquito, flea, bacillus, and microbe.*
> —AMBROSE BIERCE

IDEA 51

Save for a House or Save for Retirement?

If you're planning to buy a home, you're faced with a quandary. Should you save for a house or contribute to retirement savings plans? Despite the advertisements for no-money-down mortgages, you're probably going to need a hefty sum to buy a house or condo, not to mention additional money to pay moving costs and the cost of the accoutrements that make a house a home. In fact, given the recent spate of foreclosures that were due to risky lending practices, it's likely that would-be home buyers will have to ante up more of a down payment than previously.

Temporarily suspending retirement-plan contributions to build up your housing fund is something that shouldn't be taken lightly, but buying a home is such a smart financial move that it may be justified. Before dropping your contributions entirely, however, keep in mind that to help finance a home purchase, it's possible to tap into almost all types of retirement savings plans, including:

◆ Traditional IRA

◆ Roth IRA

✦ Workplace retirement plans, including 401(k), 403(b), tax-sheltered annuity (TSA), and Federal Thrift Savings Plans (TSP)

Depending on the plan, money can be either withdrawn or borrowed for purposes of buying a first home.

Strategies

❑ If your contemplated home purchase is still a few years away, divide your money between retirement plan contributions and savings.

❑ If you're within a year or so of buying a house and need to boost your savings, temporarily curtail or suspend your retirement contributions. Invest the savings conservatively, however, since you're going to need the money fairly soon (see Idea 35 on page 110). Also, get back to making retirement contributions as soon as possible after you've moved into your château.

Other sources of down-payment money. Here are a couple of additional ways to add to your down-payment ante:

❑ **Life-insurance-policy loans.** Borrow from life insurance policies that have a cash value (*term* policies do not—you have to die to get any money from a term policy, in which case you won't need a home).

❑ **Family largesse.** Last, but by no means least, request parental or grandparental assistance. If it's still some time before you buy the house and you have any well-off relatives, send them birthday and holiday cards as well as periodic flowers and chocolates so they'll know what a wonderful person you are.

For more information on the rules specific to withdrawals or loans from the various retirement plans, visit the reader Web site. www

If you're saving for a house, you may not have to forgo retirement plan contributions to build your savings, since most retirement plans can be tapped into for a home purchase.

■

It takes a heap of other things besides
A heap o' livin' to make a home out of a house.
To begin with, it takes a heap o' payin'.
—OGDEN NASH

IDEA 52

Should You Pay Off Your Mortgage Early?

Much to the disgust of a lot of people, I have long encouraged that, under the right circumstances, they should plan to pay off their mortgages early by making extra payments against principal. You don't have to start doing it now—the time may not yet be right. On the other hand, do you really want to spend thirty years paying off your mortgage? Or if you have taken out an interest-only mortgage, do you want to make payments for the next thirty years and still owe your original loan principal? So before you join the others who tell me this is a terrible idea, allow me to review the pros and cons of making extra payments against your mortgage.

Advantages

✦ Paying off your mortgage early saves a lot of money because the total amount of money you spend to pay off the mortgage will be less—sometimes far less—than it would if you took the full thirty years. Even though your tax deductions are reduced if you accelerate the mortgage payments, you're still ahead financially, because for every dollar of mortgage interest you pay out, you save only a small fraction of that dollar in taxes.

✦ If you can pay off your mortgage by the time you retire or shortly thereafter, you'll need a lot less income to support yourself in retirement than do those people who are either renting or still making mortgage payments. Moreover, your tax situation after you retire may be such that you will not receive as much benefit from a mortgage interest deduction as you did during your working years.

Drawbacks

✦ If you're in the highest tax brackets, the tax advantage of the mortgage-interest deduction may outweigh the advantages of making extra payments.

✦ The extra payments reduce the amount of money that you have to invest.

✦ If you can earn an average investment return in excess of the interest rate on the mortgage, making extra payments is not as financially efficacious as investing the money.

"Stocks Do Better." This is the argument advanced most vehemently by the don't-prepay-your-mortgage crowd. They believe that you'll come out ahead by stretching out the mortgage and investing the money instead. That argument pretty much assumes that this money will be invested in stocks, and stock returns—even in the go-go years—are far from certain. For example, you know for sure how much "return" you're getting by making a payment against, say, a 6 percent mortgage. But the return on stocks is less clear-cut. If you're confident that, over the long term, you'll earn more on stocks than the interest you're paying on your mortgage, then you're better off not making any extra mortgage payments. But here's another way of looking at the dilemma: if you're investing in a diversified manner—not only in stocks, but also in bonds and short-term investments such as money market funds, CDs, and savings accounts—then you're better off making extra payments against your mortgage by using money that would otherwise be invested in bonds or short-term investments. The interest rate on your mortgage is almost certainly higher than the return you'd get on a money market fund or other short-term investments and could be higher than the return on a bond or bond fund.

"I Need the Tax Deduction." Other opponents of prepaying a mortgage aren't stock market fanatics. Rather, they argue that they need the tax deduction for the mortgage interest. Every extra payment reduces the deductible interest on the loan. That argument may have some validity for those in the top tax brackets (although they could have so much income that their mortgage-interest deductions may be reduced by other tax rules). But tax theoreticians (Mothers, don't let your children become tax theoreticians) say that you have to be in a tax bracket that's at least 35 percent to make any tax deduction financially worthwhile. Few of us, however, are in such a lofty income tax bracket, which is assessed on those fortunate souls with federal taxable incomes around or in excess of $350,000. Most of us are in the 25 percent tax bracket. If so, and you pay $10,000 in mortgage interest this year, you're going to save $2,500 in taxes. Is that such a great deal? Shell out $10,000 to save $2,500 in taxes, and do that year in and year out? Mortgage interest deductions are nice, but they're hardly a reason against prepaying a mortgage, because as the next table shows, making even small extra payments can add up to big total-cost savings.

Prepay Your Mortgage If . . .

So, in reckless defiance of the criticism that's been heaped upon me, I still urge you to make extra payments against your mortgage, but if and only if:

✦ You've contributed generously to your available retirement plans, including your retirement savings plans at work and an IRA. While there are lots of financial benefits to reducing your mortgage sooner rather than later, tax-advantaged retirement savings plans offer better ones.

✦ You've paid off all other higher-interest loans, including credit card loans and car loans. It makes no sense to make extra payments against your, say, 6½ percent mortgage while you've got an 11 percent car loan and 18 percent credit card balances.

Are you a believer? There are numerous ways to prepay a mortgage, and all of them work. They range from the very informal to refinancing your mortgage to a shorter maturity. If you want to find just the right way for you to prepay your mortgage, you're in luck. Just visit the *Grow Your Money!* reader Web site for explanations and illustrations of the many ways to prepay your mortgage. **w w w**

A LITTLE EXTRA GOES A LONG WAY— THE BENEFIT OF MAKING EXTRA PAYMENTS ON YOUR MORTGAGE

$150,000, 30-year mortgage with 6% interest. Monthly payment of $900.

AMOUNT OF MONTHLY EXTRA MORTGAGE PAYMENT	MORTGAGE WILL BE PAID OFF IN	TOTAL PRINCIPAL AND INTEREST PAYMENTS
$ 0	30 years	$325,000
100	23 years	280,000
200	19 years	250,000
300	17 years	235,000
Biweekly payments*	24 years	285,000

* A biweekly mortgage involves making one-half the standard monthly mortgage payment every two weeks, for a total of twenty-six payments per year, the equivalent of thirteen monthly payments. Biweekly mortgages are particularly convenient for those who are paid every two weeks.

> Under the right circumstances, prepaying your mortgage makes a lot of financial sense.
>
> ■
>
> *If medical science continues to prolong life, some of us may eventually pay off the mortgage.*
> —ANONYMOUS

IDEA 53

Appeal Your Property Tax Bill

Are you among the hordes of homeowners who are paying more in property taxes than they have to? Chances are you don't know, but investing some time could result in a reduction in your property taxes, which, over the years, can amount to noticeably more money in your pocket (or, preferably, in your investment account). Here are some steps and tips to follow that will help you through the process of, first, finding out if your property tax bill is too high and, second, successfully appealing your assessment to the powers that be.

Investigating the fairness of your assessment. Doing the legwork to find out if your assessment is fair is tedious, but not as onerous as most homeowners believe. If you truly don't have the time, you may want to hire a consultant to do the work for you.

◆ **Time is of the essence.** Most localities impose deadlines for appealing. The local tax assessor's office will provide the information. If you missed the deadline, you'll have to wait until the following year or, in some instances longer, before you can appeal.

◆ **Building your case.** There are a couple of ways to make your case. First, the town may have made a mistake in the valuation placed on your house, and second, comparable homes may have a lower assessment.

- **Incorrect valuation.** Double-check the description of your house, including square footage and number of rooms. Check the description against any appraisals that you may have. It might also pay to have a new appraisal. If there are any changes in the property or the neighborhood that might diminish its value, this might affect your valuation.

- **Lower-valued comparables.** You can visit the town assessor's office to compare your assessment with similar homes in your neighborhood. Gather data on several homes to see if you have a valid argument that your home is over-assessed. Try to identify specific factors that reduce your home's value compared with others situated nearby.

Appealing your assessment. Once you have gathered up the necessary information, it's time to appeal. This is usually at two-step process.

✦ **Informal meeting at the assessor's office.** First, try to arrange a meeting at the assessor's office. This may or may not be permissible, depending upon town rules. Make sure you have your ducks in a row before the meeting, then lay out your case. You may be pleasantly surprised to find that the assessor agrees, although you may not be happy with the amount of the reduction. It may be smarter to accept this informal offer than to take the case to the next step, but it's up to you. If the assessor rejects your case altogether, then, unless the assessor convinces you that your case has no merit, you should take it to the next level.

✦ **Request a hearing.** Find out from your friends at the assessor's office (well, they might not be good friends if they rejected your request) when the next hearings are scheduled and request one for yourself. Organize your presentation so that it's easy for the board that's hearing your request to quickly understand your arguments. Photos and well-organized analyses will convey the seriousness with which you take the proceedings.

Is it worth the time and effort? Hey, real money is involved here, and if you think you've been wronged, it's worth the effort. Also, the odds of getting a reduction aren't bad. Real estate professionals say that nearly half of the people who appeal their property tax assessments end up getting a tax reduction. If nothing else, it will be a lesson in civics. Come to think of it, bring the kids along to the hearing.

If you think your property tax bill is too high (who doesn't?), try to get it reduced by appealing your assessment.

■

My parents didn't want to move to Florida, but they
turned sixty and that's the law.
—JERRY SEINFELD

IDEA 54

Move or Improve?

There may come a time (and that time might be now) when you're in a quandary about whether you should improve the home you're now in or move to more desirable quarters. Whatever your choice, this is an expensive and enervating decision that merits careful consideration. Let me help you "ponder" this momentous decision.

Times have changed. While owning a home has long been the American dream, the way we view home ownership has changed over the generations. In the old days, our forebears bought a home, raised their families, retired, and then passed on the property to their heirs at death. The homes were maintained, but substantial improvements were rare. Living in a house that has been passed down for generations is the exception these days, rather than the rule.

But now we're less emotionally attached to the family home, so the decision to make major home improvements or to move is one that needs to be carefully deliberated. A move or a home improvement project are time-consuming and take a lot out of you and your loved ones. Mistakes are costly and not easily undone. Here are some issues to weigh if you are ever confronting the "move or improve" conundrum:

General considerations.

❏ Evaluate the physical layout of your current home. Are there limits to how much can be added to the house without running afoul of local zoning regulations or greatly diminishing the size of your yard? If an addition is out of the question or very difficult, can you work within the existing dimensions of your home?

❏ Obtain a cost estimate for the remodeling project and add at least 10 percent to the estimate, because that's reality. Then add the cost to what you think your home is worth now. Will the total still be in line with neighborhood housing prices? You never want to live in the most expensive home in the neighborhood. On the other hand, if the proposed remodeling cost results in a house that is still modestly priced by neighborhood standards, the project could be financially sound. As unpleasant as it is, one scenario to always keep in mind is what kind of return you would receive if you had to sell the house right after you finished the remodeling, because of, say, a job change, illness, or other event.

Matters that favor remodeling . . .

❏ The most compelling reason to stay put and remodel is that you really like the community and neighborhood in which you live and plan to live their indefinitely—five years at least.

❏ Remodeling is expensive, but it may pale in comparison to the substantial costs of moving (over and above the cost of the new home), including real estate commissions, closing costs, moving costs, draperies, and endless other costs associated with whipping the new home into shape. Property taxes on the new home may also be considerably higher. In contrast, well-thought-out home improvements could add almost as much to the value of your home as they cost. (See "Best home remodeling projects," which follows.)

Matters that favor moving . . .

❑ Although you may like your current home, the possible remodeling you envision may still not make the house as livable as you would like. If you can afford it, moving into a new manse may be preferable.

❑ If you're in an older home that's beginning to require a lot of maintenance, moving into a newer structure may well outweigh modeling an old house, particularly if you are retired or nearing retirement age.

❑ Living in the midst of a construction site is a dreadful way of life, one that you and your family may not be prepared to endure. You'll be sharing your house with strangers, things will go wrong, and your home life will be disrupted. Idea 55, on page 176, offers some hints on surviving a home-improvement project.

Best home remodeling projects. If you do decide to improve your home, you need to balance your own needs and desires against how much the improvement adds to your home's value. In the best situations, most of the money you invest in your remodeling will be recouped when you eventually sell the house. However, some elements of the project that are important to you may not be of much value to the next buyer, and you need to consider this possibility when planning the project. For example, spending $10,000 on a sauna may not add any value to your home, but if a sauna is important to the comfort of the family and you expect to stay in the house (not necessarily the sauna) indefinitely, this may be a small price to pay, particularly if the alternative is to move to a house that already sports a sauna. Here is a list of the best home remodeling projects based on the expected percentage of cost they will add to the value of your home. Each is estimated to recoup at least 80 percent, but regional and other variations may affect the percentage.

✦ Siding

✦ Bathroom remodel

✦ Kitchen remodel

✦ Bedroom remodel

✦ Deck addition

✦ Basement remodel

✦ Window replacement

✦ Bathroom addition

✦ Roofing replacement

✦ Family room addition

✦ Master suite addition

The *Grow Your Money!* Web site offers some Internet resources that will help you evaluate a contemplated remodeling project. **w w w**

Deciding between selling your house and moving or remodeling the house you're in requires careful deliberation.

■

A man's home is his hassle.
—ANONYMOUS

MONEY TIP

Find Out If You're Still Required to Pay for Private Mortgage Insurance

If you buy a house with less than a 20 percent down payment, most lenders require private mortgage insurance (PMI)—and the premiums, typically ranging from $25 to $100 per month, are taken out of your hide. But you are not stuck with PMI forever. Once your equity exceeds 20 percent of the home's value (in some instances, the percentage may be more), your lender is required to let you drop the coverage. So if you've paid down enough of the principal and/or if your home has appreciated sufficiently to increase your equity to more than 20 percent—you should be able to avoid those annoying PMI premiums. Here's how:

If you purchased your home after July 1999. When the remaining balance of your mortgage equals 80 percent of the original value of the property (an appraisal will probably be required), you may request in writing that the PMI be canceled. When the balance of the mortgage equals 78 percent of the original value of the property, the lender must automatically terminate the PMI, provided that mortgage payments are current.

If you purchased your home before August 1999. It's up to you to contact the lender and prove that you qualify for termination of the PMI according to the lender's stipulations. The lender is required to provide an annual written statement detailing the rights of the borrower to cancel the PMI should the qualifications be met.

Whatever your situation may be, if you have PMI, it's in your best interest to make sure you aren't among the many homeowners—millions, according to some articles—who are needlessly paying PMI premiums.

If you're saddled with PMI, the special reader Web site offers more guidance on ridding yourself of this annoyance sooner rather than later. **www**

> ■
>
> *I hate housework! You make the bed, you do the dishes—*
> *and six months later you have to start all over again.*
> —JOAN RIVERS

IDEA 55

Surviving a Home Improvement Project

The reason so many home improvement projects end up being such a miserable experience is that so much effort is expended up front—budgeting, selecting materials, selecting and negotiating with the contractor—that there's no energy left to plan for surviving the experience itself. But investing a little time establishing some ground rules and some reasonable expectations can help you and your family cope with having strangers in your house, not to mention numerous other disruptions, for a period of weeks, if not months. The first step is one that may be crucial to how well the project proceeds, and that is selecting the contractor.

Selecting the contractor. Here are some dos and don'ts pertaining to the all-important process of selecting a contractor:

❑ **Consider at least three contractors.** Make sure each contractor is currently registered with your state. Referrals are helpful, but always ask for and check references. Find out if a contractor has a complaint or judgment history by checking with the Better Business Bureau. Agencies in your state may also maintain records on complaints. Never agree to give a job to someone unsolicited who simply arrives at your door. Be wary of pricing that seems too good to be true.

❑ **Before you sign a contract**, get a detailed, written estimate that includes price quotes for all special materials, installations, and labor. Ask for proof that the contractor carries insurance to cover your project. Make sure that the contractor applies for and obtains a building permit if one is required.

❑ **Review the contract carefully.** It should include the contractor's registration number, a street address (not a post office box), the dates work is to begin and is to be substantially completed, the total amount agreed to be paid and a payment schedule, a list of materials to be used and their specifications, and provisions for changes or "extras." Don't hire a contractor who won't agree to a written contract, no matter how small the project.

❑ **Payment schedule.** Don't pay a substantial portion of the total cost up front. Many state laws limit the percentage of the project that can be collected up front.

❑ **Late completion penalty.** If it's crucial to you that the work be completed on time, try to negotiate penalties for late completion or a bonus for timely completion.

❑ **Understand consumer protection laws.** Check your own state laws to see what protections exist for consumers versus contractors, including contract-cancellation periods, and dispute arbitration.

Once the contractor has been selected and all of the paperwork is completed to your satisfaction, it's time to prepare for the onslaught.

Coping with the project. The more time you devote at the outset to establishing ground rules for your family and the workers, the better able you will be to cope with the inevitable disruptions in daily routine.

❑ Find out what the workers' schedules will be—arrival and departure times.

❑ Determine who will have keys to your home.

❑ Remind family members to stay away from the work area, particularly when workers are present. If you have youngsters, constantly remind them of this.

❑ Secure valuables in the house and remove not-so-valuable items from the work area.

❑ Making coffee and soft drinks available to the workers through-out the day will be appreciated.

❑ Establish a plan for communicating with the contractor at regular intervals. Make all of your phone numbers available to the contractor, who should do the same for you.

❑ Immediately resolve any concerns that you have with the contractor. Don't let concerns fester.

❑ Try your darndest to stick with your original plan. Changes have a way of mounting up to the point where your $40,000 kitchen project rivals the cost of the kitchen on the *Queen Mary*.

Don't be at all surprised if every day the project is in process you rue the day you decided to undertake it. But if you heed the preceding guidance, six months after completion, you'll look back on it as merely a minor inconvenience.

Home improvement projects are never pleasant, but by following some straightforward guidelines, you can reduce the disruption.

■

The trouble with owning a home is that no matter where you sit, you're looking at something you should be doing.
—ANONYMOUS

MONEY TIP

Think Thrice Before Buying an Appliance Service Contract

One of the joys of homeownership is the constant trafficking between your domicile and the appliance store. It seems that retailers offer service contracts on just about anything you buy. It's really heartwarming to hear the salesperson or cashier encouraging you to purchase a service contract. He or she must really care about you. Or could it be that there's a hefty commission involved? Pardon me for harboring such cynical thoughts.

While the contracts may seem inexpensive, they're probably just a waste of money. None other than the Federal Trade Commission asserts that millions of consumers pay for protection they don't need. Before sinking good money into a service contract, consider the following:

✦ The product probably has a warranty already. Any major problems are likely to arise during the warranty period.

✦ The appliance or electronic gadget is probably pretty reliable in the first place.

✦ If the product is electronic, how soon is it likely to become obsolete? Why have a three-year service contract on something that will be obsolete in two years?

✦ If you must, examine the agreement carefully, and not at the point of purchase. You'll probably soon discover that the terms of the contract are very limited.

✦ Many credit card companies give extended warranty coverage to cardholders who purchase a product on their card. If your credit card doesn't, it might be worthwhile opting for one that does.

What about automobile service contracts? While automobile service contracts may be worthwhile in some instances, government regulators have found that they are often very misleading and duplicate manufacturers' warranties. As with any service contract, rather than succumb to the well-honed pitch of the person who is trying to sell it to you, you need to take the time to read the terms of the contract outside the presence of the salesperson.

The reader Web site provides a checklist of important matters to consider when reviewing an appliance or automobile service contract.

■

The best way to realize the pleasure of feeling rich is to live in a smaller house than your means would entitle you to have.
—EDWARD CLARKE

IDEA 56

Vacation Home Follies

Depending on how well the real estate market is performing, between 10 and 20 percent of home sales in the U.S. are of vacation homes. Sooner or later, if not already, you may get a hankering to buy a second home. At the risk of throwing cold water on a wonderful thought, herewith is a checklist of questions and matters that will help you approach what will be a major and lengthy financial outlay with the objectivity of an ascetic accountant.

❑ **Can you afford it?** Don't let the allure of a dream home in an idyllic setting get in the way of your good financial judgment. While the price of a second home may seem cheap compared with housing prices in your own locale, you are well advised to assess the true cost (including travel costs) to own and maintain the property. In addition, some financially challenged municipalities and states are beginning to view nonresident (and nonvoting) homeowners as a convenient source of revenue through taxes and fees that can be construed only as discriminatory.

❑ **Where will you get the down payment?** The primary reason most second homes are purchased amid frothy real estate markets is that homeowners feel flush with all the equity they have built up in their homes. Many tap into that equity to finance the down payment. Lenders typically require hefty down payments for vacation homes. Using home equity to finance a second-home purchase may be risky, however. Real estate markets don't rise forever, and if your timing is off, you could end up with a heap more housing indebtedness right before housing prices take a hit. But using home equity to partially finance a second home is a far sight better than using another source of down payment money that a surprising number of vacation-home buyers utilize—selling IRAs, which usually involves paying hefty taxes, not to mention a reduction in resources for retirement income. But everyone's situation is different, and if you can easily afford to use home equity or rifle part of your retirement money, you'll be okay. But the *best* way to come up with the down payment is to start setting money aside well in advance of buying your home in Shangri-la, or perhaps use a portion of any financial windfall—an inheritance, for example—for the down payment.

❑ **Assess local real estate market conditions.** Demand for vacation homes is strongest in ebullient real estate markets and wanes when housing prices weaken. Thus, just like investors following the herd when buying stocks, second-home buyers prefer to purchase when prices are high. This is particularly unfortunate, since vacation-home buyers can usually take their time before buying. If you can, wait until the local market slows down. Also, avoid looking for houses in high season. You'll find much more motivated sellers when all the tourists have flown the coop.

❏ **Have you spent time in the area during low season?** A lot of second homes are located in areas that have idyllic climates in high season. But if you envision using the home throughout the year, have you gotten a taste of the climate in low season, when the temperature reaches triple digits above or below zero? Incidentally, the locals are more likely to accept you if you're willing to suffer along with them when the weather is frightful and the tourists are long gone.

❏ **How much will you use the second home?** Do you fully intend to use the second home enough to justify its expense? It's easy to conclude that you will, but reality has a way of disrupting your good intentions. I say that from personal experience. My wife and I used to visit our second home throughout the year, but then the children arrived on the scene. They get to an age when the idea of accompanying their parents to a pastoral retreat—actually accompanying them anywhere—is a dismal prospect. The upshot? We have used the home a total of twenty-four days—in the last five years. I've told the kids that the cost of maintaining the property is greater on a per diem basis than the cost of staying in the Presidential Suite at the Waldorf-Astoria in New York, to which the ingrates responded: "We don't want to go to the Waldorf-Astoria with you and Mom either."

❏ **Be realistic if you plan to rent the property.** Don't buy a vacation home thinking that you'll get a lot of money renting it. Sometimes it works as a rental, but usually it doesn't pan out very well, despite the breathless attestations of the owner or broker who is desperate to unload the property. If it's a seasonal property, the primary rental period is likely to coincide with the time you want to use it. If the seller claims that the property fetches a lot of rent, ask to review the records and make sure he or she wasn't "renting" it to relatives and friends.

❑ **How easy will it be to sell the vacation home?** Unless you're absolutely, positively sure that you're going to keep the vacation home forever, you should at least consider how easy, or difficult, it might be to sell should you have to, perhaps for financial or health reasons. In flat or declining real estate markets, homes in vacation areas tend to lose more value and take longer to sell than houses in residential areas. In short, it's risky to view your vacation home as an investment with enormous appreciation potential.

❑ **Do you have plans to retire there?** Perhaps the most compelling and sensible reason to buy a second home is that you eventually intend to move there, perhaps after you retire. If you are currently a homeowner, the intention to sell your primary residence later on and use the proceeds to pay down the second-home mortgage makes the second-home purchase more financially viable. By the way, if you fully intend to move to a particular locale after retirement, but can't afford to buy a proper home there, you might consider purchasing a building lot now. Then if home prices rise significantly between now and the time you move there, you already have a stake in the ground with your building lot, which, undoubtedly, will have appreciated smartly in value.

There is a more economic alternative. My intention here is to encourage you to make an objective assessment of the viability of buying a second home before you take the plunge. I don't want to discourage you; rather I want you to assess it coolly and thoroughly. Too many people end up regretting the decision to buy a second home and take a financial beating when they sell the property. So if the preceding checklist gave you pause, remember that there's probably no rush to buy. Take your time, but in the meantime, renting during high season is always a sensible and more economic alternative.

It's preferable to view a vacation home more as an investment in your mental health than as a sound financial investment.

■

Home is the place where, when you have to go there,
they have to take you in.
—ROBERT FROST

CHAPTER 9

Paying for College and Other Big-Ticket Items

L ife sometimes seems to be a series of big-ticket items. You may have finished college with a tuition-loan-payment book that was thicker than the Los Angeles phone book. Then it's on to buying cars and a house and paying tuition now for your children, with lots of smaller big-ticket items along the way, like painting the house and car repairs. The more you can prepare in advance for these inevitable exactions, the better off you and your purse will be.

■

It doesn't matter how much you paid for the car, they all look the same after the wreck.

—ANONYMOUS

IDEA 57

Big-Ticket Items Tell a Lot

How people handle big-ticket items is often a reliable indicator of how well-off financially they will be. As discussed in chapter 3, the amount of wealth you accumulate is not a function of how much you earn. Sure, the more you earn the more likely it is that you will be able to become wealthy. (That's why I devoted an entire chapter— chapter 2—to profiting from your career, your best investment by far.) But there are a lot of people who aren't *earning* a ton of money who end up *having* a ton of money. You probably wouldn't know it by the size of their house or the cost of their car.

Perhaps the most reliable indicator of financial well-being is the family home. While they may have been struggling financially when the home was first purchased, the temptation to trade up was resisted, so by the time these singles or couples of widely varying financial circumstances reached middle age (MIDDLE AGE: *n.*, "anyone who is ten years older than you"), all live in homes whose payments are way below what they could afford. The same applies to renters. In short, as incomes rose, the inclination to move into a more expensive home or a fancier apartment didn't arise or wasn't acted on. For example, one couple had always had a modest income. By careful saving and smart investing, they had eventually accumulated almost $1 million in retirement and nonretirement investments. But their mortgage-free house was now worth only a bit more than their annual income. They had bought a modest home many years earlier and had been quite content to stay put, even though their income had grown to the point that they could have moved into a far larger and more luxurious domicile.

Another couple who enjoyed many years of six-figure incomes, had paid off all their debt, had about $2 million in investments—and a $225,000 house. If you applied the usual lending rules of thumb to this couple, based on their income they could afford a house worth well over $1 million. A third example, a single person getting ready for retirement, was earning $50,000 per year, but was paying only $500 a month in rent—only 10 percent of his income. He was fifty-six years old and had saved enough to be able to retire right then and there. It's hardly a coincidence that these people live in housing that is way below what they can afford. Their modest housing expenses allowed them to accumulate large amounts of money. None of them had the slightest desire to trade up. None of them lived in shabby circumstances, either.

Dream-house dreamers. Contrast the preceding examples with others who enjoyed similar incomes. One couple in their late forties had just bought their fourth house—their "dream house," although I suspect the first three houses were dream houses as well. Every time they traded up, they increased their mortgage. I realize that trading up is one of the American dreams. However, after almost twenty years of home "ownership," this couple had a mortgage that was triple the size of the one they had when they bought their first home. After twenty years of mortgage payments, they still had thirty years to go on their current mortgage. Their high-spending ways were reflected in other areas of their financial lives, notably two late-model cars with fat car loans. This couple's two children were about to enter college and being able to pay those costs was going to be a challenge. Student loans and a home-equity loan will probably be necessary to foot college bills. But worse, their combined savings—retirement and otherwise—were less than their annual income. This family is leading the good life, but they're sacrificing their financial future in the process.

The three basic money groups. Why is it that some singles and families have made so much financial progress while others have not? It isn't just a case of some people being a victim of circumstances. Certainly, some people are dealt tough cards in life and end up suffering financially as a result. But among people who have otherwise similar financial circumstances, who have the same income history and the same number of mouths to feed, the reason is as simple as how well—or how poorly—they have learned to distinguish among the three basic money groups: *necessities, luxuries,* and *saving for the future.* Those who have succeeded financially have, more than anything else, been able to distinguish between necessities and luxuries and spend accordingly. Despite growing incomes, the notions of buying trophy homes or always owning late-model cars don't even enter their minds.

The choice is yours. It's up to you to decide what kind of financial life you want to enjoy. *Enjoy* is the operative word. All of us have been bombarded with messages telling us that the more you spend the more you will enjoy life. But there are a lot of people who have found tremendous enjoyment without falling for that vacuous message. Of course they aren't the ones we see living in grand mansions and driving exotic cars (those are the people I worry about). The next time you envy someone who is driving an expensive car, ask yourself the question, Will owning a $50,000 car make me twice as happy as owning a $25,000 car? The mere idea of spending $50,000 on a car is enough to make some people very *unhappy.* But whatever your age, you have a choice going forward. You can lead the good life, but sacrifice your financial future, or you can lead the good life and prepare for a wealthy financial future. It all depends on what it costs to make you happy. Ponder that for a moment.

You can tell a lot by how people spend their money. There's often an inverse relationship between the value of a person's house and car and the amount of his or her wealth. After all, the wealthy usually get that way by not spending money.

■

Not everyone wants to be a millionaire; many are content just to live like one.
—ANONYMOUS

IDEA 58

Why College and Cars and Other Costly Necessities Are So Expensive

Paying for big-ticket items is a struggle, and not just because they're expensive. A big contributor to the problem is that you have to earn a lot more than the price to have enough left over after taxes to pay it. Here's a quick illustration: Say you have a $500 monthly car payment. That may not seem like a big bite considering your income, but you have to earn more than $500 in order to have enough left over to write out the $500 check. Let's say you're in the 25 percent federal income tax bracket, state taxes account for another 2 percent, plus you're probably also subject to Social Security taxes to the tune of almost 8 percent. So, in this example, if taxes on your earnings amount to 35 percent, you have to earn a bit over $750 in order to pay your $500 car loan. Here are some examples, using the same assumptions, that show how much gross income is needed to pay for various big-ticket items.

Item	Cost	How Much Gross Income Is Needed to Pay for It
Credit card loan[1]	$ 10,000	$ 18,000
Car[2]	25,000	43,000
College[3]	100,000	150,000
House[4]	250,000	720,000

[1] *Credit card balance at 15 percent interest paid off over two years.*

[2] *Three-year automobile loan at 7 percent interest.*

[3] *College costs paid out of income. Amount would be higher if borrowed money is involved.*

[4] *Thirty-year mortgage at 6 percent interest, less tax savings from interest payments.*

> No wonder it's so tough paying back loans. You have to earn a lot more than the loan payment, thanks to taxes.
>
> ■
>
> *Our national flower is the concrete cloverleaf.*
> —LEWIS MUMFORD

IDEA 59

Saving for College

I have lost track of the amount of sleep I've lost over what it's costing us to educate our kids. When I add it up for all three, the total looks more like the federal deficit than college tuition. But all families can manage to overcome the challenge. To the extent parents or grandparents can afford to part with the dough, there are various tax-wise ways to save for college, led by the 529 plan. A 529 plan is a state-sponsored investment program, available in all states, that offers tax breaks for families that are saving for college.

❑ **Don't try to save all of it.** Don't even think about trying to save every last cent that it's going to cost to educate your abecedarian. It will require putting aside more money than you can possibly afford. If you set your college savings sights too high, if you find that you can't save what you set out to, you may become discouraged and not save at all. Instead, plan to set aside an amount that you can reasonably afford—perhaps enough to cover one-third of the cost. Just having the student out of the house may save you almost enough to pay the tuition out of pocket.

❑ **Keep saving for retirement.** Don't begin saving for college unless you can at the same time keep up with your retirement plan contributions. In other words, don't reduce your retirement savings in order to save for college. While it's great to save for tuition costs, it's more important (and more financially advantageous) to put money away in retirement plans. See page 199 for an example of the financial damage caused by forgoing retirement savings in favor of college savings.

The best places to invest college money. Unless the child is very near college age, a 529 plan is probably the best alternative for college savings. It is certainly the most tax advantageous. But you have to be careful, because many 529 plans are weighed down with high fees and expenses, and have been generating lackluster investment results as well. That's not a good combination.

✦ **Consider a 529 plan first.** While some 529 plans are not worthy of your money, others are. It just takes some digging. Every state offers at least one plan, and your own state's plan may—or may not—be the best choice. Here's how to find a good one:

> ❑ If your own state offers tax breaks (about half do), opt for this plan unless the expenses are high or the performance is mediocre.

> ❑ Whether your home state offers tax incentives or not, compare the expenses and performance of your own state plan against the plans of other states.

> ❑ If you're comfortable making your own decision, select a 529 plan on your own. This will save you money. If not, ask an investment adviser for help.

✦ **Opt for age-based investing.** Unless you'd really prefer to select your own investments in the plan and move money around, choose instead the "age-based" 529 plan investment alternative. The age-based option will automatically but gradually change the investment mix as the pupil nears college age. The younger the child, the higher the percentage of money in the plan that will be invested in stock. As the child nears college age, the percentage devoted to stock will gradually be reduced, which makes a lot of sense because the last thing you want is to lose a lot of money from a stock-market tumble just before tuition bills arrive. The age-based approach is how most parents should be handling the money anyway, so rather than add "Worry about 529 plan investments" to your already extensive to-do list, simply choose the age-based alternative.

✦ **Alternatives to 529 plans.** Custodial accounts—investment accounts set up by parents or grandparents for minor children or grandchildren—were once the mainstay of college investment accounts, but no longer. In fact, the 529 is usually so much better that parents and grandparents are transferring custodial money into 529 plans. You might want to do so as well. You first have to sell all of the custodial account investments, because the 529s will accept only cash. This could trigger a tax on the sale of the custodial account investments, but it's not likely to be very much.

A couple of other alternatives to 529 plans are described later in this chapter, including a homemade 529 plan (see Idea 61, on page 195), as well as a strategy for saving for retirement and college in the same account (see Idea 62, on page 197).

For updates on college savings alternatives, click on the reader Web site. **w w w**

The 529 plan continues to be the best college savings account for parents and grandparents who can afford the contributions.

■

You seem to think that everyone can save money if they have the character to do it. As a matter of fact, there are innumerable people who have a wide choice between saving and giving their children the best possible opportunities. The decision is usually in favor of the children.

—ELEANOR ROOSEVELT

IDEA 60

Preparing for Annoying but Inevitable Expenses

Irregular expenses (those that happen all the time but usually not each month) and unplanned expenses (those that will arise, but you don't know when) don't amount to very much individually, but in the aggregate they are clearly a big-ticket item that must be planned for. In the past, your budget has probably been pinched because of these unpleasant surprises—an insurance bill, vacation expenses, a car repair, for example. The best way to prepare for them is to put some money aside each month in a separate savings or checking account—as if it were an escrow account. The following summary can be used to identify and quantify these expenses. You'll probably be shocked by how much they add up to. That's why many people who haven't set money aside to pay the darn things have trouble paying them off on time.

IRREGULAR AND UNPLANNED EXPENSES SUMMARY

This checklist will help you summarize the various budget-busting expenses that befall you on an irregular or unplanned basis. The trick is to set aside enough money regularly to pay for them. While you know when you're going to have to pay irregular expenses, you don't know when unplanned expenses will arise. It's preferable to put money set aside for unplanned expense in an investment account to give it a chance to grow before it needs to be tapped.

IRREGULAR EXPENSES

❑ Property taxes $_____

❑ Insurance   _____

❑ Seasonal fuel/electricity   _____

❑ Vacation   _____

❑ Tuition/school expenses   _____

❑ Holidays/gifts   _____

❑ Charitable contributions   _____

❑ Club membership dues   _____

❑ Estimated income taxes   _____

❑ Retirement plan contributions   _____

❑ _____   _____

❑ _____   _____

❑ _____   _____

            Total irregular expenses $_____

UNPLANNED EXPENSES

❑ Car repairs $_____

❑ Home maintenance   _____

❑ Home repairs   _____

❑ Helping out financially strapped relatives   _____

❑ _____   _____

❑ _____   _____

❑ _____   _____

            Total unplanned expenses $_____

Special note to retirees and soon-to-be retirees: It's difficult enough to cope with unanticipated expenses when you're employed, but those expenses can be downright disastrous when you're retired, because you don't have as much flexibility in your spending after retirement. So it's doubly important to both anticipate and budget for both irregular and unplanned expenses.

Expenses that are paid quarterly or annually as well as unplanned expenses can wreak havoc on your cash flow.

■

If you stay in Beverly Hills too long you become a Mercedes.
—ROBERT REDFORD

IDEA 61

Create a Homemade 529 Plan Without the Hefty Expenses

The 529 plans are the most popular plans for college savings and often for good reason. (See Idea 59, on page 190.) While they have to be funded with after-tax dollars, withdrawals (including all appreciation in value) used to pay for a family member's college expenses are usually tax-free. But many 529 plans are sapped by fees and expenses and have poor investment choices. If you're comfortable investing college money on your own, setting up a homemade 529 plan can solve both of these problems. Here's how:

✦ Set up a brokerage account in a parent's name and invest in index funds and exchange-traded funds that pass on very low capital gains. (See Idea 38, on page 121.) Also consider putting individual dividend-paying stocks into the account. You have complete control over how the money in your homemade college savings plan is invested and distributed. There are no restrictions.

✦ Any capital-gain distributions and dividends paid out before college should be subject to a low capital-gains rate. If the college money is invested in index funds, ETFs, and stocks, most of the capital gains will be made when the investments are liquidated to pay for college. But, so long as the child is not a bloomin' genius who goes off to college before reaching age eighteen, you can gift the money to a child age eighteen or older and the child's tax rate on capital gains will likely be much lower, probably just 5 percent.

✦ Also consider establishing a Coverdell Education Savings Account (ESA). You probably qualify to set one up, unless you have a high income. Although the annual contribution limit is only $2,000 per college-bound child (not per parent and grandparent), all withdrawals to pay for college are tax-free. Since you set up your own Coverdell account, you have a much broader investment choice compared with what a 529 plan offers. Also, in addition to paying for college, money withdrawn from a Coverdell ESA may be used to pay for primary- and secondary-school education costs, from kindergarten through twelfth grade.

✦ If, for whatever reason, the money in your homemade college savings plan will not be used for college, no problem. You're in total control.

For a list of some low-cost investment alternatives that might be right for your homegrown 529 plan, click on the *Grow Your Money!* reader Web site. **w w w**

> You can create your own college savings plan without the costs and restrictions of the more traditional plans.
>
> ■
>
> *Knowledge accumulates in universities, because the freshmen bring a little in and the seniors take none away.*
> —ANONYMOUS

IDEA 62

Save for College and Retirement in the Same Account

Parents of youngsters have at least two major financial hurdles to overcome: college and retirement. Saving for retirement is more important, but contributing to an IRA may help you save for college and retirement in a single account.

The strategy. Both parents should contribute as much as they can to IRAs, ideally the Roth IRA, but traditional IRAs can work as well. You can withdraw IRA money penalty-free to pay for college expenses even if you're under age 59½. But you will probably have to pay income taxes on all or a portion of the money you withdraw, although withdrawals from Roth IRAs will usually result in lower taxes than withdrawals from traditional IRAs. The high limits on annual IRA contributions allow savers to sock away quite a bit of money over the years.

Flexibility when college costs loom. While the IRA funds will be available when college tuitions have to be paid, if you can come up with all or most of the money from other sources (an inheritance, financial aid, grants, and/or scholarships, for example), then you can leave the IRAs intact for their intended purpose. But if necessary, they can be accessed as needed.

> IRAs can be used for education savings, since IRA money
> can be withdrawn to pay college expenses.
>
> ■
>
> *If a man empties his purse into his head, no one can*
> *take it away from him. An investment in knowledge*
> *always pays the best interest.*
> —BENJAMIN FRANKLIN

IDEA 63

Cutting College Costs

College is a frightfully expensive proposition. But families can manage to overcome the challenge. Sure, the student may be saddled with some student loans, but that may provide him or her with an added incentive to find a job after graduation.

Scholarships to the (partial) rescue. One too often overlooked way to reduce college costs is to search out college scholarships. A multitude of scholarship opportunities exists. Private scholarships—that is, those offered by nonacademic organizations, for academic, athletic, and leadership achievement—are very common. Parents and students should also consider any military, company, union, trade, civic, religious, or ethnic affiliations they have that could lead to other sources of funds. Leave no stone unturned. Particularly diligent families have been able to cobble together several small scholarships, $500 here and $1,000 there, to reduce the cost of college. Every little bit helps, and many scholarships go ungranted for lack of qualified candidates or, more likely, for lack of any applicants, since no one knew of the scholarship. Your child doesn't have to excel at something to win a scholarship. Thousands are available for young people who have just about any interest or ambition. Thus, scholarships are available for hobbyists, community volunteers, and those seeking to major in a particular subject.

A one-two punch. When you begin to search for scholarships, take a two-pronged approach:

1. **Look for scholarships in your community.** The first place to look is in your local community. Civic groups, businesses, and churches often have small scholarships for townies.

2. **Research scholarships nationwide.** There are seemingly several trillion scholarships available nationwide, but the Internet can help you manage the search. You shouldn't have to pay a fee for a search. If you do, make sure it's a legitimate college scholarship search service.

Someone has to receive these scholarships. You might as well get your share, and your student should take the lead in the research effort. In so doing, he or she will receive a valuable lesson in financial responsibility too.

> As college approaches, don't just resign yourself to paying the huge tuition bills. Apply for one of the numerous available college scholarships.
>
> ■
>
> *Three words that strike fear into the minds of college seniors (and invigorate their job searches)*—Student Loan Payments.
> —ANONYMOUS

MONEY TIP

The Peril of Sacrificing Retirement Savings to Save for College

Here's an example of the "cost" of reducing retirement savings in order to put money away for college:

EXAMPLE: A parent is anxious to save for his child's college expenses, so in lieu of making a $4,000 annual Roth IRA contribution, he contributes the same amount to a college savings plan for ten years, until his daughter enters college. At the end of ten years, he resumes making annual Roth contributions. While his intentions are noble, he is sacrificing retirement income by forgoing a decade of IRA contributions. In fact, assuming that he's fifteen years away from retirement when she goes to college, his retirement income will be about $13,000 less per year compared with what it would have been had he continued the Roth contributions. Had both parents suspended Roth contributions, the diminished yearly retirement income would have lost twice that, or $26,000.

Now, it's easy to argue that by not suspending the Roth contributions for a decade, the family would have had to come up with the shortfall somewhere else to pay for college. That's true. But preparing for retirement is always more important than preparing in advance to meet college costs. Families almost always manage to surmount the formidable challenge of paying for college. But, as noted in chapter 5, annual contributions to retirement plans are a "use it or lose it" proposition. Every year you forgo making a contribution is a year you can't make up for in the future.

■

You're only young once, but you can always be immature.
—ANONYMOUS

IDEA 64

If You Hate Cars, Buy New; If You Love Cars, Buy Used

My reputation may precede these remarks, but I should mention at the outset that I harbor considerable disdain for cars, because they are a huge drain on the typical family's finances. I'm also tired of being told by my children never to appear on the school grounds driving my beloved and, by my standards, late-model 1995 Volvo.

My car study. Cars are a colossal expense and, depending on your car ownership habits, you can save literally hundreds of thousands of dollars to spend on other things in life, like retirement. Years ago, much to the chagrin of the car industry, which hated the study but couldn't refute its findings, I published an analysis of car ownership costs over a typical forty-year career. The study compared someone who bought new and traded a car every three years with someone who bought new and traded (*scrapped* is probably more accurate) every ten years. At the end of forty years, the person who traded every decade had total ownership costs that were several hundred thousand dollars less than the costs of the frequent trader, even after factoring in a lot of money for repairs. In fact, the infrequent trader saved enough money to be able to afford to retire five years earlier than the frequent trader.

After consideration of my work on car ownership habits, I have concluded that it's better for people who don't really care much about cars to buy them new, while those who are devoted to their steel-and-plastic masters should buy used. Sounds perverse, but here's my rationale:

Why should car lovers buy used cars? Because they want to trade cars frequently and that habit is particularly expensive if you buy new. If you think you're going to trade your car in less than five years, buy a used car that's at least a couple of years old. If you're worried that your reputation as an automotive bon vivant will be sullied, keep in mind that many carmakers change the external appearance of their cars so little with each new model year that your friends and neighbors probably won't know your "new" car is actually a couple of years old. But most important, let someone else suffer the big depreciation in value that occurs over the first couple of years of ownership. True, you won't have the self-satisfaction that comes with a new set of wheels, but you also won't sink your finances with titanic car costs.

Why should car loathers buy new cars? If you view a car as a source of transportation, rather than as a mobile phallic symbol, why buy new? If you're likely to hold on to a car for a long time—ten years or more—buying a new car and running it into the ground is often a sensible and low-cost way to go. You can maintain the car so that it will serve you well for a long time.

The best of all worlds. If you're intent on cutting your car ownership costs to the bone, short of buying cars as I do, with over 100,000 miles on them, the best strategy is to buy a four-year-old car and hold on to it for four years.

> Here I go again, making you feel guilty about your car ownership habits.

TOP FIVE REASONS YOU KNOW IT'S TIME TO TRADE IN YOUR CAR:

1. *Instead of an air bag, there is a whoopee cushion taped to your steering wheel.*

2. *Fifteen-minute Jiffy Lube needs to keep your car for three days.*

3. *Thieves repeatedly break into your car just to steal "The Club™."*

4. *Traffic reporters start referring to you by name when discussing morning tie-ups.*

5. *While sitting at a stoplight, people keep running up to you and asking if anyone was hurt.*

IDEA 65

Ten Money Savers That Will Save You Thousands of Dollars in Car Ownership Costs

☐ 1. **Keep your cars longer.** There's no reason why you can't keep a car for seven to ten years or even longer. Those who trade in their new cars every three, four, or five years are simply throwing money away. Sure, a late-model car feels good, and you probably think people are impressed by one. But is it worth the cost?

☐ 2. **Buy a used car rather than an expensive new car.** The quickest way to lose $2,000 is to drive a new car off the dealer's lot. So many people are obsessed with frequently trading in their cars that many excellent used cars go begging. If you get into the habit of buying used cars, you'll save literally tens if not hundreds of thousands of dollars over your lifetime.

☐ 3. **Do your homework.** The only way to assure yourself a good deal from a car salesperson is to march into the showroom heavily armed with facts and figures. You should know exactly what the dealer has paid for the particular car you want to buy new. You can obtain information on dealer cost by referring to the many Web sites that carry this information. Lot's of useful information is available for used-car devotees as well. Let's face it: it's you against the dealer, and if you don't have the right information, you're at a big disadvantage.

☐ 4. **Finance over three years or less.** Some people never manage to get out from under their car loans. Ideally, you should pay cash (see my strategy for getting yourself into a position to pay cash in Idea 66 on page 205). If you can't afford to finance a car over two or three years, perhaps you can't afford that car. If you must finance a car, never tell the dealer how much you can afford in monthly payments, because if you do you'll then be sold a car whose payments are equal to that. Get the best deal you can instead and let the dealer tell you what the monthly payments will be.

❑ **5. Avoid cars that are more costly to insure.** Insurance companies aren't dummies. They maintain extensive records by car model on the claims that they have to pay out. Don't waste money buying a car that, for whatever reason—perhaps it has 24 cylinders and 300 valves and can exceed the speed of sound—incurs higher premiums than more ordinary vehicles. Bland is better.

❑ **6. Don't get frivolous options.** A "loaded" car means two things. First, it is loaded with all the available options. Second, it is going to be loaded with problems as each option starts to fall apart. When you next buy a car, evaluate your "need" for each option. Some of them cost a lot of money and serve no apparent purpose. Not only does a loaded car cost several thousand dollars more up front, you will end up paying dearly to keep those options functioning.

❑ **7. Don't buy the dealer's "extras."** Such extras are commonly called "packs." They are as close to worthless as anything you could ever buy. They include items such as undercoat, overcoat, racing stripes, and of course, the infamous fabric protector. If the dealer asks if you would like to add any of these packages to your gleaming new car, just laugh. If you think they're worthwhile, have your head examined. If the salesperson informs you that they have been added to the car, thank him or her kindly and then say you're not going to pay extra for them.

❑ **8. Sell your old car yourself.** Chances are that you can sell your old car for quite a bit more money than the dealer would give you for it as a trade-in on a new car or a newer car. Sure, it takes a little effort, but the time is well spent if you can make a little extra money to put toward your next chariot. (If you keep your cars as long as I do, however, only the junk dealer will buy it.)

❏ **9. Perform routine car maintenance yourself.** Have you noticed the labor charges for car maintenance and repairs lately? While not quite equal to a neurosurgeon's fee, they're getting there. You can perform more routine maintenance tasks on your car than you think.

❏ **10. Find a good mechanic.** Auto dealers don't have a monopoly on good mechanics. As a matter of fact, some of them don't have any good mechanics. Like locating any other competent professional, word of mouth is often your best resource.

Unless you're so in love with your car that you'll spare no expense, heed some commonsense advice on ways to reduce car ownership costs.

■

Never lend your car to anyone to whom you have given birth.
—ERMA BOMBECK

IDEA 66

Dr. Jonathan's Car-Loan-Addiction Elixir

One part of your financial planning should be to get into the habit of paying cash for your cars if you have heretofore borrowed to pay for them. This will have the benefit of lowering your car ownership costs both during your remaining working years and throughout your retirement.

My car-loan-addiction elixir illustration on the following table assumes that you buy your next car with a four-year car loan and keep it eight years. Follow the strategy and you should have enough saved to pay cash for the next car.

This example assumes a four-year loan for $25,000 at 7 percent interest, resulting in $600 monthly payments or $7,200 per year. The strategy is: after paying off the loan, you put the same monthly payment into a 4 percent interest-earning savings account.

STRATEGY FOR ERADICATING CAR LOANS

YEAR	TOTAL CAR PAYMENTS	TOTAL CONTRIBUTED TO CAR SAVINGS ACCOUNT	BALANCE IN CAR SAVINGS ACCOUNT AT END OF YEAR
1	$7,200		
2	7,200		
3	7,200		
4	7,200		
5		$7,200	$ 7,430
6		7,200	15,400
7		7,200	23,960
8		7,200	33,125

Voila! You'll have $33,000 available to buy your next car. And once you pay cash for a car, I'll bet you dollars to doughnuts you'll *always* pay cash for a car. Now, that's a healthy addiction!

My car-loan-addiction elixir will eliminate car loans forever.

■

The only way to solve the traffic problems of the country is to pass a law that only paid-for cars are allowed to use the highways.

—WILL ROGERS

CHAPTER 10

Giving Uncle Sam His Due, and Not One Cent More

What's the biggest item in your family budget? Most people guess that it's housing, but for the majority, the biggest expense is taxes. Finding ways to reduce your tax bite is one of the easiest ways to cut your cost of living and, hence, increase your wealth.

Taxes are a dour subject. The tax regulations are a nightmare. Some of the smartest people in the world can't figure out many of the tax code's provisions. To show what we're up against, here is an excerpt from the "Infernal" Revenue Code that applies to the sale of a personal residence. By the way, this is one sentence:

In the case of a sale or exchange to which this subsection applies, the ownership and use requirements of subsection (a), and subsection (b)(3), shall not apply; but the dollar limitation under paragraph (1) or (2) of subsection (b), whichever is applicable, shall be equal to the amount which bears the same ratio to such limitation (determined without regard to this paragraph) as (B)(i) the shorter of the aggregate periods, during the 5-year period ending on the date of such sale or exchange, such property has been owned and used by the taxpayer as the taxpayer's principal residence; or the period after the date of the most recent prior sale or exchange by the taxpayer to which subsection (a) applied and before the date of such sale or exchange, bears to 2 years.

There's no easier (or more satisfying) way to cut your expenses than finding sensible ways to reduce income taxes (or property taxes, as explained in Idea 53, on page 169). And as complex as most of the tax rules are, one thing has remained true: actions you now take to reduce your taxes will enhance your financial well-being. The ideas and tips in this chapter will help you save money on taxes and make thinking about taxes less onerous.

■

The taxpayer: Someone who works for the government but doesn't have to take a civil service examination.
—RONALD REAGAN

IDEA 67

Ten Top Tax-Savings Ideas

There are a lot of ways to cut your income tax bill. Some aren't worth the effort (see page 217), but others should be front and center in your planning. Here are ten important tax-savings ideas that could lop off literally thousands of dollars a year in income taxes. Always keep them in mind.

1. **Maximize contributions to retirement plans.** This is tax-saving rule numero uno for all working-age people, and the maximum amount you can contribute to these plans is rising.

Not only do you save taxes in the current year, but you also save taxes every year thereafter as the money grows tax deferred. Even when you don't receive a current tax deduction (a Roth IRA contribution, for example), you'll still enjoy lower taxes in the future. See Idea 26, on page 83, for some help on deciding which retirement plans are best for you.

2. **Consider a Roth IRA conversion.** Converting your traditional IRA into a Roth IRA doesn't save money in the year you do it. In fact, it costs money. But it's well worth it in most circumstances, because the taxes you will save later on are enormous. Roth IRA conversions are discussed in Idea 28, on page 88.

3. **Own a home.** The tax benefits of home ownership, notably the deductibility of mortgage interest and property taxes for those who itemize their tax deductions, can often allow renters to buy a home that doesn't cost a whole lot more than the rent they were paying. While a big tax deduction for mortgage interest isn't something you want to maintain indefinitely (see Idea 52, on page 165), there are many more benefits to owning a home. Think of the tax deductions as icing on the cake. Check out chapter 8 for some ideas for both homeowners and those who want to buy a home. If and when you eventually sell your abode, you'll be able to put a substantial amount, if not all, of any gain into your pocket, free of taxes.

4. **Pay attention to how your investments are taxed.** Putting as much money as you can into retirement accounts alleviates the problem of investment taxes, since the money inside the accounts is not subject to taxes until you begin withdrawing it in retirement. But, as explained in Idea 71, on page 221, taxes can be saved by judicious timing of the withdrawals from retirement plans after you retire. In the meantime, if you have money in nonretirement accounts, be sure to take maximum advantage of the low tax rates accorded most dividends and capital gains

from stock held for at least one year. As explained in Idea 12, on page 43, using your knowledge of how investments are taxed can provide a nice bonus to your investment balances over the years.

5. **Make tax-wise charitable contributions.** Heaven knows that charities can benefit from your beneficence, and you save taxes to boot. Cash is gratefully received, but you should also donate any usable but unneeded clothing and furniture. If you donate appreciated stock that you've held for at least one year, you get a deduction for its full value without having to pay a tax on the gain. Finally, if you can afford to donate at least $10,000 in cash or appreciated securities, you can receive a lifetime annuity income as well as a partial tax deduction for the amount donated. These are called "charitable gift annuities," and if you call your favorite charity to inquire, they'll be more than happy to fill you in on the details.

6. **Make the most of your employer's fringe benefits.** Employer fringe benefits are almost always tax-free, and your employer may offer a variety of benefits, including flexible spending accounts, which allow a fixed amount of pre-tax dollars to be set aside to pay qualified expenses, including uncovered medical expenses and child care. It behooves you to understand fully how these various benefits and plans work so that you can take maximum advantage of them.

7. **Own a business.** While you shouldn't start a business solely for the tax breaks, if you ever own a business, even a sideline enterprise, you'll be glad to know that the powers that be bestow many tax blessings on small business owners, including some very generous retirement savings plans, as described in Idea 30, on page 93.

8. **Look for tax credits.** Tax deductions are nice, but tax credits are the holy grail of tax-saving opportunities. For example, a

$1,000 tax deduction will save you $250 in taxes if you are in the 25 percent tax bracket. A $1,000 tax credit, on the other hand, reduces your tax bill by $1,000 no matter what tax bracket you're in. Sadly, a lot of taxpayers who qualify fail to take advantage of them. Examples of available tax credits include the adoption credit, the child-care and dependent-care credits, earned income credit, credit for the elderly and disabled, retirement savings contributions credit, and credits for college tuition. You'll have to do a little digging to find out if you qualify for any, but it's a crying shame to miss out.

9. **Look for deductions available for nonitemizers.** Contrary to popular opinion, tax deductions aren't just for fat cats. There are a number of deductions and credits available for those who don't itemize deductions. (Most of these deductions are also available to itemizers.) Deductions include those for retirement plan contributions, student loan interest, job-related moving expenses, self-employed medical insurance, college tuition deductions, and alimony paid. Many of the tax credits enumerated above in tax-saving idea number 8, above, are also available for nonitemizers.

10. **Timing is everything.** Finally, the timing of various tax-related transactions can make or break a tax deduction. Whether it's deciding on which tax year to make a tax-deductible payment, when to sell your home, or when to make retirement-plan withdrawals, to name but a few, don't let a poorly timed decision cost you tax payments that could have been avoided.

See also Idea 72, on page 226, for a list of late-year tax-cutting strategies.

The special reader Web site contains more ideas and Internet resources that will help make sure you don't pay one cent more in taxes than you have to. **w w w**

MONEY IN YOUR POCKET — TAX-SAVINGS IDEAS

1. Maximize contributions to retirement plans.
2. Consider a Roth IRA conversion.
3. Own a home.
4. Pay attention to how your investments are taxed.
5. Make tax-wise charitable contributions.
6. Make the most of your employer's fringe benefits.
7. Own a business.
8. Look for tax credits.
9. Look for deductions also available to nonitemizers.
10. Timing is everything.

Taking advantage of tax-saving strategies can put more money in your pocket and less in Uncle Sam's.

■

I'm proud to be paying taxes in the United States. The only thing is—I could be just as proud for half the money.

—ARTHUR GODFREY

IDEA 68

News Flash: Congress Isn't Going to Tinker with Your Tax Breaks

A lot of people are being advised by their tax and financial advisers (who ought to know better) or their acquaintances (who are ignorant of such matters) to avoid making a sensible financial decision because, they assert, the tax rules are going to be changed. I guess these people must have an inside track on the precise tax-rule changes that Congress is going to enact over the next twenty years. Come on! Even Congress doesn't know what changes will be made in the tax rules—not twenty years from now, not even next year.

Any time you start fiddling with your financial decisions based on what you or your adviser thinks is going to happen to the tax regulations in the future, you're going to make the wrong decisions. For example, I've heard countless people say they're not going to make a Roth IRA contribution or Roth IRA conversion because the rules are going to be changed and Roth distributions will be taxed. I've been around long enough to recall that skepticism abounded when the original IRA was established. Another favorite is: "I've got a big profit in a stock, but I've got to sell it now before they raise capital gains taxes." And this is my all-time favorite: "I've got to start collecting my Social Security benefits as soon as possible because Congress is going to cut the benefits. If I start collecting now, I'll be able to lock in a higher benefit." Actually, that one is a lot more upbeat than what many working-age people say who think that Social Security benefits won't be curtailed, they'll be terminated altogether.

Here's my advice: never avoid making an otherwise sensible financial decision based upon what Congress **might** do. No one can predict what Congress will do for us or, more likely when it comes to taxes and Social Security, to us. The trend over the past decade has been to enhance tax breaks, particularly for retirement savers (for example, the maximum allowable IRA contribution has at least doubled) and retirees (IRA withdrawal rules have been significantly liberalized). This happy trend is far more likely to be enhanced than curtailed in the future, regardless of which party controls the Congress and the White House.

Don't let anyone dissuade you from making an otherwise sensible money decision based on their imagined changes in future tax regulations.

■

It has often been said that the only two certainties in life are death and taxes. But at least death doesn't get worse every time Congress convenes.
—ANONYMOUS

IDEA 69

Increasing Investment Returns by Decreasing Taxes on Investments

You can accumulate a lot more money over the years by increasing the gains you earn on that money, as the next table illustrates. That's obvious. But another way to increase investment returns year in and year out is not so obvious. That's a shame, because it's easy to do, but it's too-often overlooked by do-it-yourself and professional investors alike.

The rules. Once you understand how investments are taxed, you will become a tax genius simply by putting particular investments into your various accounts according to the following two rules:

1. **Put tax-FRIENDLY investments into accounts on which you have to pay taxes every year.**

2. **Put tax-UNFRIENDLY investments into accounts that are not subject to yearly taxes, mainly retirement accounts.**

A short course on investment taxes. Investments vary in the way they're taxed. Tax rates can vary from nothing to as high as 35 percent. That's a big difference, so it behooves all investors to understand how the various investments that they want to own are taxed. By paying attention to these mundane matters, you could end up with a lot more money than your neighbor who doesn't care about—or, more likely, doesn't understand—the distinction between tax-friendly and tax-unfriendly investments.

Here are some explanations of the terminology used in the next table:

- Most *dividends* are subject to low federal income taxes, although there are exceptions, including dividends from real estate stocks.

- Most *interest* from bonds, money market funds, and other interest-paying investments is subject to high federal income taxes (equivalent to your tax rate on other income), with the exception of municipal bond interest.

- *Capital gains* taxes on investments that are sold are either *short-term* if the investment is sold within a year or *long-term* if sold after a year. Long-term gains are taxed at a much lower rate than short-term gains

Type of Investment	Taxes on Capital Gains, Interest, and/or Dividends
Tax Friendly— *Best Investments for Accounts That Must Pay Annual Taxes*	
Individual stocks	No taxes due until stock is sold; dividends usually subject to a low tax rate
Index funds and exchange-traded funds	Most distribute small capital gains; dividends usually subject to a low tax rate
Tax-managed mutual funds	Managed to minimize taxable distributions

Municipal bonds and municipal bond funds	Interest generally exempt from taxes
Mutual funds that distribute primarily long-term capital gains	While not classified as tax-managed, many funds have a policy of distributing low-taxed long-term capital gains

Tax Unfriendly—
Best Investments for Retirement (Tax-Deferred) Accounts

Mutual funds that distribute considerable short-term capital gains	Short-term capital gains are subject to high tax rate
Corporate bonds and corporate bond funds	Interest subject to high tax rate
Government bonds and bond funds	Interest subject to high tax rate

While it's okay to put tax-friendly investments into retirement accounts (with the exception of municipal bonds and muni bond funds, whose interest is tax exempt from the get-go), **avoid putting tax-unfriendly investments into currently taxable accounts.**

See Idea 11, on page 38, for the ways really rich folks use the tax rules to their everlasting financial benefit.

For more help on minimizing taxes on your investments, including resources for finding out about the tax friendliness of a particular mutual fund you're considering, refer to the *Grow Your Money!* reader Web site. **w w w**

TAX-WISE INVESTING PAYS OFF

The table shows the everlasting advantage of minimizing income taxes on your investments. It assumes that an investor starts with $25,000 and saves an additional $5,000 per year for the number of years indicated. The assumed annual returns after taxes are taken out are 6 percent for the investor who doesn't pay attention to how investments are taxed and 8 percent for the tax-wise investor.

NUMBER OF YEARS	TAX-UNWISE INVESTOR (6%)	TAX-WISE INVESTOR (8%)
10	$ 110,000	$ 125,000
20	265,000	345,000
30	540,000	820,000
40	1,030,000	1,840,000

Decrease the tax bite on your investments by simply paying attention to how various categories of investments are taxed.

■

The problem with being a breadwinner these days is that the government is in for such a big slice.
—MARY MCCOY

MONEY TIP

Many Tax-Saving Strategies Aren't Worth the Effort

The value of tax-wise investing notwithstanding, don't let the siren song of reducing your tax bill cloud your otherwise sound financial judgment. In the olden days, tax rates were a lot higher than they are now. It wasn't unusual back then to find yourself in the 50 percent— or even 70 percent—income tax bracket. At those tax rates, finding ways to reduce income taxes was more important. But now, most of us are in the 25 percent federal income tax bracket, while few are taxed at higher than 30 percent. At these levels, the benefit of reducing taxes is more limited. If you are in the highest income tax bracket, you may be able to derive some benefit from tax deductions. But for the rest of us, don't conclude that you're a tax genius by undertaking some complex tax-savings strategy that only results in saving about $3.98 in income taxes.

> ■
>
> *The United States is the only country where it takes more brains to figure your tax than to earn the money to pay for it.*
> —EDWARD J. GURNEY

IDEA 70

Getting a Tax Refund Is Bad News

The average federal income tax refund is over $2,000. Perhaps that's a nice surprise, but it constitutes an interest-free loan to the U.S. government. On the other hand, if you don't have enough taxes withheld and owe more than a pittance on your tax return, does Uncle Sam give you an interest-free loan on the money? Of course not, and that's all the more reason why getting a tax refund is bad news, particularly when you can easily avoid it.

Tinker with your withholding exemptions. The trick is to claim the number of withholding exemptions that will result in withholding an amount that is close to what you're going to owe. You may not recall, but when you signed up with the payroll department, you filled out a form that declared a number of withholding exemptions that in turn told the payroll department how much to withhold from your paychecks. In order to adjust your withholding, you'll need to file a new W-4 form with your employer. It looks daunting, but the instructions are actually rather helpful.

Since a lot of things can change vis-à-vis your income tax situation, a couple of times a year you should check to make sure that there's an adequate amount being withheld. One of those times should be in October or November of each year, so there's time to increase the amount withheld if it looks as if you're going to come up short.

Besides the prospect of receiving a big tax refund or having to pay a lot of money with your return, there are a few other situations that may require you to adjust your withholding, including:

❑ Changes in your family status, notably marriage, the arrival of children, or no longer being able to claim a dependent that you had been claiming (increase or decrease withholding exemptions)

❑ Paying out significant medical or other expenses that are wholly or partially deductible (increase withholding exemptions)

❑ Buying a home (increase withholding exemptions, which will help you make those breathtaking mortgage payments)

If you have not been itemizing deductions in the past, keep in mind that changes in your financial situation, such as buying a home, may mean that you'll benefit from itemizing.

What to do with your increased take-home pay? After you adjust your withholding to eliminate or at least reduce your refund, you'll soon notice a loftier paycheck. Deciding what to do with the extra money is one of those proverbial "nice problems to have." It's up to you, of course, but if I had my druthers, I'd recommend that you not take home your increased take-home pay. Instead, put it away for the future either by increasing your retirement plan contributions at work or by arranging to have the extra money transferred automatically to a retirement or investment account.

Rather than wait to receive a tax refund, increase your cash flow each payday by increasing your withholding exemptions.

■

Did you ever notice? When you put the two words
"The" and "IRS" together it spells: "THEIRS."
—ANONYMOUS

MONEY TIP

Prepare Your Own Income Tax Returns

It's shameful that our elected officials have created and countenanced a tax system that is so complex that most Americans feel compelled to pay someone else to fulfill their civic duties. There are a couple of reasons why you might want to do so. First, your tax situation may be so complex that there's no way you could ever figure out what's going on. Second, you're more than happy to pay for the peace of mind of having someone else prepare your taxes who is able to represent you in the unlikely event the IRS comes knocking. Thanks to the evolution of tax-preparation software and Web-based services, though, you might want to consider doing your own taxes, even if your tax situation is nontrivial. Here are four choices for would-be do-it-yourselfers:

❏ **Prepare it by hand.** This is the old-fashioned way, which, before the invention of tax software and Web sites was the only available choice. But thanks to a round after round of "tax complification" legislation, few of us (save our high-school- or college-age children) can easily and confidently complete the returns by hand.

❏ **Tax-preparation software.** Fortunately, the tax-preparation software has evolved to the point that anyone with a modicum of computer knowledge can complete and e-file even very complex federal and state tax returns. The software leads you through the return preparation process in a simple Q&A format, and the cost of the software is a fraction of what it would cost to pay someone to do your returns.

❑ **Tax-preparation Web sites.** Rather than purchase and install the software, you can access tax-preparation software remotely on any of a number of Web sites that also use a convenient interview method to walk you through your return. You can also stop when you want and continue where you left off at a later time.

❑ **Free tax-preparation services.** The IRS Web site (*www.irs.gov*) provides a list of free tax-preparation-service providers. Depending on your particular situation, these providers may be able to take care of your tax-preparation needs for free. But be sure to read the fine print on these offers.

There's an additional benefit to preparing your own taxes in addition to the obvious money savings. Rather than relying on your tax preparer to give you ideas about ways to save taxes, by doing them yourself, you'll be better able to understand your own situation and what strategies may help you pare down your impost.

For the latest information on the various tax-preparation services, visit your *Grow Your Money!* reader Web site. **w w w**

IDEA 71

Managing Your Tax Bite After You Retire

No good deed goes unpunished. Here's a sad story, with you playing the lead role: You do the right thing during your working years by contributing to retirement savings plans. Then you're walloped with income taxes when you start withdrawing from them after retirement. But there may be some ways to control your taxes, particularly if you have money set aside both inside and outside of retirement plans.

If all or most of your money is in retirement plans. If all or most of your money is in retirement accounts, there's not much you can do to avoid the tax bite unless the retirement money resides in a Roth IRA account since withdrawals from a Roth are usually tax free. Don't feel bad, though, because you did the right thing during your working years by putting as much money as possible into tax-advantaged retirement plans. There may be a couple of tax-reducing opportunities, however.

❏ Since most of your income will be taxable, be assiduous in identifying any and all tax deductions for which you qualify.

❏ Be particularly careful about your income tax bracket. If you find that your planned withdrawals from traditional IRAs will put you into a higher tax bracket (from the 15 percent to the 25 percent bracket, for example), look for ways to avoid a late-year IRA withdrawal, to keep you in the lower bracket. You could use credit cards toward the end of the year, but you'll want to repay them early in the following year. If your end-of-year expenses are particularly high—perhaps you're buying me a particularly expensive holiday gift—you can borrow from your IRA. So long as you replenish the amount withdrawn within sixty days of withdrawal, you don't have to pay taxes on the borrowed money. (See page 75.) If you have a Roth IRA, you could withdraw from that account rather than a traditional IRA, to avoid moving into a higher income tax bracket.

If you have money both inside and outside of retirement plans. More tax-planning opportunities exist for those who have both retirement plans and money in nonretirement accounts (brokerage accounts and bank accounts, for example).

❏ In your early years of retirement, you'll probably be able to reduce your taxes—perhaps considerably—simply by withdrawing money from your nonretirement accounts before tapping into your retirement accounts. The math is simple, and compelling. If you need

$24,000 per year for living expenses and you're in the 25 percent income tax bracket, you'll need to withdraw $32,000 from retirement accounts in order to have $24,000 left over after taxes. Withdrawals from nonretirement accounts, on the other hand, are subject to much lower taxes, if any. For example, you would need to withdraw only $24,000 from a money market fund—or slightly more, to account for taxes on the interest—to net the needed $24,000. So the rule of thumb is:

[Withdraw already taxed (nonretirement) money first.]

Following this strategy may place you in a position of owing little or no income taxes. There is one exception to this rule, however: if you come up to the end of the tax year and find that you're due to pay zero tax or you're in the lowest tax bracket, take advantage of your low bracket by withdrawing enough money from your retirement account to have it taxed at the lowest tax rate.

EXAMPLE: A newly retired couple has been living off maturing CDs, so they have very little taxable income. In fact, an additional $20,000 in taxable income would be taxed at only 15 percent. So rather than using the CD money to pay living expenses, they withdraw $20,000 from their IRAs in order to take advantage of the low tax bracket. They argue that eventually, when they have to take minimum required distributions, it will be taxed at 25 percent or more, so they might as well take advantage of their low tax bracket now with some of their retirement money.

❑ If you have abundant money set aside outside of retirement plans and you're in a low income tax bracket, consider converting some of your traditional IRAs into Roth IRAs, using the nonretirement-plan money to pay the income taxes. If you qualify for them, Roth conversions are often very advantageous, even for retirees. For more information on Roth conversions, see Idea 28, on page 88.

❑ If you still have considerable nonretirement money once you reach age 70½ and have to begin withdrawing from your retirement accounts, strive to make only minimum required distributions (MRDs). This will allow the money in your retirement accounts to continue to grow tax deferred. While we don't want to contemplate your demise, current tax rules are very favorable for transferring retirement accounts to younger-generation family members.

Income taxes don't go away after you retire, but there are ways to reduce taxes by deferring retirement-plan withdrawals.

■

It's hard to believe America was founded to avoid high taxation.
—ANONYMOUS

MONEY TIP

How Long Should You Keep Your Tax Returns?

Many people, including my nonagenarian mother, think there is no substitute for keeping your tax returns and their supporting records forever. True, if you've been filing grossly fraudulent tax returns or not filing at all, your good friends at the Internal Revenue Service can go back to the time you were in diapers in search of income to tax. But if you are fundamentally an honest taxpayer, you don't need to keep decades of past tax returns.

❑ **If your tax situation is very straightforward.** The minimum required time to keep your income tax returns and supporting documents is three years from the return's original due date, including extensions. If all or most of your income comes from wages and investments, and you have no unusual tax transactions, such as a home sale, you should be okay adhering to this schedule.

❏ **If your tax situation is more complicated.** Save all of your tax returns and documents for at least six years. For example, do so when you have income from self-employment or have substantial investment gains or losses or simply have some doubts about the accuracy of past tax returns. The reason for keeping the records longer is that the three-year time limit doesn't apply to taxpayers who fail (intentionally or not) to report a substantial amount of taxable income.

❏ **The stuff to hold on to indefinitely.** There are some documents that should be kept in a separate file indefinitely, including:

- **Records supporting the cost basis for investments** such as stocks, mutual funds, and collectibles. You'll need to hold on to these until you sell the investments, in order to prove how much you paid for them. Incidentally, you generally don't need to maintain such records for investments you hold in retirement accounts, since the capital gains and losses in these accounts are not taxed. The only income taxes you pay on retirement accounts are generally assessed when you make withdrawals and are not based on an investment's cost.

- **Records supporting your home purchase and home improvements.** Finally, hold on to all records pertaining to the original purchase of your home, including the closing statement, as well as any improvements you have made to your manse. These may come in very handy when you eventually sell your home.

> ■
>
> *Money isn't everything; in fact, after the tax collector*
> *gets through, money isn't anything.*
> —ANONYMOUS

IDEA 72

Last-Minute Tax-Savings Ideas

While planning ways to cut your tax exaction is best done early in the year, procrastinators still have time to prune their taxes even in late December. Here are a list of last-minute opportunities, along with a to-do list for early next year:

❑ **Make charitable contributions.** Cash, appreciated securities, clothing, furniture—any of these can be donated at the last minute. (The charities will not take children, however. I've tried.) If you truly wait until the last minute, so long as your check is dated and sent by the end of the year, you're entitled to a deduction even if the check clears in the new year.

❑ **Sell losing investments.** If you have any stocks or other investments in a taxable investment account (not a retirement account) that have losses, you can sell the shares, take the loss, and use that loss to offset any capital gains, including gains in mutual funds. Also, once you've used your losses to offset all of your gains, you can use up to an additional $3,000 in losses to offset your job and other income. If you have a significant loss, any losses that you cannot use can be carried forward to future tax years. Good deal for an investment gone bad.

❑ **Boost contributions to workplace plans.** Contributions to your workplace retirement plans (401(k) and 403(b) plans, for example) usually must be made throughout the year, but some plan administrators allow for "catch up" contributions in December if your contribution level is less than the maximum allowed. This is a good way to save taxes at the last minute. If this is not allowed, put this into your mental to-do list: come January, ask the plan administrator to boost the percentage of your salary that's going into the plan.

❏ **Set up a self-employed retirement plan.** You can do so if you have income from self-employment, even part-time self-employment. The regulations impose a December 31 deadline for setting up most, but not all self-employed plans, even though you can fund them in the following year. For more information on these plans, see Idea 30, on page 93.

❏ **Do a Roth IRA conversion.** The rules surrounding Roth IRA conversions often necessitate a late-in-the-year evaluation of your financial and tax situation, but be forewarned that any money that is converted to a Roth for a given tax year must be transferred by the end of that year.

❏ **Review flexible-spending accounts.** Depending on your employment situation, a review of any flexible-spending accounts available through your employer might reveal last-minute strategies that will help you take maximum advantage of benefits.

❏ **Avoid late-year mutual fund purchases.** Many investors unwittingly pay an unexpected capital gains tax by purchasing a mutual fund in a nonretirement account shortly before it distributes its realized capital gains, typically late in the year. Postponing the purchase until immediately after the distribution, which may be as late as the end of December, will avoid unwelcome tax consequences in the current tax year.

❏ **Make tax-deductible payments with your credit card.** If you want to make tax-deductible payments late in the year, including charitable contributions, but lack the cash, you can use your credit card to make the payment this year, take the deduction this year, and pay your credit card bill next year. No wonder they call America the "land of opportunity."

New Year To-Do List

❑ **Contribute to retirement accounts.** Depending on the type of retirement account you have, you can usually make contributions for the prior tax year as late as the due date of your tax return. In the case of self-employed plans, the due date is generally even later if an extension has been filed.

❑ **Organize your tax records.** Don't wait until the last minute to organize the records you or your tax preparer will need to prepare your tax returns. As tax-related stuff arrives in the mail, put it in a folder right away. The better organized you are, the less taxes you'll pay. It's a simple as that.

❑ **File early if you're owed; file later if you owe.** Our friends at the IRS don't pay any interest on money owed to us, so if you're due for a refund, file as soon as you can in the new year. (If you always receive a refund, go to Idea 70, on page 218 for help on doing away with what amounts to an interest-free loan to the federal government.) On the other hand, if you owe some money, but won't be subject to any penalties and interest, there's no rush to send in your return. File and send in your money on April 15.

The *Grow Your Money!* Web site will offer more guidance on ways to reduce your tax bill at the last minute. **w w w**

PROCRASTINATOR'S CHECKLIST—END-OF-YEAR TAX-SAVINGS IDEAS

Late-Year To-Do Items

+ Make charitable contributions.
+ Sell losing investments.
+ Boost contributions to workplace plans.
+ Set up a self-employed retirement plan.
+ Do a Roth IRA conversion.
+ Review flexible-spending accounts.
+ Avoid late-year mutual fund purchases.
+ Make tax-deductible payments with your credit card.

Items to Attend to in the New Year

+ Contribute to retirement accounts.
+ Organize your tax records.
+ File early if you're owed; file later if you owe.

It's never too late in the year to take action to cut your tax bill.

■

Don't tax you, don't tax me, tax that fellow behind the tree.
—RUSSELL LONG

CHAPTER 11

Securing the Future for You and Your Loved Ones

t's time to get serious about securing the future for you and your loved ones. A single oversight in your insurance coverage, for example, could cause a large outlay of money. Insurance is one of the most expensive items in the family budget, but there are several ways to reduce insurance costs. Out-of-date estate-planning documents—if they've been prepared at all—could lead to major problems for your survivors. Aging family members may eventually depend on you for help in managing their day-to-day financial affairs. This chapter offers ideas and tips that address these and other areas so that you can rest assured that if adversity strikes, you're covered.

> ■
>
> *If I had my way I would write the word "insure" over every door of every cottage and upon the blotting book of every public man, because I am convinced that, for sacrifices that are conceivably small, families can be secured against catastrophes which otherwise would smash them for ever.*
> —WINSTON CHURCHILL

IDEA 73

Filling Gaps in Your Property Insurance Coverage

A single gap in your property insurance coverage could wipe out years if not decades of hard-earned savings. Here is a list of the more common gaps in insurance coverage:

❑ **Personal liability.** Here are some frightening scenarios: Your new-driver daughter borrows your car and promptly rear-ends a Bentley. Or, your uninsured housepainter gets stung by a bee, falls off a ladder, and is seriously injured. Unless you're one of the tiny percentage of people who can afford to self-insure against such calamities, you need *umbrella liability insurance* coverage, also called *extended personal liability insurance.* Generally, this type of insurance runs $200 to $300 annually for $1 million worth of coverage. Higher limits are also available. This coverage kicks in if you're sued and you've exhausted the limits on your car and homeowner's or renter's insurance policies. Here's a comforting statistic: 94 percent of all lawsuits filed in the world are filed in the United States. Think about it. You could spend all of your money just defending yourself against a lawsuit, not to mention paying any adverse judgment. To get umbrella insurance, you generally must carry a minimum of

$250,000 of liability insurance on your auto insurance policy and $300,000 on your homeowner's policy.

❑ **Valuables.** The coverage provided by your homeowner's or renter's policy for valuables is pitifully low. For example, you're probably limited to $1,000 to $2,000 of coverage for all jewelry and furs. If you have jewelry, art, antiques, and collectibles, you need a rider on your homeowner's or renter's insurance policy. Think of it this way. If the burglars have any class, what are they going to take first? With a so-called *floater policy,* if your valuables are stolen, lost, or damaged, you are covered based on what it would cost to replace those items at retail. The amount of coverage for each item is based upon sales receipts and appraisals you have provided to your insurance company when you obtain the extra coverage. How much you pay depends on what you are insuring, but it will be nothing compared with having to replace it on your own dime.

❑ **Safe-deposit box.** Do you have a bank safe-deposit box? The contents are probably not insured by your bank, so you may wish to consider extra coverage for safe-deposit box contents if you store any valuables therein. It's a lot cheaper to insure any collectibles that are stored in a safe-deposit box, so if you've got valuables at home that you don't use or display, consider putting them in your safe-deposit box.

❑ **Replacement cost on household possessions.** Replacement-cost coverage is a low-cost option that is added to your homeowner's or renter's insurance policy. This provision will replace your belongings at today's prices and is far preferable to the standard actual-cost coverage, which factors in depreciation and reimburses you for substantially less.

❑ **Hurricanes and earthquakes.** If you live in a hurricane or earthquake zone, or just want to be extra careful if you're on the fringes of such a zone, make certain you have added coverage for those perils. This is an enormous risk that many homeowners simply choose to overlook. Sure, the coverage is expensive, but that's just a manifestation of how much risk you're taking by not having it.

❏ **Flood.** If you live in an area prone to floods, consider getting reasonably priced federal flood insurance. Also, even if you live in an area that has never had a flood, that doesn't mean it can't in the future.

The reader Web site is filled with additional guidelines and helpful information on closing any gaps you may have in your insurance coverage. **w w w**

Closing any and all gaps in your property insurance coverage will prevent any uninsured losses that could jeopardize your financial well-being.

∎

Needing insurance is like needing a parachute. If it isn't there the first time, chances are you won't be needing it again.
—ANONYMOUS

IDEA 74

Surprise: You're Probably Overinsured

You should close any gaps in your insurance coverage, as described in Idea 73, on page 231. This will cost you more money, but you can pay for it by eliminating unneeded or excessive coverage. See also Idea 78, on page 244, for insurance to avoid. The main culprits and what you might do to lower premiums include:

❑ **Your homeowner's or renter's insurance.** Increase deductibles; eliminate nonessential coverage.

❑ **Your aging car.** If you have an old car—worth under $4,000— eliminate collision and comprehensive coverage; increase deductibles; for your newer cars eliminate nonessential coverage like towing and substitute transportation.

❑ **Your aging life insurance policies.** Life insurance needs often decline as you age, and some insurance might be able to be eliminated; replace a term insurance policy if cheaper coverage can be obtained. (See Idea 75 on page 235.)

❑ **Duplicate health coverage.** If both spouses have health insurance, they probably need only one policy that covers both.

❑ **Private mortgage insurance.** Cancel PMI if you have at least 20 percent equity in your home (see page 175).

❑ **Changes in your financial or family situation.** Review policies to make sure they reflect your current situation. For example, if you have children away at school who aren't driving, you may be able to remove them temporarily from your auto policy during school terms.

❑ **Earn discounts by purchasing insurance coverage from one company.** Many insurance companies offer discounts to customers who purchase multiple policies from them, such as automobile, homeowner's, and umbrella liability.

❑ **Inquire about discounts.** Many insurers offer discounts for homeowners who take protective measures against fire and burglary. You may also qualify for discounts from your automobile insurer, but you need to inquire.

❑ **Comparison-shop for coverage.** By all means ask your insurance agent to shop for lower-cost coverage, or do it yourself. The Internet can be an excellent way to compare premiums.

Chances are that you're overpaying for your insurance coverage, but there are many ways to lower your premiums.

■

A nickel ain't worth a dime anymore.
—YOGI BERRA

IDEA 75

The Straight Scoop on Life Insurance

If you're married, partnered, and/or have dependent children, you need life insurance, probably a lot of life insurance. If you're a breadwinner and, to be blunt, you die, your loved ones will likely have enormous difficulty making ends meet. Ditto if you take care of kids or other family members at home. Single people's life insurance needs may be modest, perhaps enough just to cover what are euphemistically called "final costs." Your life insurance policy at work may be more than sufficient to cover those. On the other hand, look into the future to determine if there may be situations where a more than minimal coverage may be necessary. Perhaps your parents will eventually need financial support or your siblings aren't very well off financially and, had you survived, you might have been able to help them pay college costs for your nieces and nephews. In these instances, you may need more than a small amount of coverage.

How much life insurance do you need? The rule of thumb is to buy about five to eight times your current wages. If you make $50,000 per year, that equates to $250,000 to $400,000 of life insurance coverage. Another approach would be to secure enough coverage to meet major financial obligations, enough to pay off the mortgage(s), plus pay for the kids' college educations. On top of that, an additional sum could be provided to help the family transition from the loss of your income.

Term or cash-value life insurance? There are two primary types of life insurance:

1. **Term insurance** is just plain insurance with no bells and whistles, and generally is cheapest—particularly for younger people. You can buy *annually renewable* term insurance or *level* term insurance, which charges the same premium over a fixed term of say five, ten, twenty, or even thirty years.

   The downside of level term insurance is it provides protection for only a specified period. If you die during that period, that's great—from the standpoint of collecting on the policy. Hopefully, though, you'll live a long life, and when the term expires, you'll have tons of money saved, the mortgage will be paid off, and the children will be out of the nest (if they ever leave the nest), so you won't need the insurance.

   On the other hand, you can keep renewing an annually renewable term policy, but beware:

   ✦ The annual premium will most likely rise and eventually become prohibitively expensive.

   ✦ Some insurance companies may require you to take a medical exam before letting you renew coverage. If you have a medical condition, you could find it tough to get insurance or the cost of your insurance may rise substantially.

2. **Cash-value life insurance** policies come with more than insurance and they generally provide lifelong coverage. They give you protection with savings. There are several types of cash-value policies, including:

   ✦ **Whole life** lets you lock in your premium payments for permanent protection. Your payments go both to a specific death benefit and a cash-value savings account, which grows income tax-free. With whole life insurance, you get dividends, which may be used to buy more insurance, to pay premiums, or to slash the number of years you pay premiums. The downside: whole life usually pays relatively low interest rates that are set by the life insurance company. You can do better investing on your own. Hence the often bandied, "Buy term and invest the difference." But that doesn't mean whole life or other cash-value insurance shouldn't be purchased, as discussed below.

✦ **Universal life** lets you adjust your premium payments. This can be attractive if you're in a career or business that has periods of unusually high or low income. But when interest rates are low, the investment component of your policy usually earns less than whole life's. Also, if you slack off on payments, your policy could be canceled.

✦ **Variable universal life** insurance also lets you make flexible premium payments. But it also lets you invest the cash value in a selection of investments, including stock and bond mutual funds. The downside: if the stock market plummets, as it did from 2000 to 2002, you could see your stock-fund holdings within the policy decline substantially. In fact, you might need to cough up some additional cash to keep the policy in good standing.

Optional extras. *Riders,* which range in cost from $50 to several hundred dollars annually, can fine-tune your insurance coverage. Depending on your situation, some may be worth the extra money, but most are probably not. Here are the most common:

✦ **Guaranteed insurability rider:** Lets you increase your insurance coverage without taking a medical exam or buying a new policy.

✦ **Disability income rider:** Provides some disability insurance coverage if you're unable to get it elsewhere.

✦ **Accelerated death benefit:** Also called a *living benefit,* it will pay the life insurance proceeds while the insured is still alive but is terminally ill.

✦ **Double indemnity or accidental-death benefit:** Lets your beneficiaries collect double the death benefit if you die in an accident.

✦ **Automatic premium loan provision:** Covers your premium payments in the event you cannot or choose not to pay a premium. The insurance company pays the premiums as a loan against the policy's cash value.

✦ **Waiver of premium:** Covers your life insurance premiums if you get injured or disabled. It's not designed, however, to be a substitute for disability insurance, which covers your income.

✦ **Family rider:** Lets you buy term insurance for other members of your family with your whole life coverage.

Which type of life insurance is best for you?

❏ **How long you'll need the coverage.** The primary life insurance question to resolve is how long you expect to need the coverage. If your life insurance needs are likely to decline at some point in the future, when the kids get out of college, for example, then term insurance is the answer. On the other hand, if you expect your life insurance needs to continue indefinitely, to help support your spouse or partner in retirement, for example, then cash-value insurance, aptly called "permanent insurance," is the safer choice.

❏ **Affordability.** Cash-value policies are very expensive if you need a lot of coverage. If cost is a problem but you may need insurance for a long time in the future, it's probably better to buy a long-duration level term policy, say thirty years.

❑ **Part term, part cash value.** Like most dilemmas in your financial life, choosing the best kind of life insurance coverage for you is not an either/or decision. You may want to opt for term insurance for temporary needs and cash-value coverage of indefinite-duration insurance needs.

❑ **Better investment returns available elsewhere.** Finally, the investment feature of a cash-value life insurance policy should *not* be considered the foundation of your lifelong investment program. While you can build up substantial values within many policies, they should not be viewed as a substitute for saving and investing the old-fashioned way, as described in chapter 5.

Shop for coverage. If you're in the market for life insurance coverage, be sure to shop, or ask your agent to shop for the best deal offered by a financially strong life insurance company. Premiums for essentially identical coverage vary widely, and this is one area of insurance coverage where price is a major consideration. If you already have a term policy, you may benefit from shopping for new coverage. See Idea 76, on page 240.

Life insurance tips for empty nesters and retirees. If the children are on their own, if the mortgage is paid off, and/or if you're in excellent financial shape, you may not need to continue some of your life insurance coverage. But this is a decision that shouldn't be taken lightly. Also, if you're well into retirement, it could pay to tap the cash value of a policy you've had for a long time. This may be attractive if it's paid in full or "endowed" and you already have substantial assets. Evaluate the suitability of taking out a low-interest tax-free policy loan. Then, put the money to work elsewhere or, better yet, take an expensive cruise.

For more information on securing the right kind of life insurance coverage for you, including sources of low-cost coverage, visit the *Grow Your Money!* special reader Web site. **w w w**

Life insurance is a family necessity, and choosing the right amount and type of coverage is actually quite straightforward.

■

Whoever created the name life insurance *had to be the sales genius of all time.*

—ROBERT HALF

IDEA 76

Is It Time to Trade In Your Term Life Insurance Policy for a Newer Model?

Whether you already have term life insurance, need more, or are shopping for the first time, this is a great time to buy term insurance—which is plain ole life insurance with no expensive savings or investment features. For most people, this type is the lowest-cost life insurance you can buy, and low price is an important consideration when buying a lot of life insurance or perhaps replacing an older, more expensive policy. After all, think about what has to happen in order to collect on a life insurance policy.

Insurance premiums for term insurance are about one-half of what they were a decade ago. That's because people are living longer and the longer everyone lives, the less you typically pay for life insurance. Say you're a forty-year-old male nonsmoker in good health. As I write this, you can buy a $500,000, twenty-year level term life insurance policy—which means your premiums stay the same for twenty years—for just $340 annually.

Sitting on a higher-cost policy? It could pay to consider switching. Or, if you have a family and need more life insurance, consider buying more.

Here are some guidelines to follow if you decide to switch or need more coverage:

❏ Consider having a life insurance agent or financial planner determine how much coverage you really need. It's important to buy enough, so that your family needn't worry. On the other hand, you don't want to be shelling out more money than necessary.

❏ Buy enough insurance to replace any existing individual life insurance you have unless your needs have declined.

❏ Compare prices of several companies.

❏ Note on the application that you plan to replace an existing policy.

❏ Don't cancel your old term insurance policy before you get your new one. Even though you'd never know about it, you don't want to die without coverage!

❏ You may be required to take a medical exam. If you're not in good health, your insurance premiums could be higher or your application could be declined. But you still have the old policy in hand.

❏ When you obtain a new insurance policy, there typically are "incontestability" and "suicide" clauses. This generally means your insurance company may contest claims made only during the first two years, for example, if you didn't disclose known health problems.

❏ Consider adding a rider that lets you get more life insurance coverage later without taking a medical exam.

❏ Always check the financial strength of the insurance company you are considering. The strongest companies are rated A++ and A+ by A.M. Best and AAA by Standard & Poor's.

Costs of term life insurance have declined so much in recent years that you may be better off trading in your existing term policy for a cheaper model.

■

Love conquers all things except poverty and toothache.
—MAE WEST

IDEA 77

Long-Term-Care Insurance?
Not for Everyone

Whether to get long-term-care (LTC) insurance, which provides health care if you become chronically ill or disabled, is a real dilemma. It's expensive. Meanwhile, if you are one of the estimated 50 percent of the population that will never require home or nursing-home care, you'll never collect on the policy.

On the other hand, if you must enter a nursing home, and you don't have long-term-care insurance, consider whether you can afford to shell out upward of $80,000 annually for your care. That adds up to at least $300,000 over four years, and if you enter a nursing home ten or fifteen years hence, those costs could be doubled.

The older you are, the more expensive LTC coverage gets. A seventy-year-old could easily pay $3,600 a year for a basic LTC policy; double that for a couple. Plus, even at these astounding prices, you'll still have substantial out-of-pocket expenses, because even the best policies probably won't come anywhere near paying the total cost of coverage when you eventually need it. One disturbing trend among some long-term-care providers is to hike the premiums substantially later on when the insureds can hardly afford it. If you buy an LTC policy and discontinue it or let it lapse, you lose all your benefits. So it's important to carefully evaluate all aspects, including how easily you'll be able to afford the premiums. It may be easy to afford the premiums if you acquire an LTC policy while you're still employed, but how easy will it be to pay them after you retire and your income declines?

The bottom line. Not everyone needs long-term-care insurance. So analyze your own situation before shelling out the big bucks. Weigh your answers to these questions:

✦ **Are you worth over a million dollars, excluding your home?** In that case, you probably can afford to pay for home health care and nursing care out of your own pocket.

✦ **Do you have a limited income and less than $500,000 in investments, excluding your home?** You probably can't afford long-term-care insurance.

✦ **Are you somewhere in between?** Have more than several hundred thousand dollars, but aren't quite a Rockefeller? Long-term-care insurance could be worth the price, particularly if you're married or in a partnered relationship. If you're single . . .

✦ **Are you single?** The major protection offered by long-term-care insurance is preventing nursing-home costs from impoverishing a surviving spouse or partner. If you're single and are not really anxious to pass on your estate to someone, then if you can afford to be placed in a top-quality nursing home and then spend-down your investments, you may not need this coverage.

The best time to obtain long-term-care coverage. Be sure to get coverage when you're younger and healthy. It's usually advisable to obtain coverage in your fifties or early sixties. The premium will be as little as one-third the amount it would cost you to buy a similar policy at age seventy, and that assumes health problems haven't intervened.

Shopping tips. If you're shopping for long-term-care coverage, you should consider:

❑ Inflation protection that provides for your benefits to increase 5 percent annually.

❑ Guaranteed renewable policies, so that the company can't cancel you.

❑ Waiver of premiums once you start collecting benefits.

❑ Third-party notification in case you forget to pay a premium.

❑ A provision that lets you keep a lesser amount of insurance in force if you let the policy lapse.

❑ Restoration of benefits, which insures that your benefits are reinstated under certain conditions if they lapsed due to an oversight on your part.

Decide once and for all if long-term-care insurance is right for you.

■

If anything can go wrong it will, and at the most inopportune time.
—MURPHY'S LAW

IDEA 78

Insurance to Avoid

Avoid buying insurance that you don't need. Insurance is usually one of the top four expenses in the family budget, and it's a fruitful area for cutting back on unneeded coverage (see Idea 74, on page 233), as well as avoiding unnecessary coverage in the first instance: Chances are you need life, health, auto, disability, homeowner's or renter's, and, perhaps, long-term-care insurance. But don't buy into sales arguments that you need other more costly insurance that provides you with coverage for only a limited range of events. It's always preferable to acquire broad coverage.

Here's a rundown of coverage that you can probably do without:

❑ **Rental-car insurance.** You probably don't need rental-car insurance, despite the often vigorous efforts by the rental agent to sell you this costly coverage. Most personal auto insurance covers accidents involving a car you rent for personal use. In addition, most major credit cards also cover rental-car damage when you use a credit card to rent the car. Check with your auto insurance agent and credit card provider for more details.

❑ **Travel insurance.** It usually pays to skip airline insurance to cover lost or stolen items when you travel. Again, your homeowner's or renter's insurance should cover you. In addition, airlines typically reimburse passengers up to $3,000 for lost or stolen domestic baggage. Did you pay for your ticket with a credit card? You may already have additional lost-baggage coverage.

❑ **Trip-cancellation insurance.** You don't need travel-cancellation insurance anytime you travel. Most airlines will let you change your plans for a fee, say $50 or $100, depending on the carrier. Trip-cancellation insurance might be a good idea, however, if you are planning to take an expensive cruise and are concerned you may have to cancel.

❑ **Critical-illness insurance.** Stay away from a critical-illness policy if you already have health insurance and, perhaps, long-term-care insurance. These policies protect you only in the event some specific illness befalls you, like cancer. They're a waste of money.

❑ **Mortgage insurance.** Avoid insurance that will pay off your mortgage if you die, unless you're ineligible for term life insurance. Reason: Mortgage insurance coverage declines as you pay down your mortgage, yet the premium stays the same. By contrast, the value of the death benefit on term life insurance doesn't decline and is usually far cheaper. In fact, the commission on some mortgage insurance policies is over 90 percent of the premium cost.

❑ **Non-medical life insurance.** You may get a solicitation in the mail offering you life insurance that doesn't require a medical examination. If you're near death, its a great deal. Otherwise, this coverage is shamefully expensive.

❑ **Identity-theft coverage.** Generally, you can forget identity-theft insurance—or credit-report-monitoring services, for that matter. Many homeowner's insurance policies already cover identity theft. As for the credit-report-monitoring service: you're already entitled to one free credit report annually. Plus, there are a number of other circumstances under which you may get a free credit report— including, if you're an identity-theft victim.

❑ **Appliance and auto service contracts.** Last on the list of coverage that's probably worth a lot less than it costs is a service contract for an appliance or car. For a rundown on why such contracts are usually a waste of money, see page 179.

A lot of heavily touted insurance policies are too limited in what they cover and outrageously overpriced.

■

Happiness has many routes, but none more important than security.
—EDWARD R. STETTINIUS JR.

IDEA 79

Estate Planning—Ignore This If You Dislike Your Heirs

This is a deadly topic, but not as deadly as it will be for family members if you fail to set up an estate plan before you become incapacitated or die. The cornerstones of an estate plan include:

- ❑ **A will.** This legal document tells who will manage your estate, who will get your belongings, and who will become guardian of your minor children when you die. Die without a will and the state makes these decisions—often at an added cost to those you love most.

- ❑ **A durable power of attorney.** This delegates the power to legally handle your business and financial affairs should you become incapacitated. Without this, no one may be able to access your bank account, securities, or any other property in your name without lengthy legal proceedings.

  A *living trust* may be required by financial institutions in lieu of a durable power of attorney. (More about this in Idea 80, on page 249.)

- ❑ **An advance directive.** This is a catchall term that refers to a health-care directive, a living will, a health-care (medical) power of attorney, and other personalized directives, all of which let you legally express your preference for continued health care should you later become physically or mentally incapable of doing so on your own or terminally ill. A *health-care power of attorney* (also called a *designation of health-care surrogate*), names a spouse or trusted relative to make health-care decisions for you if you can't.

- ❑ **Letter of instructions.** A letter of instructions is an informal document that gives your survivors information concerning important financial and personal matters that must be attended to after your demise. You don't need an attorney to prepare it. Although it doesn't carry the legal weight of a will and is in no way a substitute for a will, a letter of instructions clarifies any special requests to be carried out upon death. It also provides essential financial information, thus relieving the family of needless worry and speculation. Just as with other estate-planning documents, be sure your loved ones know where your letter of instructions is located.

Important matters to be included in the letter of instructions include:

✦ A list of information you'll need to know in the event of an emergency

✦ Information on medical insurance plans; Social Security number; date of birth; names and phone numbers of doctors, lawyers, accountants, and brokers; veteran discharge dates; and marriage dates

✦ Locations and information on life and disability insurance policies, the deed for the home, the car title, stocks and mutual funds, bank certificates, and prepaid funeral receipts

✦ A list of the contents of any safe-deposit boxes

✦ The location of the checkbook and ATM card

Other estate-planning strategies for the very well-off. If you're fortunate enough to be worth a few million dollars, you need to consider ways to cut estate taxes. Although estate taxes are slated to be eliminated altogether, many expect them to be reinstated. Also, many states have estate taxes—some even more onerous than the federal tax.

Here's how federal estate taxes work for married couples: Your spouse inherits your assets estate-tax-free. But once the second spouse dies, assets above a certain level ($2 million, in 2008) may be taxed. Heirs may also need to pay income taxes on certain retirement accounts after estate taxes have been paid. You'll want an attorney to help you figure out how to cut the impact of taxes on your estate. Common options include making gifts to family members and charities. Consult an experienced estate-planning attorney and, perhaps, insurance agent before you make this move. Professionals also should consider the impact of your estate plan on long-term-care decisions.

Spread the word. Make certain loved ones have copies of all important estate-planning documents. Periodically review them to make sure they're up to date and laws haven't changed.

The *Grow Your Money!* special reader Web site provides additional details on preparing and keeping up to date the various estate-planning documents. It will also keep you apprised of changes in estate-planning regulations and strategies. **w w w**

> It's never too early to prepare essential estate-planning documents, but it can be too late.
>
> ■
>
> *I owe much; I have nothing; the rest I leave to the poor.*
> —FRANÇOIS RABELAIS

IDEA 80

Do You Really Need a Living Trust?

The virtues of a living trust are often overhyped by lawyers, financial advisers, and insurance agents. Yet there are situations where you need a living trust.

Definition. A *living trust*—officially it's called a *revocable living trust* and is also known as a *family trust*—is a trust that's established while you're living and is revocable, so you are able to make changes whenever you want during your lifetime, including revoking the entire trust. The document describes how your property in the trust should be managed while you are alive and how it should be distributed upon your death. Provisions for how your property is to be handled if you become incapacitated are also provided in the typical living trust.

Some people set up *irrevocable* living trusts, whose provisions can't be changed during their lifetime. These are complex arrangements and are usually employed by those with beaucoup money or people who don't have a lot of money but are hell-bent on giving it to their greedy children rather than paying it to a nursing home. Having "impoverished" themselves, they then qualify for Medicaid, which means the government (in other words, your and my tax dollars) pays their nursing-home costs. I think you can deduce my opinion of that scheme.

Advantages of a living trust. A living trust can help you avoid probate—the court-administered legal process of settling an estate. It can also keep your financial matters private, since a will is, in effect, a public document. A living trust can also speed the transfer of your estate to your heirs, which may be particularly helpful for people who have no immediate family members capable of settling their estate. Plus, it is increasingly relied upon as more financial institutions are reluctant to accept powers of attorney, owing to fraud. If you anticipate any acrimony among your heirs, a living trust is more difficult to contest than a will. Finally, one situation where a living trust is usually very necessary is if you own real estate or business interests in more than one state.

Living trust disadvantages and alternatives. Privacy is often cited as a reason for establishing a living trust, but if you don't have millions, you might not care if your financial information is available to the public. Chances are no one is going to seek out that information anyway. Avoiding probate may not be an issue, because probate rules or costs may not be particularly burdensome in your state. Another disadvantage is cost. Creating and administering a living trust can be expensive, a lot more expensive than preparing a will. A lawyer may charge a flat fee, an hourly fee, or a percentage of assets. There also may be fees to administer a trust once it's set up. Plus, assets, for example, real estate, must be retitled inside the trust, a very common oversight. And fees may be charged by area governments to record the document. Then, there's always the risk that your appointed trustee may not act in your interest. Finally, it's impossible to put all of your assets into a living trust, so you'll still need a will.

If avoiding probate and speeding the transfer of money to your heirs is a concern, there are other low- or no-cost options that also avoid probate, including:

✦ Joint accounts, which allow assets to pass directly to the other joint account holder

✦ Payable-on-death accounts, in which you designate beneficiaries to whom funds in the accounts will pass upon your death

✦ Life insurance, by which you designate a beneficiary to receive policy proceeds

One common misconception about the living trust is that it saves income taxes and estate taxes. It doesn't.

The upshot is that while people with complex and sizable estates and family issues may benefit from a living trust, most others will not benefit enough to offset the cost and inconvenience. But laws and family situations keep changing, so it's always best to talk with an estate-planning attorney in your state about a living trust. *Don't* rely solely on the opinion of an attorney who advertises and/or offers seminars that ballyhoo the virtues of the living trust. An objective attorney should analyze all the pros and cons of a living trust and quote you a price for creating one.

> Before going through all the gyrations of establishing a living trust, find out if you really need one.
>
> ■
>
> *A millionaire is a man who gathers a fortune he doesn't need to leave to people who don't deserve it.*
> —ANONYMOUS

MONEY TIP

Where Should You Store Your Will?

Although your family members or close acquaintances should have photocopies of your will, only one original version should exist. Deciding where to keep that important original document can be perplexing, so let's evaluate the options so you can resolve this here and now.

✦ **Options.** A home safe, business safe, bank safe-deposit box, your lawyer's office, or the clerk of your local probate court, who will hold it for safekeeping in a sealed envelope.

✦ **Potential problem with a bank safe-deposit box.** Before you decide to store the will in a bank safe-deposit box, consider state and local probate law. Many laws require that a bank safe-deposit box be automatically sealed upon your death. This can result in messy complications.

✦ **Home safe.** The best bet often is to purchase a good-quality home safe. The safe should be able to withstand temperatures up to 1,700 degrees in case of fire. Place the safe in the basement if you have one, so if there is a fire, it can't fall through the floor. The safe should always be locked. Be certain someone you trust has a key or the combination. If you have other valuables in a home safe, consider an alarm system or obtain professional help to make it burglar resistant.

✦ **Don't keep the location a secret.** Most important, family members or close friends should know the location of your original will.

✦ **If you prepare a new will . . .** If a new will is drafted, ask the attorney who prepares it whether you should destroy the old one.

> ■
>
> *Where there's a will, I want to be in it.*
> —ANONYMOUS

IDEA 81

Helping Older Family Members Cope with Their Finances

As parents (or you, if you're a parent with adult children) age, younger-generation family members should be aware that the oldsters could become more dependent on others to help them cope with their finances. Here are some matters that sooner or later may require the assistance of a younger-generation family member or acquaintance—first, for active seniors, and second, for seniors who are in declining health.

Keeping an eye on active seniors. Here are four particularly important matters to attend to as your parents age:

1. **Insurance.** Make sure your parents keep and maintain the right kind and amount of insurance. Some seniors either are victimized by unscrupulous insurance agents who sell them unneeded coverage or go out on their own and buy narrowly defined coverage (cancer insurance, for example) that's a waste of money—or they simply drop needed policies.

2. **Health care.** Make sure the seniors in your life are getting the quality of health care that they deserve and are entitled to and that they maintain the appropriate Medicare supplemental and drug coverage. It's difficult enough for a younger person to navigate the health-care maze. Sometimes a younger-generation family member will have to assist or intervene to make sure that the senior is receiving appropriate health care.

3. **Housing.** As they age, some retirees, including perhaps your parents, seem reluctant, if not downright obstinate, about deciding that a change in housing may be desirable. "Change in housing" may mean selling a too-large and/or too-tough-to-maintain house and moving into something more manageable. It could also mean moving into assisted-living housing or even the dreaded nursing home. But it is incumbent upon a responsible child to look for signs that their parents can no longer comfortably and safely live in their current housing. It may take some prodding to advance the notion of a change in venue, and be prepared for them to vigorously oppose your suggestions. Enlist the help of your siblings or close friends of your parents. Sometimes a gentle show of force will prove decisive.

4. **Day-to-day money concerns.** Finally, be alert for situations where there might be problems handling money. A change in spending habits, late filing of tax returns, late payment of bills, may indicate that a senior is simply unable to maintain his or her day-to-day finances. It doesn't necessarily mean that a parent is having trouble making ends meet, but the assistance of a child or another family member or acquaintance is probably necessary. Another matter to be wary of is that seniors are all too often the victims of scam artists. For help on avoiding scams, see Idea 88, on page 278.

When health declines. If you are responsible for taking care of the financial affairs of a parent or another family member or an acquaintance whose health or mental acuity is declining, take this quiz:

> ✦ Do you know where his or her financial records are?
>
> ✦ What investments does he or she have?
>
> ✦ How about income taxes?

Drawing blanks? If so, here are some important items to attend to:

❏ **Estate-planning document review.** Examine the person's will and durable power of attorney (which appoints someone to handle his or her financial affairs), and advance directive (which provides information for end-of-life care). See Idea 79, on page 247, for more information on these essential documents. Make certain that information is current, you have a copy, and you know where the original signed documents are located. Ideally, you, as the power of attorney designee, should live nearby. Be certain that the power of attorney adequately covers every possible situation, including the handling of taxes and retirement plans. If your senior has debt problems, make sure that the durable power of attorney gives you the right to be served a summons if the bank forecloses on his or her home or condo. You may also need power to make arrangements for long-term care.

❏ **Access to important documents.** Obtain a key to the senior's home, as well as safe-deposit box. Be sure the bank has your signature on file, along with permission to access the safe-deposit box. If it has not yet been prepared, assist in preparing a letter of instructions (see Idea 79, on page 247).

    While you're at it, revise or prepare your own letter of instructions.

❏ **Record keeping.** Check the senior's tax records to make certain that the proper documents are being saved in files. If you're noticing that bills aren't being paid or financial statements are suddenly missing, consider working with the senior or obtaining assistance. Most communities have services that can assist in bill payment and organizing tax records. You might buy a folding file box with pockets in alphabetical order. When a bill is paid, have the senior put the statement in the appropriate folder, such as "E" for electric bills. Be certain he or she is filing away bank statements. You may need this information to track direct deposits, income tax deductions, and charitable contributions.

❑ **Income taxes.** Set up a tickler file to remind your senior of income tax deadlines. Quarterly income tax estimates are due April 15, June 15, September 15, and January 15. Remind the senior about state tax payments and the April 15 income tax filing deadline. Contact the senior's tax preparer to make sure returns are being filed timely and request a copy of the tax return. Having a tough time getting cooperation from your family member? Ask him or her to take all the tax documents as they arrive in January and February, except personal correspondence and checks, and file them in a large envelope. At the end of February, the envelope can be mailed to the tax preparer.

Be prepared to help your parents or other older relatives and close friends to manage their financial affairs as they age. It's the right thing to do.

◼

True, you can't take it with you, but then, that's not the place where it comes in handy.
—BRENDAN FRANCIS

CHAPTER 12

Making Smart Money Decisions a Family Affair

You're all in the same financial boat, so it behooves family members of all generations to row together. Selecting the right financial professionals to help you make the right decisions about all areas of your financial life may be indispensable. Learning to cope with your spouse's or partner's financial peccadilloes will foster domestic tranquility. Devoting some time and perhaps some money to helping your children become financially responsible may lower the probability that you'll be supporting them for the rest of your life. You and other family members, particularly those in the older generation, will do well to be ever mindful of any efforts by scalawags to separate you from your money.

> ■
>
> *Misers may be tough to live with, but they make great ancestors.*
> —ANONYMOUS

IDEA 82

Picking the Right Professionals to Advise You, If You Really Need Their Advice

It's often helpful to get some objective professional advice on financial matters from time to time. The challenge is to find the right advisers for you—those who will put your own interests above their own. True, some insurance agents, attorneys, investment advisers, and financial planners have a well-deserved bad reputation. But with a little digging, you can find financial professionals who will serve you well. Finding the right advisers is well worth the effort. There is no single ideal way to identify the cream of the crop, but word-of-mouth recommendation is often the most effective way. Ask acquaintances of similar age and in financial circumstances similar to yours for recommendations. If you already have an adviser that you are happy with, ask him or her to recommend professionals in other areas where you need assistance. Hopefully, there will be no referral fees involved, but it doesn't hurt to ask.

Insurance agent

Insurance is a complicated business, so you probably want to use an agent for all or most of your coverage needs. The better agents will review your coverage with you at least annually, shop around for appropriate policies, and go to bat for you when necessary. If you're having difficulty securing some needed coverage—for example, because of a health problem—a good agent will work hard to find you the necessary insurance at the best possible price. To assure a good relationship, you must keep your agent informed of changes in your circumstances. If necessary, insist on a periodic review of your coverage.

Should you buy insurance on your own? The serious do-it-yourselfer can obtain insurance without using an agent. Many Web sites offer comparison shopping services, and some major insurance companies sell policies directly to individuals as well as through agents. You may be comfortable doing that, or you may not. A good agent can provide you with guidance that is very difficult and time-consuming to acquire on your own. On the other hand, you may be able to save money by going direct. Remember also that the decision to use an agent or to buy insurance on your own is not an "either/or" decision. You may want to buy some of your coverage—term life insurance, for example—direct and obtain your automobile and homeowner's insurance through an agent.

Here are some key times when you need to either check in with your agent or, if you obtain coverage on your own, review your coverage:

- ❏ Any change in family, job, health, or financial circumstances

- ❏ Before retirement, in order to evaluate any needed changes in coverage

- ❏ Coverage should be reviewed annually, under all circumstances, to determine if any changes are warranted

Attorney

You may not yet have a family attorney. But you'll need one at least to prepare necessary estate-planning documents, such as wills. (See Idea 79, on page 247.) It's best to have an attorney who is roughly your age or younger. You'll probably use the same attorney over the years, and you don't want to be burdened with having to find a new lawyer when your current one retires. Don't try to prepare legal documents yourself. Even when you can get away with doing that, how will you know when you need to make changes? While most attorneys are up to the task of preparing basic estate-planning documents, if your financial or family situation is particularly complex, you may need an attorney who specializes in estate planning, particularly since the estate tax environment is likely to change in the near future. But whomever you select, he or she should be responsive to your needs and should conduct work on your behalf in a timely manner.

Here are some situations that often require a consultation with an attorney about the adequacy of your estate planning:

❑ **To prepare a will and other essential estate-planning documents.** Don't try to prepare these important documents without the assistance of an attorney.

❑ **Any change in your family situation,** including the arrival of children or grandchildren, divorce, and entering into a partnered relationship.

❑ **Any change in your financial status,** both positive and negative, may require a change in your estate planning

❑ **Periodic checkup.** In the absence of any changes in your life, you should check in with your estate-planning lawyer every few years to make sure there have been no changes in regulations or the estate-tax rules that may require a tweaking of your documents.

Investment Adviser

Investment advisers are in the business of giving advice about securities. Most *financial planners* are investment advisers, but *not* all investment advisers are financial planners. Selecting someone to help with your investments is a critical decision, particularly since almost anyone can call themselves an investment adviser, even though they do have to be registered with state or federal regulators. Be sure to inquire about experience, educational background, how they are paid, the kinds of investments they select for their clients, and how they would envision handling your investments.

You should expect the following from your investment adviser, at a minimum:

❑ **Periodic verbal updates** on your investments and plans for any changes therein over the near future

❑ **Written analysis** of investment performance and comments, at least twice a year

❑ **Prompt responses** to any questions or concerns you may have

Financial Planner

You are your own best financial planner, but that doesn't necessarily mean you shouldn't retain the services of a financial planner. While financial planning is a service everyone could use, many people don't benefit significantly from the services of a financial planner. You may do quite well on your own. Too many people think the planner can turn their finances around. But financial planners aren't miracle workers. Also, many financial planners are actually insurance agents or investment advisers, who may not be capable of or interested in dealing with the multiplicity of matters that affect a person's financial well-being, including loans, taxes, pensions, retirement planning, and estate planning. They may understand a lot about the products they sell, but they may not be well versed in other important financial-planning areas.

When it's most important to take a close look at your financial situation. Even if you prefer to manage your own finances, there are times in your financial life when the services of an independent financial planner may be very helpful, if for no other reason than that he or she can attest to the fact that you are on track, including:

❑ **Shortly after starting your career,** in order to help you get on the road to saving and selecting the best ways to save for retirement and other needs

❑ **Preparing for major financial outlays,** including buying a house or meeting college costs

❏ **Mid-career,** twenty or so years into your career, to gauge your progress toward meeting your retirement goals

❏ **A couple of years before retirement,** to begin to plan for changes in your financial life and needs when you retire

❏ **A couple of years after retirement,** to make sure your investments and retirement budget are on track

Finding a good financial planner. What constitutes the right kind of planner for you depends on your needs. If you want to be assured of getting objective advice, use a fee-only planner—but be prepared to pay for the service. A fee-only planner usually, but *not* always, is in the business solely to provide you with independent advice. That's often all that you need, particularly if you use a financial planner infrequently. That doesn't mean a planner who earns commissions should be avoided, so long as you understand that there may be a conflict of interest. Look around; there are many excellent financial planners—both fee-based and commission based—in your community.

If it's not working out. If you're unhappy with one of your advisers, it may be because you have not taken an active role in the relationship. First, try to resolve the problem, but if it persists, don't hesitate to make a change. It's amazing how many people dislike or distrust their advisers, particularly their investment adviser, yet continue to do business with them.

The special reader Web site has more guidance for selecting and working with financial professionals, as well as some useful Web sites for do-it-yourselfers. **w w w**

Whether or not you want to manage your financial planning on your own, selecting top-notch financial professionals and an attorney can be indispensable to achieving your financial goals.

■

The minute you read something you can't understand, you can almost be sure it was drawn up by a lawyer.
—WILL ROGERS

IDEA 83

Domestic Financial Felicity Need Not Be an Impossible Dream

They say two people can live as cheaply as one. But it may not be worth the savings if you don't talk about money before you get to that point. Avoiding the subject, as too many do, can hurt both your relationship and your financial well-being.

Start simply by analyzing your respective money habits. Do you tend to spend your money or do you save it? What about your significant other? There's no right or wrong answer. However, extremes in any situation can spell trouble.

Fortunately, there also are solutions if you discuss your habits and compromise over them early in your relationship. (Remember that cute habits of profligacy or penury during your courtship many not be so cute when you set up a household and combine finances.)

+ A spender and a saver, for example, might consider separate checking accounts, plus a joint account to pay bills.

+ Two spenders could work together to set up a plan that has money automatically taken out of their paychecks and invested. Or, they might pay cash for most everything—an automatic way to spend less.

✦ Never have any fun because you both save a lot? Understand the importance of setting aside fun time for yourselves, before you begin living together.

If marriage or cohabitation is in the cards, you need to get down to hard numbers. Talk about how you plan to manage your assets as a unit.

✦ First gather your statements and financial records. Write down how much each of you has in cash, investments, property, insurance, other assets, and debts. If one of you is in debt, better to decide beforehand whether one or both of you will pay it off.

✦ Examine health-care coverage. Does one of you have a better or lower-cost plan at work? If so, the other might enroll in it after marriage.

✦ Check whether you have duplicate investments. Some may need to be redeployed. It's important to be well-diversified, but you won't be able to know whether you are until you combine your respective investment and savings accounts, including company retirement savings plans.

✦ Analyze how marriage will impact how much tax you'll pay.

✦ Do you both have life and disability insurance? If not, can you get the coverage at work?

✦ You may need to consider revising your wills, durable powers of attorney, and advance directives to recognize your new status. If, as is often the case, you haven't yet prepared these documents, it's definitely time to do so now that you're a grown-up.

✦ What about your plans to raise a family, buy a house, send kids to college, and save for your retirement? Discuss what you both want, how much it will cost, and how you'll save for it.

Should you prepare a prenuptial or cohabitation agreement?

Now that you've done the hardest work, it could pay to discuss whether a prenuptial agreement is necessary. Don't choke! All prenups do is override state laws, which, for example, provide that a certain amount of assets must go to a spouse in the event of a death or divorce. They may also provide for alimony.

Prenuptial agreements are particularly important when one of you has a whole lot more money or property than the other. These are some other examples of when a prenup could be worthwhile:

✦ This is a second marriage, and one or both of you want children from a previous marriage to inherit your assets rather than your spouse.

✦ You live in a community-property state, like California, in which any property a spouse acquires during a marriage is jointly owned.

✦ One of you is giving up a paycheck.

✦ One of you has a family business.

If you do decide to get a prenuptial agreement, each of you must hire your own attorney. Recognize also that the following could invalidate a prenuptial agreement:

✦ Failure to disclose all assets

✦ Commission of fraud

✦ Signing the agreement near your wedding day or under duress

If you're already married, but think some kind of agreement might be desirable, speak with an attorney about preparing a postnuptial agreement.

Cohabitation agreement. If marriage is not in the cards, but a long-term relationship is, you should consider a cohabitation agreement. A cohabitation agreement, more informally called a "living-together contract" spells out the terms of the relationship and often addresses financial issues and how property will be divided if the relationship ends. While considerable latitude is permissible, the typical cohabitation agreement will cover the following areas:

✦ Distributing property in case of death or breakup

✦ Obligating financial support during the relationship or upon its dissolution

✦ Handling the payment of debts

✦ Dividing the residence upon breakup or death of one of the partners

✦ Determining the right to serve as guardian in the event of incapacity

✦ Establishing the right to make medical decisions

✦ Defining various rights if there are minor children in the relationship

Communication is key. Communication is at least half the battle when it comes to dealing with money issues between spouses or partners. So if you've followed these suggestions as a couple, your relationship is off to a positive start!

For more information on ways to improve domestic financial felicity, particularly if one of you is a saver and the other is a spender, check out the companion Web site. **w w w**

> If you're talking about marriage or a domestic partnership with your special someone, discussing financial matters and what your plans will be after the merger can get the relationship off to a good financial start.
>
> ■
>
> *Money cannot buy love, but it can put you in a good bargaining position.*
> —ANONYMOUS

IDEA 84

Advice for Twentysomethings: Something Your Parents and Grandparents Know for Sure

You're now at an age when you have a newfound respect for the wisdom of older people, after many years of giving short shrift to any advice proffered by anyone over thirty, particularly your parents and grandparents. I have been authorized to speak on their behalf on the matter of saving. If you can get into the habit of saving now, later on in life you'll avoid a tremendous amount of angst about whether you'll have enough money to buy a home, educate any progeny that grace your portals, and retire in style. It all starts with saving—living beneath your means—then investing those savings smartly, as described in chapters 6 and 7. Why risk spending many years or decades of your future fretting about your finances when putting away just a little bit now will avoid those travails?

Here's my entreaty, which is wholly supported by your parents, grandparents, and the many other old people who care about you: if you can start putting money away in your twenties and keep it up, it's almost a slam dunk that you will enjoy a rich financial future, just as it's almost a certainty that your parents will heed my advice to baby boomers and other elderly folks that they should plan to spend all their money after they retire, leaving nothing to their children. That means you.

Consider the following table that shows how a young but habitual saver can stockpile a stupendous amount of money over forty years with an average annual investment return of 7 percent. The table also shows forty years' worth of savings if you can manage to increase your savings by 5 percent each year, not an onerous amount, but it amounts to an enormous sum by the time you retire.

A LIFELONG LESSON FOR THE YOUNGER GENERATION

| | ACCUMULATED BALANCE IN 40 YEARS | |
ANNUAL SAVINGS	CONTRIBUTE SAME AMOUNT EACH YEAR	INCREASE SAVINGS 5% EACH YEAR
$1,000	$215,000	$425,000
2,000	430,000	850,000
3,000	345,000	1,275,000
4,000	860,000	1,700,000

Heed the advice of your parents and grandparents just this one time and start putting money away for a more secure and worry-free future.

■

When I was a boy of fourteen, my father was so ignorant I could hardly stand to have the old man around. But when I got to be twenty-one, I was astonished at how much he had learned in seven years.
—MARK TWAIN

IDEA 85

Dual-Career Parents of Youngsters: Does That Second Paycheck Really Help the Family Budget Very Much?

Most parents of young children confront the dilemma of whether both parents must work outside the home during their children's early years. Many are greatly conflicted by the choice that involves one partner interrupting a career, not to mention a financial sacrifice, and a great number of parents conclude that they simply cannot afford to live on one paycheck. But a closer inspection of the amount of money that the second paycheck adds to the family coffers may be revealing. Consider the following example:

A couple has two preschoolers. Each spouse grosses $52,000, for a total family income of $104,000. With all their expenses, they can't foresee any way that one of them could leave the workforce. But before making a final decision, they did some number crunching to determine how much the second-paycheck earner actually brings home, given day-care expenses and the other costs of having both parents work. Here's their analysis:

PARENTAL DILEMMA: HOW MUCH IS A SECOND PAYCHECK WORTH?

Weekly gross income from second paycheck:	$1,000
Less income taxes:	
Federal at 25% (all of the second paycheck will, in effect, incur federal income tax at that rate, since it is incremental to the first paycheck. In other words, the first paycheck moves the family into the 25% bracket, so all additional income from the second paycheck will be taxed at 25%.)	(250)
Social Security at 8%	(80)
State at 4%	(40)
Total income taxes	(370)
Weekly after-tax income	630

Less expenses associated with both parents working outside
the home:

Day-care for two children (less tax credit)*	(350)
Other work-related expenses that could be avoided if one parent leaves the workforce (work clothes, commuting, meals at work, etc.)	(75)
Total expenses	(425)
Weekly income provided by $1,000 second paycheck	$205

* Average day-care costs are $160 a week per child, but, depending on locale, range from a low of around $100 a week to over $300 a week.

Depending on our family's financial circumstances, the second paycheck may still be a financial necessity. But this couple, like many others who have performed a similar analysis, are startled by how little the second paycheck actually brings home. In this example, only about one-fifth of the income ends up with the family.

So there may be a lot of compelling reasons why both parents of young children want to work outside the home, but for many, the additional money that the second paycheck brings home is not as great as it may seem at first glance.

While many parents of young children have to bring home two paychecks to make ends meet, some are surprised at how little the second paycheck actually adds to the family budget after day-care costs and taxes are factored in.

■

My hair stands on end at the cost and charges of these boys. Why was I ever a father! Why was my father ever a father!
—CHARLES DICKENS

IDEA 86

Teach Kids About Money

Stop your children from making the same financial mistakes you probably made. Or if you have always been a diligent financial manager, don't rely on genetics to engender similar habits in your progeny. Start teaching them about money early and continue well into their teen years. Here is a list of ideas:

❏ Television doesn't exactly help the cause—particularly when children's favorite characters try to convince them to buy everything under the sun. It's a tall order, but you need to counter the impact of television commercials on your children's spending. When your kid comes to you to buy him or her the latest gizmo, explain that you have only a certain amount of money. So you must prioritize. Money first needs to be routed to the items one needs in order to live—like clothes, shelter, and food. Also explain the importance of finding the best-quality goods at the lowest possible price. That may or may not be the item advertised. Never be reticent to tell the little wastrel that "we can't afford it."

❏ When you shop, encourage the child to help clip grocery coupons and assist you when it comes to finding the item you need. Offer a "salary" of half the savings from the coupons you use. Help the child understand that even with coupons, buying items you don't need is wasteful.

❏ After your child has learned to add and subtract, consider conducting the following exercise together. Sit down with paper, pencil, and a calculator. In one column, list all the clothes and school supplies your child needs. In a second column, list the quantity of each. In a third column, write down the item's price. Then, have your child, perhaps using the calculator, total the cost of everything on the list. Because you may not have money to afford everything, help him or her figure out ways to cut down both the list and the prices.

❑ Based on what you can afford, it could be a good idea to start giving your child a periodic allowance, perhaps starting between ages five and ten. The amount should not be tied to routine chores, which are allotted to all members of the household. Help your child divide up the allowance. Go with the child to open a savings account at a credit union or bank. Explain that, to get the most bang for the buck, at least one-third of an allowance should be saved for the future, perhaps to buy something big that cannot be afforded with the weekly allowance (like one of those damnable iPods). A portion of the rest may be given to charity. The child can spend the remaining amount as he or she sees fit.

❑ When giving your child money, give one-dollar bills instead of a larger bill. This way, it's easy to divide it into categories—savings, charity, and current spending.

❑ With the youngster in tow, go to the bank or use the Internet to purchase U.S. savings bonds. Show him or her that the $50 invested now may be worth a lot more in several years, thanks to compound interest.

❑ When shopping at stores or on the Internet, encourage your child to comparison shop to discover the best values.

❑ If you're using credit cards, take advantage of the opportunity to explain how credit works. Show the child how to verify charges. Explain how to calculate the tip on a restaurant bill and where to write it. Make certain he or she understands the cost of added interest that comes from not paying the credit card bill within the grace period.

❑ Be sure to convey to teens the concept of how short-lived fads can be very costly. You might suggest that a teen save on his or her own for a faddish item. Convey that trade-offs are necessary.

❑ Have your older child keep good records of money saved, invested, or spent. Encourage the child to keep receipts for all purchases.

❑ Teens often avoid considering the future when they spend. Your teenager needs to understand that money earned through hard work should be carefully spent.

❑ Talk about mistakes you and your friends have made with money.

❑ Help your child distinguish between needs and wants. A teen may need a car to get to work or college. He or she may really want a Mercedes (the apple doesn't fall far from the tree). Yet, going into debt for the Mercedes might require working extra hours, which would leave less time and energy for more important parts of life, such as enjoying the car with family and friends. The solution: buy a more affordable car, just like the parents.

❑ If you're a grandparent, don't subvert all the hard work that's being done by indulging the grandkids—despite your strong inclination to do so, abetted by the acquisitive grandchildren, who soon learn that grandparents are an easy mark.

Don't expect perfection when teaching your children about money. Just do your best—through education and example. Children within the same family differ, and this plays out no differently with money. Although all three of mine are still teenagers, I already know that my efforts have worked well with one, so-so with the second, and have thus far been an abject failure with the third. Same education, widely divergent outcomes.

Teaching your children about money from early childhood through their teen years can get them started on a life of financial stability.

■

If you want a kitten, start out by asking for a horse.
—NAOMI, age fifteen

■

Grandparents and grandchildren are natural allies against a common enemy.
—ARNOLD TOYNBEE

IDEA 87

IRAs for the Younger Set

You don't have to be an adult to qualify for an IRA. You just need work-related income. IRAs, particularly Roth IRAs, are a wonderful idea for younger-generation family members, because your generosity imparts some enduring lessons, including:

✦ Giving an IRA to a younger-generation family member conveys the importance you place on saving for the future, in this instance, saving for retirement, which is many decades away. This is an important lesson that could provide lifelong benefits. There is also an entirely selfish reason for contributing to their IRAs. By doing your best to inculcate good financial habits in your children or other youngsters in your life, you will hopefully not have to spend half of your retirement income supporting them.

✦ At a minimum, opening an IRA on behalf of a young person provides a chance to teach them a bit about investing and the miracle of compound growth. But more important, you will be able to convey to your child, niece, nephew, or grandchild the importance of saving for retirement even though it's many decades away.

EXAMPLE: A teenager (or, more likely, the teenager's parents or grandparents) puts $1,000 into an IRA for each of four years. If the money stays put for forty-five years (admittedly a big *if*), at an average growth rate of 7 percent, that paltry four grand will grow to $93,000 which may not seem like a lot of money forty-five years hence, but will still be a lot better than nothing. Indeed, if inflation averages 3 percent per year over those decades, the result of that $4,000 investment will have a purchasing power of $25,000 in today's dollars, enough to engender good memories about the loved ones who funded the account in the first place.

See Idea 23, on page 76 for another illustration of the great things that can happen to a small amount of money invested over several decades.

How to set up an IRA for Junior

✦ There is no minimum age to set up an IRA. If the child is a minor, many, but not all, mutual funds, brokers, and banks will allow you to set up a "custodial IRA" also called a "guardian IRA."

✦ There's no requirement that the same dollars that were earned be used to fund the IRA. You can gift the money to the child. (If my teenagers ever volunteer to fund their IRAs out of their job earnings, my wife and I will drop dead on the spot.)

✦ The major challenge for setting up IRAs for children, especially young children, is the earned-income requirement. The income must be related to work. Investment income doesn't qualify. That doesn't necessarily mean that the child has to actually pay tax on the income. Even though the total amount of income may be small enough that an income tax return does not have to be filed, it will still qualify for an IRA contribution. A lot of informal work for pay will qualify, including babysitting, mowing lawns, or similar tasks, as well as part-time or summer jobs in high school or college.

✦ What about earnings from household chores? The IRS has not yet ruled on this issue. Some tax experts indicate that, so long as the child actually does the chores, this qualifies as earned income. Many others caution against it, so before you set up an IRA funded on the basis of an allowance or payment based on household chores, it's prudent to check with a tax professional.

Roth or traditional IRA? A Roth IRA is almost always preferable to a deductible IRA for the same reasons as delineated in Idea 26, on page 83. Another argument for a Roth IRA is that the child's income is likely to be so small that no taxes are due and, hence, there could be no benefit from a tax-deductible IRA. If the child can hang on until retirement age, the ultimate advantage of a Roth IRA is that all of the money will be able to be withdrawn tax-free.

Other considerations

✦ Whichever IRA is established, the child or grandchild will not necessarily have to wait until retirement to make good use of your largess. Subject to some limitations, tax rules permit IRA money to be withdrawn without penalty to help pay for a first home purchase. If the money is in a Roth, the child will probably be able to withdraw more of it for a home purchase than is possible with a traditional IRA.

✦ Putting money in a child's name is usually not advantageous if there's a chance the family will qualify for college financial aid. But IRAs are not considered in financial-aid applications, so an IRA account should not jeopardize qualification.

✦ Keep in mind that money in a child's IRA belongs to the child. Hopefully, the child will hold on to the money, but there's always a chance that he or she will do otherwise. Of course, if Junior cashes in the IRA to take a vacation, this might serve as a valuable indicator of how you should eventually pass on your estate to him.

✦ Finally, once a younger-generation family member joins the workforce (a joyous family event, to be sure), your generosity can also provide a lasting money lesson. You could offer to help him or her make contributions to a workplace retirement savings plan, like a 401(k) or 403(b) plan. It's a struggle for people who are starting out in their first real jobs to contribute to these plans at a meaningful level without a little help from the relatives.

Giving money to the younger people in your life that is earmarked for a retirement that is decades away empowers both the kids and you. They're empowered because you have shown them how to become financially well-off. You're empowered because by raising financially savvy children you no longer have to be concerned about passing an inheritance on to them. Thus, once you retire, your primary financial strategy will not be inheritance maximization; rather, it will be spending maximization.

Please check out the special reader Web site for any updates on the use of IRAs for children and other minors. **w w w**

Giving a younger-generation family member an IRA can convey an important message about the importance of saving regularly for retirement, even though it's decades away.

■

Blessed are the young, for they shall inherit the national debt.

—HERBERT HOOVER

IDEA 88

Avoiding Financial Scams

Some of our nation's wealthiest have fallen victim to financial scams. Don't let it happen to you. Here are some common ploys:

✦ **The old "Ponzi scheme".** A so-called broker or financial professional promises that you can make 50 to over 100 percent on your money in some overlooked investment. But rather than invest your money, the scammer uses it to pay off another investor. This practice is repeated—until all of the investor money finally runs out.

✦ **High-yielding investments or promissory notes.** You make what seems to be an attractive investment and never see your money again. Always keep in mind that any investment that purports to pay interest that is far higher than conventional investments is a disaster waiting to happen.

✦ **Free lunches.** You get invited to a free lunch or dinner, but get hard-sold on an annuity, stock-trading program, or high-priced get-rich-quick scheme.

✦ **Mortgage foreclosure scams.** Are you overextended on your mortgage? If making your mortgage payments is getting tougher, a scam artist may offer to take title for a year or two and make the payments. Once he or she gets title, your property is sold out from under you with the scam artist pocketing the cash.

✦ **Authentic-looking but fake communications** from well-known financial institutions and government agencies, such as the IRS or FDIC, requesting personal information. Once you provide it, the information is used for identity theft.

✦ **Fraudulent Medicare prescription drug plans.** Unsavory characters have been targeting persons with disabilities and asking for money and checking account information to get them to enroll.

✦ **Free but fraudulent online investment newsletters** falsely claim to independently research stocks they profile. They either spread false information or promote worthless stocks. Some drive up the price of a stock with their recommendations and sell their own holdings for substantial profits. You're left holding the bag.

✦ **Work-at-home schemes.** You answer an ad, often in reputable newspapers, offering money simply for evaluating a company's customer service. You're sent a check upfront to deposit in your checking account. You're then encouraged to write a check out of your account for an item or service, and mail it to a respected company. But the check is sent to the scam artist's address and he or she cashes it. To make matters worse, the check you've deposited in your account is bogus. If it doesn't clear, you could be liable to your bank not only for that amount, but also for overdraft fees.

✦ **Gift cards** have sometimes had the personal identification number scratched off and used by thieves. Keep the original receipt for any card you buy, in case you learn its value has already been used.

✦ **Fake valuables.** A lot of jewelry, art, and historical artifacts that have been sold have been fake.

How to stay financially scam-free. Here are some rules of thumb that will help you and other family members avoid being scammed:

✦ On the computer, don't click on hyperlinks in or respond to e-mails from your financial institution, or from anyone you don't know. Call the sender directly instead, verifying the phone number via directory assistance.

✦ Keep antivirus, firewall, and spyware protection up-to-date on all home computers.

✦ Never use the same password online that you use for your ATM card, and change your passwords periodically. Include both letters and numbers in your passwords.

✦ Don't do business with any individual or financial company without first checking them out thoroughly. Check licenses with proper state and federal regulatory agencies. Check the Better Business Bureau for complaints. Check online search engines for consumer feedback.

✦ Don't access personal accounts from public computers.

✦ Check a Web site's privacy rules. Look for evidence of encryption, often symbolized by a lock. This means the information you are keying in is scrambled so that it can't be read if it's intercepted.

✦ Don't invest in anything you don't understand.

✦ Know the entity to which you send money. Research that it truly exists as something legitimate.

✦ Hang up on telemarketers and enroll in the National Do Not Call Registry by visiting www.donotcall.gov or by calling 1-888-382-1222.

✦ When you buy good jewelry or another collectible, always obtain a detailed appraisal from the seller, and keep a receipt indicating how much you paid for it.

✦ Do business online only with a major credit card. If you haven't received merchandise by the time payment is due, dispute the charge.

Help older family members avoid scams. If you have a parent, grandparent, other relative, or close acquaintance who is getting up there in years, you can help them avoid being ripped off. Sadly, seniors are all too often the victim of scam artists. They are easy marks and are often too embarrassed to complain to anyone. Suggest that the senior in your life check with you before making any major expenditure. Whether it's an investment, a driveway paving job, or whatever, encourage the senior to get your independent opinion. Just telling the salesperson that one has to check with a relative before making a decision is enough to make most reprobates flee. We have a "$500 rule" in the Pond family. If one of our parents is going to spend more than $500 on anything that someone else has suggested, they first check with one of the adult kids.

Taking precautions and using a healthy dose of skepticism will help you and your family avoid becoming victims of a financial scam.

◼

It's morally wrong to allow a sucker to keep his money.
—W. C. FIELDS

CHAPTER 13

Enjoying a Great Retirement

Everything you do in your financial life throughout your working years should be geared toward one goal: being able to retire comfortably. This is a chapter for both those who are still working and those who are retirees. It covers important strategies and decisions that have a major bearing on how well you'll be able to live after you retire.

+ If you're already retired, you know well that one's financial concerns don't end with retirement. The only difference is that you now have more time to pay attention to your finances, which can be a big help.

+ If you're within a decade or so of retirement, this could be the most important chapter in *Grow Your Money!* because it's definitely time to get serious about your retirement planning if you haven't already.

+ Even if retirement is a long way off, the ideas contained in this chapter can help point your financial life in the right direction.

You might also be better able to advise your parents as they approach or enter retirement. After all, you want them to be well off enough in retirement that (1) you won't have to support them and (2) there might be a little left over for you (despite my encouraging them to do otherwise).

> ■
>
> *I've got all the money I'll ever need if I die*
> *by four o'clock.*
> —HENNY YOUNGMAN

IDEA 89

Can You Get There From Here?
Finding Out Where You Stand

One of your most important annual tasks, no matter what your age may be, is to find out where you stand financially. There are plenty of free Web sites that will do the number crunching for you. Don't avoid preparing projections because you think your situation is so dire that there's nothing you can do. That's not the case. Sure, you may have some work to do, but the purpose of forecasting is to give you a basis for a plan of what you need to do. Otherwise, you'll probably lose a lot of sleep not knowing where you stand. Some suggestions for preparing useful projections follow.

✦ **If you're a member of the working class.** You'll want to plug in the information necessary to find out what you need to save per year in order to close the gap between what you now have in savings and investments and what you're going to need when you reach retirement age. If you don't like what you see, try delaying your retirement date by a few years or cutting back on your expected living expenses. If you can't yet save what the damnable computer says you should save, don't fret. You can always build up to that savings level over the next few years.

✦ **If you're retired.** Retirees still need to run projections in order to find out if the amount they're currently withdrawing from their retirement savings and investments puts them in danger of running out of money. To find out, you enter your current withdrawal rate and the computer should tell you how long that money will last.

Retirement-projection caveat. Future projections of your retirement nest egg are just estimates. They inevitably make some assumptions that are not going to turn out as planned. Inflation, life expectancy, and particularly investment returns will vary from your estimates. Other uncertainties include how much you're going to be able to save from now until you retire and how much you're going to spend when you retire. Even if you're already retired, it's well-nigh impossible to predict how much you'll be spending five or ten years from now. But despite the inherent inaccuracies, preparing these projections is a whole lot better than doing nothing at all and simply hoping for the best. Obviously, your projections are only as good as your assumptions, so here are three important assumptions I strongly recommend you use:

1. **Inflation.** Use 3 percent. While there's a chance that inflation will continue to be quite low, you shouldn't risk your financial future on it. If you use 3 percent and actual inflation averages less than that, then you'll probably be in better shape when you retire than the projections will show. Better to beat your projections than come up short.

2. **Life expectancy.** Assume you'll live to age ninety-five, and I hope you do. That seems like a long time to most people, and it is. Nevertheless, the odds are pretty good that you'll make it to ninety or more. So, while you may not be attracted to the idea of becoming a nonagenarian, you'd better plan financially for such

an eventuality. Here are my recommendations for estimating your life expectancy:

❑ **If you're over forty.** Assume a life expectancy of age ninety-five unless your forebears have had methuselian life spans. If so, use one hundred.

❑ **If you're forty or under.** The way life expectancies are advancing (in 1960 the average life expectancy was only sixty-four), you'd be smart to assume that you'll live to one hundred.

❑ **If you're over ninety-five.** First, congratulations. Second, add ten years to your age and then strive to beat that estimate.

3. **Investment gains.** This is the most perilous estimate, because overstating investment returns could lead to big problems later on. Use 6 to 7 percent to project your average annual investment gains. Hopefully they'll be better than that, but don't wager your retirement ranch on it. If you overstate your estimated investment returns, you will probably be confronted with Hobson's choice later on: either curtail your retirement budget or work longer than you had anticipated.

4. **Retirement spending budget.** This is a toughie, particularly if you're a long way from retiring. You might simply use a percentage of what it's costing you to live now, adjusted for any changes between now and the time you retire, like an empty nest or paying off the mortgage. Also, take inflation in living expenses into consideration. The nearer you are to retirement, the more work you should devote to homing in on your actual living costs. Idea 91, on page 290, will help you with this chore.

You may be tempted to fiddle with my suggested assumptions, increasing investment returns or lowering life expectancy, for example.

But avoid too much tinkering. While I hope you're optimistic about your financial future, don't let that optimism cloud your sound judgment in planning. I want all of your future financial surprises to be pleasant ones!

Consider a less-than-rosy scenario. While you're at it, you might also change some of your assumptions to consider how you would fare if, as can happen, (1) you have to retire earlier than planned, (2) you live longer than you're estimating, (3) inflation increases, and/or (4) your investment returns aren't as robust as you had predicted. If you find that you'll be okay under these more dire assumed circumstances, you know you're on track for a good retirement. Here are some comparative assumptions you might want to consider:

	Normal Assumptions	Worse-Case Assumptions
Retirement age	Your choice	5 years earlier
Life expectancy	95 to 100	100 to 105
Inflation	3%	4%
Investment returns	6 to 7%	4 to 5%

Your *Grow Your Money!* reader Web site contains further help on preparing retirement-income-and-expense projections, including Web sites and a retirement-budget worksheet. **w w w**

Preparing a forecast of your retirement income and expenses will help you determine what you need to do to achieve your retirement goals if you're still working. If you're retired, a forecast will show you if your current spending level is reasonable.

■

The trouble with retirement is that you never get a day off.
—ABE LEMONS

IDEA 90

Achieving Early Retirement

While the trend among working-age people, particularly baby boomers, is toward late retirement, a large number of people still aspire to retire early. Early retirement is possible. There are two ways to achieve it:

1. **The easy way.** Perhaps you are in line to receive a substantial windfall, like an inheritance, although with long life expectancies, you may not receive it in time to retire early. Or you're already a trust-fund baby. Another technique is to marry a lot of money (pardon me, I mean marry a wonderful person, the love of your life, who coincidentally is blessed with more money than the GNP of a small country). Please, if you're married already, don't even think about the last alternative.

2. **The old-fashioned way.** If you plan far enough in advance, you should be able to accumulate enough money to retire early, but as the following table illustrates, the earlier you start planning the better. Say you would like to retire at fifty and need $50,000 a year (in today's dollars, and adjusted for inflation in later years). If you start at age twenty-five, it will require saving $16,000 per year, which, depending on your financial situation and your zeal to retire early, may or may not be manageable. If you wait until age thirty-five to prepare for your dream, according to the table, the yearly hit is a considerably more challenging $41,000. Starting to save at age forty-five—five years in advance of retiring—you'd better get a job at a hedge fund, because you'll need to save a whopping $180,000 per year.

   If the following table shows that retiring early is not within easy reach, you'll be pleasantly surprised to learn that delaying retirement by just a few years can significantly reduce the amount of money you'll need to save for retirement. For more tips and guidance on delaying retirement, see Idea 92, on page 293.

EARLY RETIREES SAVE EARLY

PLANNED RETIREMENT AGE	ANNUAL SAVINGS REQUIRED FOR A $50,000 ANNUAL RETIREMENT INCOME IF SAVINGS BEGIN AT AGE*		
	25	35	45
50	$16,000	$41,000	$180,000
55	10,000	24,000	72,000
60	7,000	15,000	37,000
65	4,000	9,000	21,000
70	3,000	6,000	12,000

*Assumptions: equal annual savings until retirement, 7% annual investment returns throughout, annual retirement withdrawal of $50,000 in first year of retirement (rising by 3% for inflation each year thereafter), and resources last until age 95.

Secrets of successful early retirees. While there's a lot of emotion tied up in deciding when to retire, being able to afford to do so boils down to money. Here are the strategies used by those who did it themselves the old-fashioned way, without the benefit of rich parents or huge salaries:

✦ **Eye on the prize.** Most people aren't in a financial position to decide when, say, they're age fifty to retire at age fifty-five. Successful early retirees have their eyes on the early-retirement prize decades in advance of retirement.

✦ **Modest lifestyle—before and after retirement.** Being able to retire early almost always requires some financial sacrifice both before and after retirement. A high savings level, often as high as 30 percent of income, is required during the working years. A modest lifestyle continues after retirement, but by then, you'll be used to it.

✦ **Aggressive investing.** Throw caution to the wind when you invest. You can't afford to be conservative if you're amassing a portfolio that may need to sustain you for five decades or more. While those who expect to work longer may get by with 60 percent of their money in stocks, aspiring early retirees should be looking at 75 percent or more in stocks. If the stock market doesn't cooperate, the penalty will be to delay retirement by a few years. But if history is any indicator, the odds of a stock-heavy portfolio accumulating the money you'll need to retire early are in your favor.

✦ **Part-time work in retirement.** Many early retirees don't retire cold turkey. They are content to leave an often stressful full-time job and work in a lower-pressure job, often one that allows them to pursue a passion and get paid a bit at the same time. Those who are planning to retire early are well advised to at least consider the possibility of gainful employment after "retirement." This has two advantages. First, earning even a small amount of income after leaving the full-time workforce can have a surprisingly positive financial impact, as described in Idea 92, on page 293. Second, some people find early retirement isn't as satisfying as they thought it would be. They return to the workforce, and to the extent they have something lined up when they retire or, as described in chapter 2, have job skills that are in great demand, they keep their options open.

Everyone should prepare for early retirement. You may have no desire to retire early, but it's still important to plan for that eventuality. Almost 40 percent of those who retire before age sixty-five do so involuntarily owing to job loss, health problems, caring for a family member, and other reasons, so whenever you are running your retirement-income-and-expense projections, see where you would stand if you had to retire five or tens years earlier than you would like.

The *Grow Your Money!* reader Web site offers more help for early retirement aspirants. **w w w**

If you want to retire early, follow the strategies of successful early retirees—and start preparing for retirement early.

■

Retirement is wonderful. It's doing nothing without worrying about getting caught at it.
—GENE PERRET

IDEA 91

It Will Probably Cost You Less When You Retire Than You Think

The published estimates of how much you'll need to retire are scary. They're usually stated as a percentage of your income just before you retire. Most ersatz experts suggest that you'll need at least 80 percent, and some even suggest as high as 110 percent. That's right—they say you'll need more income to survive in retirement than you did while working. Encouraging, isn't it? Forget those rules of thumb. Everyone's situation is different, and the average person who's now retired took a 30 percent income haircut upon retirement and never looked back.

A crucial number. It's always important to estimate what your living expenses will be when you retire, because this amount, above all, will influence what you'll need to do between now and retirement to accumulate the resources necessary to meet those expenses. You may think it's too early to prepare a retirement expense budget, but the further away you are from retirement, the more time you have to do the necessaries to achieve your retirement aspirations—in other words, match up your projected income with your projected expenses.

If you're within a decade or so of retirement, you should devote con-siderable effort to homing in on a pretty precise forecast of your post-retirement expenses.

Why you may be able to retire well on less. The following list and brief notes will help you identify expense areas that are likely to decline as well as those that are likely to increase when you retire. Space is also provided to estimate how much your expenses might be reduced or increased.

Expenses that may decline or be eliminated when you retire:

✦ **Savings, including retirement plan contributions.** Mercifully, you can pretty much curtail your savings, including retirement plan contributions once you retire for good. Depending on the amount you're saving before retirement, this could be 5 to 20 per-cent of your preretirement income.

  $ _____ .

✦ **Mortgage and other housing costs.** Paying off the mortgage by the time you retire could reduce the current amount you're spend-ing by 20 percent or more. If you relocate to a lower-cost locale, your housing costs will likely decline, as will many other items in your retirement budget.

  $ _____ .

✦ **Loan and credit card payments.** If you're currently saddled with debt but plan to pay it off or at least reduce the burden, that will translate into lower expenses after you retire.

  $ _____ .

✦ **Work expenses.** The cessation of clothing, transportation, and food costs associated with your job will further reduce your postre-tirement expenses. If after you can retire you can survive without your daily fix of designer latte, you'll probably enjoy a princely retirement.

  $ _____ .

✦ **Expenses associated with the younger set.** If you're of an age when children are still at home, you're probably paying out a lot, particularly for education. Hopefully, these expenses will go by the wayside by the time you retire, but that may be too much to wish for.

$ _____ .

✦ **Income taxes.** Your income taxes are probably going to decline. Even if you remain in the same income tax bracket, if you have a lower income, you'll almost always pay lower income taxes. Also, your share of Social Security and Medicare withholding taxes, amounting to about 8 percent for most of us, will no longer be paid once your job income ceases. Imagine that. After decades of paying into Social Security, you'll be on the receiving end at last!

$ _____ .

Expenses that may rise when you retire:

✦ **Medical insurance and medical care.** According to one study of retiree spending, health-care costs were the only budget item that increased after retirement. Every other spending area decreased.

$ + _____ .

✦ **Recreation and travel.** Unless you're a recluse, recreation and travel costs are likely to be higher than they were during your working years,

$ + _____ .

For help on estimating your retirement budget, including some work sheets to help you do the tallying, check out the special reader Web site. **w w w**

> You'll be surprised to discover that it will cost you less to re-
> tire than you had been led to believe.
>
> ■
>
> *Poverty is no disgrace, but it is confoundedly*
> *inconvenient.*
> —SYDNEY SMITH

IDEA 92

Last-Minute Ways to Boost Your Retirement Income

Perhaps you are approaching retirement and don't like what you see financially. Or while your estimated retirement income looks pretty good, you don't want just an okay retirement. You want a great retirement. You may be able to close any gaps by taking certain actions that can increase your retirement income or reduce your retirement expenses, often by a big amount. But these actions are not to be taken lightly, so due deliberation well in advance of retirement is essential.

❏ Downsize Your Home

Downsizing—in other words, either selling your current hacienda and buying a less expensive home either before or after you retire, or renting—makes a lot of financial sense and could be a sensible life-style decision besides. Downsizing, particularly into a newer home, could reduce the time and inconvenience of maintaining your current home. Relocating to a place that has a less frenetic pace can be attractive to some. Conversely, moving from the suburbs to the big city is appealing to others.

Financial advantages. Here are the many financial benefits of downsizing:

1. **Reduced debt.** Eliminating or reducing a mortgage that might otherwise erode your retirement budget will dramatically improve your retirement living standard.

2. **Tax breaks.** Uncle Sam rewards home sellers with a big break in capital gains taxes. Suffice it to say that you'll probably not owe any federal income taxes when you sell your home.

3. **Increased income.** If your downsizing allows you to free up capital to invest, you'll enjoy more income throughout your retirement if you invest it wisely.

4. **Reduced housing expenses.** Downsizers usually also enjoy lower housing expenses—for example, for property taxes and utilities. If you downsize into more modern quarters, maintenance hassles and costs should be lower.

All in all, downsizing can result in a financial home run, or two home runs if you combine downsizing with relocating to a lower-cost locale, which is discussed next.

❑ Move to a Lower-Cost Locale

If you live in a high-cost area, relocating to a lower-cost locale may be very rewarding financially. For example, denizens of the Northeast and the West Coast of the United States will find their cost of living drops by as much as 40 percent by moving to the Sunbelt. Those who retire overseas could save even more. Overseas retirement is a growing trend. The Social Security Administration says that over five hundred thousand Social Security recipients receive their checks outside the United States.

But relocation should not be taken lightly, particularly if it might take you to a foreign locale. Just because your favorite vacation spot looks very appealing in high season doesn't mean it's an idyllic year-round setting. (See Idea 56, on page 180, for some thoughts on buying a home in a vacation mecca.) Keep in mind that moving is never easy, and the older we become, the tougher it is to pick up stakes. You don't want to make the mistake of relocating and then finding three months later that you hate the place. Despite all those warnings, though, relocation can work wonders on your retirement budget.

❏ Delay Retirement

One of the biggest trends in the twenty-first century is the preference for many to work beyond the traditional retirement age of sixty-five. For sure, a couple of generations ago, the typical sixty-five-year-old had one foot in the grave and the other on a banana peel. But it's a lot different now. Many people approaching that age simply enjoy working and are in great physical and mental condition, so why retire? While the motivation for continuing to work may be personal, I'm here to tell you that delaying retirement has enormously positive financial ramifications as well. Consider the following case study that shows the financial benefit of delaying retirement from age sixty-two to age sixty-eight:

CASE STUDY: Betty will have $300,000 in retirement savings at age sixty-two. If she retires later, she will add $15,000 per year to her retirement savings. The following table summarizes Betty's situation if she retires at sixty-two compared with her retiring at sixty-eight. If she retires at sixty-two, she'll have a total annual income of $31,000, including Social Security and withdrawals from her retirement stash. But Betty likes her job and sees no reason to leave the workforce at sixty-two. On the other hand, Betty is wise to look at her situation in the event she has to retire early. Many of those who retire early do so involuntarily. That's an eventuality that everyone should contemplate and plan for. But with some luck, Betty—and you—will have choices about when to retire.

What a difference delaying retirement makes in the income Betty can enjoy. If she retires at age sixty-eight, rather than age sixty-two, her first year of retirement income will rise from $31,000 to $57,000— that's an 84 percent increase.

DELAYING-RETIREMENT CASE STUDY

	IF BETTY RETIRES AT	
	62	68
Social Security	$14,000	$23,000
Withdrawal from nest egg	17,000	34,000
First-year retirement income	$31,000	$57,000

84% increase!

❑   **Phased Retirement**

Phased retirement (also called "gradual retirement") has a lot of appeal for both lifestyle and financial reasons. Phased retirement means working a reducing number of hours in either the same occupation or a new vocation. A lot of workers simply can't imagine retiring completely at age sixty-five under any circumstances. The notion of working a reduced schedule has great appeal. If you possess occupational skills that are in demand, you have a good chance of being able to continue working on your terms.

The following table shows what happens financially if you delay collecting Social Security and withdrawing money from your nest egg simply by earning enough money to support yourself, without adding even another nickel to your savings. What a difference! There are two reasons why phased retirement results in so much more retirement income. First, your retirement savings have more time to grow before you begin tapping into them. Second, each year you continue working is one less year your money will be needed to fund your retirement. Also, by delaying the date you begin collecting Social Security retirement benefits, that income will increase as well.

THE BENEFITS OF PHASED RETIREMENT

	DELAY RETIREMENT		
	1 YEAR	3 YEARS	5 YEARS
Social Security income will increase	6–8%	19–26%	36–44%
Withdrawals from retirement nest egg can increase	10%	25%	40%

You can take any of several actions just before or after you retire that can significantly improve your retirement standard of living.

■

Retirement: it's nice to get out of the rat race, but you have to learn to get along with less cheese.
—GENE PERRET

IDEA 93

It's a Mistake to Collect Social Security Early

Deciding when to begin collecting Social Security is a complicated decision, and conflicting advice about it is rife. The dominant opinion seems to be: take the money as early as possible. It's bad enough that most writers on the subject espouse this, but it's worse when the representatives at the local Social Security offices by and large say the same thing. One caller to a talk show told me that after she balked at collecting benefits right away, the Social Security rep started pestering her at home with phone calls exhorting her to take the money and run.

But here's the reality, one that is at last starting to get the attention it deserves: For most people, **it's a mistake to collect Social Security benefits before full retirement age,** which is between ages sixty-five and sixty-seven, depending on your birth year. Since, according to the Social Security Administration, almost 75 percent collect Social Security retirement benefits early, a lot of people may have made a mistake. When you begin to "ponder" when to collect Social Security retirement benefits, I hope you will at least consider what Pond has to say about the matter. I realize that a lot of people who have collected benefits early will take great offense at my advice. So before firing off the hate mail, please note that if you collected earlier than you should have, this is far from a financial disaster. In the panoply of financial boo-boos, this is not a big one. But the following remarks are directed toward those who have yet to begin receiving benefits, so that you can make the decision that will give you a good chance of maximizing the benefits you'll receive over the rest of your life.

There are three key dates to consider, plus a fourth that is usually not thought about, but may be just right for you.

1. **Age sixty-two.** The Social Security Administration says that slightly over half of the workforce collects benefits the first month they're eligible. There are some, but not many, justifications for taking the benefits ASAE (as soon as eligible), including:

    ❑ You lack sufficient personal resources (retirement plan investments, savings, other income) to make ends meet without the benefits; in other words, you have no alternative but to collect early.

    ❑ You and your spouse, if any, have good reason to believe you will die early in your retirement. Simply not wanting to live until age one hundred is not sufficient reason. You need better evidence, like your doctor insisting that you pay your medical bills in advance.

    ❑ You're convinced that Social Security is going to be terminated in the very near future, so if you delay benefits, you'll never receive any. If you believe this, use the money from your first Social Security check to have your head examined.

Other than these situations, which affect many people but nowhere near the vast number of the eligible population that's collecting benefits early, you'll probably do better waiting at least until full retirement age to commence benefits.

2. **Full retirement age.** If you were born after 1942, full retirement age is no longer sixty-five. It ranges from sixty-six for those born between 1943 and 1954, ratcheting up to sixty-seven for those born in 1960 or later. Here are some arguments that favor waiting until full retirement age.

❏ If you expect to work until full retirement age, you're likely to be ineligible during that time for most or all of your Social Security benefits, since any job income beyond a minimum, which is currently around $13,000 per year, results in a loss of benefits. After attaining full retirement age, however, job income no longer results in lost Social Security benefits. On the other hand, at any age, up to 85 percent of Social Security benefits may be subject to income taxes.

❏ Even if you leave the full-time workforce before full retirement age, if there is even a small possibility that you will earn more than a paltry amount of income in the interregnum, it's best to wait to collect your benefits.

❏ If you're married and there is a disparity between your two income histories that results in a sizable difference in your respective Social Security benefits, it's often preferable for the spouse with the higher income history to delay collecting benefits. That's because a lower-income spouse is entitled to the higher-income spouse's benefits if the higher income spouse predeceases.

3. **Age seventy.** It may seem to be a bit of a stretch to delay benefits until age seventy, particularly because if you continue working after full retirement age, your benefits will not be reduced
regardless of how much you earn. But there is at least one situation where it may make sense to wait.

    ❑ For married couples where at least one of the spouses
expects to live a long time in retirement, at least into
the eighties, the best solution is for the higher-income
spouse to wait until age seventy to start Social Security and the lower-income spouse to start collecting at
full retirement age, in order, as noted above, for the
lower-income spouse to receive maximum benefits
should the higher-income spouse predecease. This
strategy is predicated on having enough savings available in order to delay Social Security payments that
long. You generally wouldn't want to exhaust a good
portion of your retirement nest egg, leaving little
money to cope with unexpected big-ticket items or financial emergencies.

4. **Somewhere in between.** Just as in many other areas of your
financial life, the decision about when to collect Social Security
is not either/or. For each month you postpone starting benefits
between age sixty-two and age seventy, you will receive a higher
benefit for the rest of your life. The increase is one-half percent
per month (6 percent per year) from age sixty-two to full retirement age and two-thirds percent per month (8 percent per year)
from full retirement age until age seventy.

The *Grow Your Money!* reader Web site contains more information
and some illustrations that will help you make the right decision
about when to begin collecting Social Security. If you've already
started Social Security early but should have waited until full retirement age, the reader Web site will show you a way to pay back the

money you have already received with no penalty, so that you can receive a higher benefit. **w w w**

WHEN TO BEGIN COLLECTING SOCIAL SECURITY

COLLECT EARLY IF . . .

✦ You don't have any other resources to support you.
✦ You, and, if applicable, your spouse anticipate that you will die early in retirement.

COLLECT AT FULL RETIREMENT AGE IF . . .

✦ You expect to work either full- or part-time until full retirement age.
✦ You're married and there's going to be a big difference in benefits between the two of you, in which case the spouse with the higher benefits should delay collecting until at least full retirement age.

COLLECT LATE IF . . .

✦ You're married, have a significant disparity in expected benefits, and can temporarily afford to support yourselves without Social Security benefits. In which case, the spouse with the higher income should consider commencing benefits after full retirement age.

Collecting Social Security before full retirement age is not a wise choice for many.

■

Retirement at sixty-five is ridiculous. When I was sixty-five I still had pimples.
—GEORGE BURNS

IDEA 94

Changes You Should Make in Your Finances When You Retire

Common wisdom suggests that retirement triggers major changes in your financial life. However, there isn't a whole lot that you need to alter, but those few areas where changes are necessary are important. After all, you have a lot less flexibility—money flexibility, that is—after you retire. While there was a lot of time to make up for a bone-headed financial decision when you were in your twenties, you don't have decades to make up for big financial mistakes during retirement. To cite a sad example, the three-year steep decline in the stock market that began in 2000 destroyed the financial security of many, many retirees who got caught up in the 1990s technology-stock boom. Had their money been well-diversified rather than concentrated in hot stocks, their money might have been pinched a bit during the three-year bear market, but they wouldn't have had to resort to working in fast-food emporia to make ends meet.

Now that you are suitably frightened, here are some important retirement matters to keep in mind. Don't wait until the day before you retire to noodle these decisions. The more time you spend deliberating in advance, the better:

❏ **Investing.** Investing wisely goes without saying. This requires a balancing act between investing for income, in order to do such annoying things as paying your bills, and investing for growth, in order to be able to keep up with inflation over the decades (because try as you may, your cost of living will continue rising). Deflation is unlikely. There's no such word as "flation," which should mean steady costs. So all we're left with is inflation. While you definitely need to invest a sizable portion of your retirement money so that it will grow, don't go overboard. On the other hand, for the first time in your life you may be able to devote some time to your investments. Do it. But it's too late to fancy yourself a tech-stock day trader.

❑ **Withdrawing from your nest egg.** Deciding how much can be sensibly withdrawn from investments at retirement strikes fear in almost everyone planning for retirement. It's a crucial consideration, of course, because the amount withdrawn in the first few years of retirement sets the course for the rest of a retiree's life. In your planning, use a 4 percent per year withdrawal rate from your retirement and other investments as a starting point. That's generally considered to be a rate that will allow you to keep up with future inflation without having to worry too much about running out of money. If running out of money is an overwhelming concern or if you invest very conservatively, 3 percent should protect you quite nicely. You may be able to stretch it to 5 percent, but anything above that is probably too much of a stretch.

❑ **Considering a reverse mortgage.** Reverse mortgages may come in handy later on in retirement for those who have a bundle of their money tied up in home equity, but that's a decision that's usually best made later, rather than sooner. See Idea 96, on page 312.

❑ **Taxing matters.** Retirees are often surprised and chagrined at the magnitude of their income taxes. Work hard, do the right thing by saving for retirement, retire, and then sacrifice a sizable portion of these savings on the government's altar. But there are some straightforward strategies that many retirees can use to reduce income taxes. See Idea 71, on page 221.

❑ **Health insurance.** If you think navigating the health insurance system is complicated enough already, are you in for a surprise when you retire. Make sure you have the necessary health insurance on top of Medicare basic coverage.

❑ **Life insurance.** Retirement is a good time to revisit any life insurance you may hold, because your needs often change once you retire. See Idea 75, on page 235.

❑ **Estate planning.** The estate-planning documents that were prepared during your working years—you have prepared them, haven't you?—should stand you in good stead, but in some circumstances, they may need to be revisited. Pay particular attention to your durable power of attorney, which takes over if you become incapacitated, and your advance directive, which directs your health care in the event of incapacitating or terminal illness. Why these, you might ask? You (and, alas, I) are no longer spring chickens, so the probability of our needing these documents is a lot greater than it was a couple of decades ago.

❑ **Housing and relocation.** While you may decide to stay put, as you approach retirement, you should give some thought to where you want to live when you retire and, if you decide to stay where you are, whether a change in housing might be worthwhile, either less expensive housing or something that's easier to maintain. If you have children, I will guarandamntee you that they are already a bit concerned about the possibility of having to drag you out of your current home some time in the distant future when you lack both the ability to maintain it and the mental acuity to realize that you need to get out of there. See Idea 54, on page 171, for more tips on relocation.

❑ **Planning what you're going to do after you retire.** This should be a pleasant exercise, but if you've been wedded to your career for decades, you should expect some angst when you retire, particularly if you don't have much going on outside your work life. Heads up if you and your spouse or partner are retiring at different times, because the relationship experts say that this can be stressful on a relationship. Be sensitive to these matters, particularly if you're the first to retire. The last thing you want at this stage in your life is to be asked to take permanent leave of the family home. As the saying goes, "Marriage may be grand, but divorce is about a hundred grand."

The special reader Web site offers more help on the important changes facing retirees. **w w w**

You probably don't need to make a lot of changes in your investment and financial planning after you retire, but there are a few important matters to attend to.

■

Retirement: that's when you return from work one day and say, "Hi, honey, I'm home—forever."
—GENE PERRET

IDEA 95

Making Sure You Never Run Out of Money

The biggest financial fear for those planning for retirement and, particularly, those already retired is of losing all their sources of income. Of course, despite the opinions of the uninformed that the program will somehow be terminated, Social Security will always provide you with an income, but for most it won't provide much more than the basic necessities. If you're fortunate enough to be receiving a pension, all the better. But the percentage of retirees who are receiving a pension is dwindling. So for the majority of those planning for retirement or who are already retired, there are two sources of retirement income: Social Security and your own retirement savings. Here are my musings on both:

✦ **Social Security.** While you may think you have no control over Social Security, you do to the extent that you carefully evaluate the best time to begin collecting benefits. Delaying the collection of benefits has the potential of increasing your Social Security income by over 50 percent. If other sources of income fail to keep up with inflation or, worse, fall by the wayside, a higher Social Security income will offer a measure of protection. See Idea 93, on page 297, for suggestions on choosing the best time to begin collecting Social Security.

✦ **Your retirement savings.** Unless you'll receive a pension, your retirement savings will probably generate most of your retirement income. Therein lies the concern over running out of money, which can happen for any reason or a combination of reasons, including:

- **Outliving your money.** You may simply live a lot longer than you had planned for financially.

- **Withdrawing too much.** Getting into the habit of withdrawing too much money is a ticking time bomb for many retirees.

- **Investment losses.** Whether through bad investment decisions—yours or those of an investment adviser—and/or bad investment markets, a nest egg can evaporate a lot sooner than anticipated.

- **Major expenses.** In addition to the most feared major expenses of requiring home health-care or a nursing home, other unplanned expenses, like the need to help support a child through a rough patch or major home improvements, can quickly erode, if not decimate, retirement savings.

RETIREMENT INCOME LINEUP

Here is a thumbnail summary of what the various sources of retirement income will and will not do for you.

	BENEFITS FOR LIFE?	BENEFITS INCREASE WITH INFLATION?
Social Security	Yes	Yes
Pension	Yes	May or may not[1]
Income annuity	Yes	Depends[2]
Personal investments[3]	Depends	Depends

[1] *Ask your pension-plan administrator if the current pensioners are receiving annual inflation kickers. Keep in mind in your forecasting and planning that even pensions that rise with inflation reserve the right to cease doing so at any time.*

[2] *You may select an income annuity that rises with inflation, but at the cost of a considerably lower initial benefit. Annuities that are tied to stock-market performance may also provide increasing benefits.*

[3] *Whether personal investments last a lifetime and can provide enough income to keep up with inflation depends on investment returns, rate of withdrawal from the investments, and your life span.*

How Should You Deploy Your Retirement Nest Egg?

Deciding how to deploy a lifetime of hard-earned savings deserves very careful deliberation. Should you invest the money, either on your own or with the assistance of an investment adviser, or should you take out an *income annuity* (also called an *immediate annuity*)? While there are several flavors of income annuity, all involve depositing money with an insurance company in exchange for a guaranteed income, usually for the rest of your life. This is a particularly important decision because the annuity decision is, for all intents and purposes, one you cannot change later on. Once you select an annuity, it will be with you for a lifetime.

Key considerations. Here in a nutshell are the key considerations when making this key decision:

1. **Investment risk.** Managing the money on your own is a big responsibility. If you lose it in unwise investments—or even "wise" ones that go sour anyway—there's no recourse but to suffer in silence. If you're confident of your own investment abilities—or those of a competent adviser—you may be better off managing the money on your own. On the other hand, if you've got more interesting things to do after you retire than worry about your investments, then why not foist that burden on the annuity company?

2. **Liability risk.** Money that you manage on your own is usually not protected from liability. The principal may have to be used to pay major medical (or other) expenses, including nursing-home costs, if the income from those investments is insufficient. This is of particular concern to couples, since the illness of one could leave the surviving spouse or partner with little to live on. Also, you can be sued for just about anything these days, and all or much of your nest egg could be lost to legal and settlement costs. While income from the annuity will need to be used to pay medical or lawsuit expenses, the annuity itself should not be subject to forfeiture. Insurance can provide some measure of protection against these risks, including long-term-care insurance (see Idea 77, on page 242) and umbrella liability insurance (see Idea 73, on page 231).

3. **Inflation risk.** While you can purchase an annuity whose payments are adjusted (at least partly) to offset the effects of inflation, many are not. The reality of a fixed-payout annuity is a steady loss of purchasing power due to rising living costs. On

the other hand, if you self-manage your money, you have a good, but by no means assured, chance of investing it so that it gains enough to enable you to keep up with inflation.

4. **Anticipated income.** Generally, annuity payments give you less income than you can make if you invest the money on your own. Reason: the payout schedules tend to be figured very conservatively to minimize the annuity company's future financial risks. On the other hand, the annuity business is very competitive, so shopping for the best deal (so long as it is offered by a financially strong insurance company) will narrow the gap between what the insurance company pays you and what you might be able to earn on your own.

5. **Longevity risk.** The main advantage of an annuity, and it's a big one, is that the insurance company is stuck with making its payments to you for as long as you live. If you're married or partnered and you wisely select an annuity that will pay both of you for life, you'll also protect against any financial misfortune that may befall a surviving spouse or partner with respect to self-managed money.

6. **Mortality risk.** While a few annuity plans provide benefits after death, most annuity plan payments cease when you do. Consequently, there's nothing to pass on to your heirs. If you manage your retirement money on your own, and the investment gods are with you, you have a good chance of being able to leave some leftover money to your heirs.

IT'S AN IMPERFECT WORLD

Here are the top three potential advantages and drawbacks to managing your retirement nest egg on your own and/or putting the money into an income annuity.

CHOICE	MAJOR POTENTIAL UPSIDES	MAJOR POTENTIAL DOWNSIDES
Self-manage	☺ Retain control	☹ Poor investment results
	☺ Keep up with inflation	☹ Outlive the money
	☺ Pass remaining investments to heirs	☹ Loss due to health-care costs, lawsuit, etc.
Income annuity	☺ Assured income	☹ Loss of control
	☺ Alleviates chore of investing the money	☹ Fixed annuity loses purchasing power
	☺ Protection from a loss due to major expenses	☹ Inability to pass on money to heirs

---

A little here, a little there. Before concluding that there is no way you can make the right decision, here is my two cents' worth of advice. Don't view the "self-manage" versus "annuity" choice as an either/or decision. It isn't, and anyone who suggests otherwise is more interested in getting a fat commission than looking out for your best interests. Purchasing an annuity is often a wise decision, particularly if any of the previously noted downsides of managing your money yourself is especially angst provoking for you. If you decide to take out an annuity, rarely should you annuitize all of your money, nor should you annuitize all of the money you want to annuitize all at the same time. Instead, you might be better advised to, when you first retire, invest half of the total money you have earmarked for an income annuity and then wait several years to invest the other half.

Be sure to check out the special reader Web site for real-world illustrations of people who have successfully achieved their desire to control their retirement nest eggs while assuring that they'll always have enough money. **w w w**

> The number one fear among retirees is of the money running out. But careful planning before retirement can alleviate that concern.
>
> ■
>
> *I advise you to go on living solely to enrage those who are paying your annuities. It is the only pleasure I have left.*
> —VOLTAIRE

MONEY TIP

The New Breed of Variable Annuity

The combination of the near-death of the traditional pension plan and a hotly competitive insurance industry means that those who are considering an income annuity when they retire will have a range of choices that are often far superior to the old-fashioned fixed-payment annuity. If you are not going to be in the market for an annuity in the near future, chances are you'll find even better annuity products later on.

Variable annuity with some attractive kickers. A *variable annuity* is one where the money deposited into the annuity is invested in stock and/or bond mutual funds. They've been around for a long time, but without the protective features of the new generation of annuity. Here are some examples of the types of variable annuity offered by several insurance companies that provide a variety of features often referred to as "living benefits." For example, someone who is several years from retirement can put money into a *deferred variable annuity* with guaranteed principal growth until the money is withdrawn at a later date. If the underlying mutual funds perform better than the guarantee, you reap the benefits. Guarantees are also available during retirement, including increases (but not decreases) in annuity payments based on the performance of the underlying stock and bond investments. Principal protection is another feature, whereby the annuitant will have money left to pass on to heirs, as opposed to the more traditional annuity where the principal went kaput with the annuitant. Of course, these added features come with added costs, but if the insurance company is adept at identifying or running top-performing mutual funds, those costs may be a reasonable price to pay.

An investment tip. If you ever decide to put some (not all, please) of your money into one of these annuities that offer great potential to increase in value but protect your principal from decline, you should select the most aggressive investment alternative. If the company offers an all-stock choice, do it. Shoot for the moon, because you'll likely benefit mightily from a rising stock market. This is no time for timidity, because you are protected from losses in your account.

The annuity business is a moving target, and it's moving in the right direction for you and your retirement needs. The *Grow Your Money!* reader Web site will keep you updated on these exciting developments. **ᴡ ᴡ ᴡ**

> Retirement is like a long vacation in Las Vegas. The
> goal is to enjoy it to the fullest, but not so fully that
> you run out of money.
> —JONATHAN CLEMENTS

IDEA 96

The Reverse Mortgage: Less Than Meets the Eye

The reverse mortgage, often criticized as being far too restrictive and expensive, is getting more attractive as an increasing number of lenders start offering it. But that doesn't necessarily mean it is or will be right for you.

A *reverse mortgage* is a loan, based on the value of your home, which you needn't repay until you move, sell your home, or die. In short, the reverse mortgage can be an added source of income if you need cash and you have no heirs, or your heirs are unconcerned about inheriting your home. At your demise (I prefer that phrase over the more commonly used "When you die"), the loan is repaid from your estate, which typically never can owe more than the home's value. Unlike traditional loans, a reverse mortgage requires no income to qualify. But it generally comes with a host of steep fees, making it more expensive than a traditional mortgage. Also, you generally must be at least sixty-two years old to qualify. The longer you wait before doing a reverse mortgage, the more money you'll be able to get out of your home.

Matters to consider:

❑ Prices are starting to drop on reverse mortgages. Secondary-market-player Fannie Mae historically had been the only buyer of reverse mortgages. That's changing. Now the loans are being sold on Wall Street.

❑ The reverse mortgage comes in several flavors, including programs that pay you a lump sum, rather than a lifetime monthly income, or give you a credit line or provide a combination of those. Be especially wary of any program that allows you to get all or most of the money up front. Let me be blunt. If you need a reverse mortgage, particularly fairly early in your retirement, it may indicate that you've had trouble managing your budget in the past. If that's the case, receiving a large sum of money may be dangerous. It's far safer to opt for the monthly payment program.

❑ Be sure to investigate the different available programs and calculate how much you might be able to obtain from a reverse mortgage. You may be in for an unpleasant surprise if you think that all your home equity is going to get you a whopping payment. That may not be the case. For example, if you own your house free and clear and it's worth $300,000, here's roughly how much you'll be able to receive from a reverse mortgage, depending on your age when you signed up:

✦ Age sixty-five: $900 per month

✦ Age seventy-five: $1,200 per month

✦ Age eighty-five: $1,800 per month

❑ If you are obtaining state, federal, or local financial benefits, evaluate (at the time you're considering a reverse mortgage) whether a reverse mortgage could disqualify you by putting you over income or asset requirements.

❑ Take advantage of reverse-mortgage counseling programs by contacting a member of the National Home Equity Conversion Mortgage (HECM) Counseling Network, which is approved by the U.S. Department of Housing and Urban Development and described on its Web site at *http://www.hud.gov/offices/hsg/sfh/ hcc/hccprof18.cfm*.

❑ Carefully evaluate whether other options—such as selling your home—might prove more attractive. While you are probably attached to your home, comparing a reverse mortgage with selling your home and using the proceeds to buy or rent new quarters is the best way to evaluate whether a reverse mortgage makes sound financial sense. While the thought of moving from the family home may be anathema, you might welcome the possibility of moving into more manageable and less costly housing. If you have children, ask for their opinions as well.

❑ As you would with most everything else you purchase, shop for the best deal. The reverse mortgage industry is evolving rapidly, so better offers may be on the horizon. Also check with state and local housing agencies. Sometimes attractive government reverse-mortgage programs are available.

My opinion. I'm not particularly high on the reverse mortgage. First and foremost, don't delude yourself into thinking of a reverse mortgage as a substitute for saving for retirement the old-fashioned way by contributing to retirement plans. So when you are projecting your retirement income and expenses (see Idea 89, on page 283), don't include your home in your ciphering. Yes, your home may well be the best investment you ever make, but it shouldn't be considered an "investment" from the standpoint of providing income during retirement through a reverse mortgage, particularly if you're many years from retirement.

I would rather consider a reverse mortgage as a "late-life trump card" for veteran retirees, say in their eighties, who are intent on staying in their home for the duration, but could use a boost in income. Certainly there are other situations where such a mortgage can work well, but the permanence of a reverse mortgage should not be taken lightly. Too many things can happen during a long retirement, and the equity in your home is like an insurance policy. Tapping into a reverse mortgage is like cashing in a life insurance policy.

The special reader Web site will keep you up to date on the reverse mortgage and provides important Internet resources if and when you want to consider a reverse mortgage. **w w w**

The reverse mortgage can provide a needed income boost later on in retirement, but it should be approached with caution, particularly by younger retirees.

■

And in the end it's not the years in your life that count.
It's the life in your years.
—ABRAHAM LINCOLN

CHAPTER 14

Savoring the Good Life— Now and Later

The preceding chapters have provided you with lots of ideas and tips designed for one primary purpose—to help you achieve and maintain lifelong financial security. That's obvious, but there's also a side benefit to growing your money. Once you are on track for a better financial future, you will be in a position to be in control of your life as never before. Even if you're a long way from being able to join the ranks of the financially independent, once you start making progress, you'll have a whole new and brighter outlook. You can start to streamline your finances so that you can spend your time on more important matters, like savoring the good life.

> ■
>
> *While money can't buy happiness, it certainly lets you*
> *choose your own form of misery.*
> —ANONYMOUS

IDEA 97

Simplifying Your Financial Life

If you're going to have the time to savor your financial future, you'll need to simplify your financial life. After all, unless becoming an investment and financial planning junkie is your idea of the good life, you don't want to waste your time on boring tasks that are easy to simplify. Here are some ways to manage your financial affairs more efficiently:

❑ **Set your records straight.** A good-record keeping system is one that is (a) complete enough to be effective and (b) simple enough that you will use it regularly. The computer can be a big help in your record keeping, although it is not essential. But even genuine computer enthusiasts will still have to maintain some paper records. Every good record-keeping "system" has three main components:

1. **A safe-deposit box** that contains important personal papers that are either impossible or very difficult to replace if lost or destroyed. Be sure to keep a summary of the contents of your safe-deposit box, in order to avoid a wasted trip to the bank looking for something that isn't there.

2. **An active file kept at home** that keeps track of personal papers and important information necessary for preparing your current year's tax returns. Because the active file needs to be easily accessible, it should be located in a convenient and pleasant location like a den. It doesn't need to be fancy; a few manila file folders purloined from your place of business should suffice.

3. **An inactive file kept at home or in storage** primarily for the purpose of documenting and supporting past tax returns. See page 224 for help on determining how long you should keep past

tax records. A few other items should also be kept in your inactive file, including the invoices and canceled checks pertaining to any home improvements and the investment statements necessary to substantiate capital gains and losses. You may also want to keep in the inactive file important papers that are not currently needed, such as family health records and proof that major debts and other contracts and obligations have been discharged.

❏ **Get rid of unnecessary papers.** Once you conclude that you'll never be elected president, you will no longer need to hoard personal papers in order to fill up your presidential library. You don't need to keep receipts and bills and bank statements for years on end. Chuck them. If they have Social Security numbers or account numbers on them, you should shred them to avoid becoming a victim of identity theft. Also, please don't hold on to anything that could be embarrassing to your children, like grammar school report cards. Many years after my stint at Bethesda Elementary School, my parents took great pleasure in showing mine to their friends and, worse, my future wife. My teachers' comments and predictions were off base anyway. I didn't spend my adult life incarcerated.

❏ **Maintain a household inventory.** Making a personal inventory of your household possessions is crucial to assuring that you get back what you deserve should you ever suffer a loss. Record any and all identifying information about your possessions, as well as a complete description of each item. Photographs of furniture, appliances, and the like will be a big help. Videotapes are even better. Make no mistake about it—taking a household inventory is one of the most boring things you'll ever do. Save it for a rainy Saturday, but don't wait too long. (And don't forget the garage.) This may seem incongruous in a discussion of simplifying your financial life, but imagine how complicated your financial life could be if you come home from work someday and they are shoveling what remains of your house into the back of a pickup truck—and you have to try to recall from memory your household possessions. By the way, store your inventory, photographs, and videotape somewhere away from your house—in your safe-deposit box or in your desk at the office. Also, remember to keep your inventory file up to date by adding receipts for possessions acquired subsequent to your initial inventory. Finally, you will probably need to secure additional insurance coverage on any valuable jewelry, silverware, and the like (see Idea 73, on page 231).

❏ **Consolidate your accounts.**

✦ **Credit card accounts.** You probably need only a couple of credit cards to indulge your need for plastic. The more cards you have, the harder it is to keep up with all the statements and the greater the chance of fraudulent card use.

✦ **Bank accounts.** If you have several accounts at several different financial institutions, you can greatly simplify your finances, reduce mail and paperwork, and perhaps even get better deals by concentrating your business with fewer institutions.

✦ **Investment accounts.** It's easy to accumulate a bunch of different IRA accounts or brokerage accounts over the years. If so, consider combining these accounts, which may also result in a reduction in account fees. You probably don't need so many accounts, particularly if you have, or can open up, accounts in the large financial supermarkets that allow stocks, bonds, as well as mutual funds from many different mutual fund companies, to be held in a single account.

❏ **Shop on the Internet.** Shopping on the Web can be both a time and money saver. You'll save time by avoiding a trip to a store, if not several stores, and you'll save money by being able to comparison shop online (the Internet is usually very effective for comparison shoppers), not to mention save the cost of traveling to said store(s). After you have found the lowest price for what you want, be sure to check out whether a discount coupon is available from the retailer. See page 53 for information on finding discount coupons on the Web.

❏ **Automate your investing.** The more you put your investing on automatic—through regular transfers from your paycheck or checking account into a retirement or investments account—the more time you save and the more money you're likely to accumulate. (See Idea 31, on page 96.)

❏ **Bank Online.** I've saved the best for last. Do you like filling out checks? Is your idea of fun standing in line at your local bank branch? If so, read no further. If not, join those who have found online banking to be almost as freeing as when you first got your driver's license. Most banks and credit unions, even smaller ones, offer online banking of varying scope.

    Advantages aplenty. Online banking offers many advantages, including 24/7 convenience from anywhere you have access to a computer, faster processing of transactions, and access in a single site to all of your accounts, including checking, savings, CDs, investments, and loans. Your banking institution may now or soon offer even more sophisticated online bells and whistles, such as stock quotes, alerts, and portfolio-management programs.

    A matter of trust. The primary impediment to online banking is a fear that somehow your data and transactions will be compromised. Keep in mind that trust is arguably a bank's or credit union's most valuable asset, and they are constantly working to maintain and enhance the security of their online banking sites. Perhaps the best thing to do if you have any concerns is to always print out a copy of each transaction that you initiate on-line. However, rest assured that your data is secure, but if it is ever compromised by an unauthorized person, the institution will make you whole.

Filling out checks by hand will soon become a relic of the past. Online banking is here to stay, and it behooves you to join those who have much better things to do than bank the old-fashioned way.

The *Grow Your Money!* special reader Web site has work sheets and more information, including the latest innovations in online banking, to help you simplify your financial life. **w w w**

Simplifying your financial life will save time and reduce hassles, allowing you more time to enjoy the good life.

■

Anyone who says money doesn't buy happiness doesn't know where to shop.
—ANONYMOUS

MONEY TIP

Always Keep the Basics in Mind

While the financial-services industry thrives on making your financial life seem a lot more complicated than it actually is, always keep the basics in mind.

✦ In order to become financially secure, you have to accumulate an investment portfolio.

✦ You can't accumulate an investment portfolio unless you get into the habit of saving regularly.

✦ In order to save regularly, you have to spend less than you earn.

✦ In order to spend less than you earn, you have to learn to **be happy with what you've got.**

The last point is crucial, but many of us have difficulty practicing it. They want a fancier car or an imported kitchen or an exotic vacation or a larger house. After all, the advertisers tell us that we have to have these things to be happy. By golly, our neighbors have some of these things that we don't have, and they sure seem happy. What a crock! The neighbors probably feel the same way about you as you feel about them. If you can be happy with what you've got, you'll find it a lot easier to save the money to make the investments that give you financial security. It's as simple as that. Don't get me wrong, however, I'm not saying that you should be resigned to your current financial situation. You should strive to advance in your career (see chapter 2), save an adequate amount of money (see chapter 3), and grow your investments (see chapters 6 and 7).

You should always have high career and money aspirations, but at the same time, you should realize that you've probably already got a lot of material things. Life is a series of choices, and as long as you think you're deprived of things, you're going to want to acquire more things. More things won't make you any happier, but more things could put a dent in your financial future.

Get rich slowly. Getting rich quickly is a one-in-a-million long shot. Judging from the plethora of seminars and infomercials that promise quick riches, a lot of people prefer immediate results, which, we all know, are rarely achieved. On the other hand, if you work hard, do what's needed to advance in your career, save regularly, invest those savings wisely, and periodically address other important personal financial matters, getting rich slowly is a sure bet. If you can be happy with what you've got now, you'll enjoy more abundance later in life.

> ■
>
> *There are no secrets to success. Don't waste your time*
> *looking for them. Success is the result of preparation,*
> *hard work, learning from failure, loyalty to those for*
> *whom you work, and persistence.*
> —GENERAL COLIN POWELL

IDEA 98

Financial Security in Thirty Minutes a Month

You may conclude from the many ideas and tips presented here that there's a lot to attend to in creating a sound financial future. That may or may not be accurate, depending on your situation. But once the basics are in place, maintaining your plan should not require much time. In fact, you should be able to keep track of your essential financial matters in just a half hour a month. Most financial-planning matters can be attended to once a year, with the exception of investing, which requires more frequent review. As the following table illustrates, accumulating and monitoring your investments should be the focal point of your overall financial planning. Investing is the moving target that requires more frequent attention.

INVESTING IS THE FOCAL POINT
OF YOUR FINANCIAL PLANNING

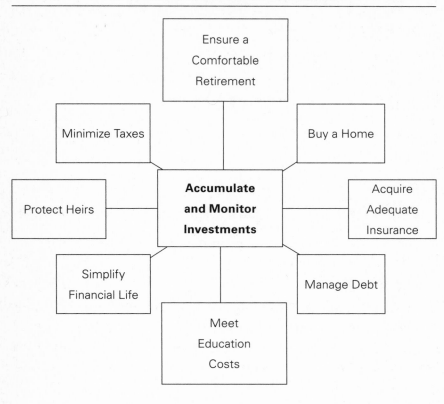

Here are the important items to consider once a year, or if indicated, twice a year. (Note, this adds up to twelve evaluations to do a year.):

❑ Evaluate your overall investment diversification and decide whether rebalancing or other changes in allocation may be necessary. (Perform this evaluation twice a year, six months apart.)

❑ Evaluate the performance of the individual investments held in each of your accounts to ascertain if any weaklings should be replaced. (Perform this evaluation twice a year, six months apart.)

❏ Check on the adequacy of your insurance coverage and estate-planning documents.

❏ Plan ways to reduce your income taxes.

❏ Look for ways to improve your record keeping and otherwise simplify your financial life.

❏ Tote up all of your debts, and plan ways to avoid adding more debt and to reduce the debt you have.

❏ Prepare a projection of your expected retirement income and expenses, whether you're working age or retired.

❏ Plan ways to improve your savings, beginning with increasing contributions to retirement savings plans.

❏ Figure out how you're going to pay for any future big-ticket items, like a home, college, or your next car.

❏ Review your progress in achieving your financial goals and decide what you plan to do differently in the next year to help reach your goals. Involve your spouse or partner, if applicable, in these deliberations.

Also, if you have a major change in your family or financial circumstances, you should immediately revisit all areas that may be affected by the change.

Thirty minutes is all it should take. You should be able to address each of these matters in a half hour. If you want to devote more time, you might benefit—up to a point. But some go overboard, particularly in the investment area, often to their detriment. For example, you may have coworkers or acquaintances who check up on their investments several times—a day. What, pray tell, can they accomplish from doing that?

See the *Grow Your Money!* To-Do Calendar in the appendix for monthly reminders of these and other financial topics that may require your periodic attention.

> Once you've got your financial life in good working order, it should take you only a half hour per month to monitor your progress and identify areas for improvement.
>
> ◼
>
> *There are two classes of people who tell what is going to happen in the future: Those who don't know, and those who don't know they don't know.*
> —JOHN KENNETH GALBRAITH

MONEY TIP

Never Underestimate the Value of Common Sense

It's easy to conclude that paying proper attention to the vast and diverse array of matters affecting your personal finances should be a full-time job. But I hope you have found that personal financial planning isn't really that complicated, despite the zealous efforts of many in the financial services industry to make you believe otherwise. All it takes is some discipline and a little time (see Idea 23, on page 76).

If successful financial planning can be boiled down to two words, they are *common sense*. If you think back on the—I'll be polite—less-than-stellar moves you have made with your money in the past (and no one is immune from these transgressions), you will no doubt find that your money calamities were caused by lapses in common sense on your part.

Here's an example. Think back on a remark that your parents probably made when you were an adolescent, "For one moment's pleasure, you could end up paying for the rest of your life." While at the time you may have thought they were alluding to something else, in fact they were talking about credit card loans. Here's what they were saying: a short-term money dalliance takes a heck of a lot longer to undo than getting into the predicament took in the first place.

There's a lot of common sense in this book. Here's something to keep foremost in mind as you get serious about your financial future: **it takes a lot less time to make the right moves with your money than it does to undo any wrong moves.**

◼

Genius, that power which dazzles mortal eyes, is often
perseverance in disguise.
—HENRY WILLARD AUSTIN

IDEA 99

Invest in Your Good Health

You've got a good chance of living to one hundred. That has enormous financial implications, of course. The longer you live, the more money you'll need. But there's more to preparing for a long life than the customary triad of saving regularly, investing those savings wisely, and eliminating debt. Taking care of your health can make a big difference in how well and how long you'll be able to savor the good life, and you can stack the odds in favor of a long and healthy retirement by improving your health habits.

What good is wealth without good health? It's well known that older Americans today are more prosperous and healthier than their forebears, and those differences are expected to increase when the first baby boomers reach retirement age. Also, the current batch of seniors is showing substantially less disability, which points to an improved quality of life, another positive trend that is expected to accelerate.

While the population as a whole is enjoying longer life, lower rates of disability, and better overall health, there are vast differences in individual outcomes. That's where taking care of your health can be so important. You want to stack the odds in your favor, and there are a few things you can do not only to greatly reduce the probability of premature death, but also make the rest of your life a lot healthier. It would be a shame to do all the right things financially to assure you're going to enjoy decades of financial security only to have your stock-pile eroded or spent on preventable infirmities simply because you didn't take sufficient care of your health.

It's never too late to improve your health prospects. The good news is that even if you've had lousy health habits in the past, changing those bad habits now can reduce future problems and lengthen your remaining life. Here's what you need to do:

❑ **Diet.** We all know the foods that make up the well-balanced diet, but that doesn't mean that we follow it. Eating fresh fruits, vegetables, whole grains, fish, and lean meats in moderation will help you maintain good health for a longer time. Consult your doctor about the food regimen that's best for you.

❑ **Exercise and stress reduction.** Moderate to vigorous exercise for at least thirty minutes several days a week will work wonders in reducing stress, improving your overall outlook (and look), and preventing or postponing later-life health problems. Be sure to include strength and flexibility workouts in your exercise regimen. Specialists advise that the older you get, the greater the proportion of your aerobic/strength exercise regimen that should be devoted to strength training.

❑ **Checkups.** You will be able to receive many diagnostic tests that were not available just a few years ago. Screening tests, as part of regular doctor visits, will help identify diseases or other health problems early, making them easier to treat. In fact, diagnostic technology, including genetic testing, is advancing so fast that it won't be too long before such testing might reliably indicate what is likely to cause future infirmity. The future direction of your health care could focus on the malady that's most likely to do you in. Unless you're not too enthusiastic about finding out such matters in advance, keep up to date on the state of the art in diagnostic tools.

The Mind Needs Work Too. You need to keep your brain in tip-top condition if you're going to savor the good life to the max.

❑ **Keep mentally sharp.** A lot of what you do to keep yourself physically fit will also promote mental fitness. One of the biggest fears we have as we age is of losing cognitive function, which many witness firsthand with their aging parents or other older relatives. Neuropsychologists urge those of us who have a few decades under our ever-widening belts to participate in cognitively challenging activities, in other words, exercising parts of your brain that haven't been used very much. Ideally, you should pursue new activities that are difficult. Learn a new language or a musical instrument (I want to learn how to play the steel drum), something a youngster could master a lot faster than you, which tells us all something about our mental acuity. Or try crosswords, Scrabble, painting, or the like. But when you get good at something, move on to something else. Forty years of research has shown that undertaking (excuse the poor word choice) cognitively challenging activities as an adult delays the onset of dementia and slows its progression. Remind your parents about this.

❑ **Keep busy.** There's no question that we're a lot busier now than were previous generations, and that helps maintain your mental health. Leading a full life doesn't cease when you retire. You'll know you've got the right stuff after you retire if you look back wistfully at your working years as a period when you had a lot more spare time.

❑ **Develop a social portfolio.** Develop and nurture meaningful relationships with family and friends. Having such people in your life is conducive to a longer, healthier life. Good relationships add to your enjoyment of life and help you better manage stress. Those who maintain a positive mental outlook will way outlive the sad sacks.

❑ **Coping with your loved one's irksome financial habits.**
Part and parcel of enjoying good health is getting used to your loved one's financial foibles. Chances are you don't always agree with your spouse's, or your partner's, money habits. I concluded long ago that such strife is inevitable, because spenders are attracted to savers, and vice versa. Each of these maladies manifests itself in obvious ways. For example, spenders actually believe that to buy something on sale is to save money. Savers, on the other hand, abhor spending of any kind, and constantly berate the spender's profligacy. But the sooner you resign yourself to tolerating your loved one's annoying financial habits, the better. Disagreements about money are natural in a relationship. But don't let them undermine the relationship. Just because the spender-love-of-your-life has non-buyer's remorse every time he or she leaves an emporium empty-handed doesn't mean he or she is unworthy of your affection, nor is the loved one who would rather live in squalor than spend a nickel. Do the best you can to cope, and resign yourself to the fact that your loved one will never change his or her annoying financial habits—nor will you. See Idea 83, on page 263, for more help on ways to encourage family financial felicity.

Taking good care of your physical and mental health will help you better enjoy a long and productive life in which you can happily spend all of your money.

■

Another advantage of being rich is that all your faults
are called eccentricities.
—ANONYMOUS

IDEA 100

Taking Advantage of the Best Financial Opportunities

As you grow your money you have a lot to look forward to. But you and/or your advisers have to stay current on opportunities as they arise. Remember, the goal is to fare so well that savoring the good life becomes a daily occurrence.

Here are ten timely thoughts on matters that will improve your well-being—if you take heed:

1. ❑ **Diversification will be the key to successful investing.** Everyone knows diversification is important, but most either don't know how to do it or don't care to do it. In the past, you could get away with an undiversified portfolio. No longer, though, since investment sectors that heretofore had only a scant presence have become performance leaders. Failure to adjust your investments to include these new sectors is a recipe for mediocre investment returns.

2. ❑ **Stocks will continue to reward investors in spite of occasional blips.** A majority of any money you're not going to need for at least a decade should be invested in stocks. Despite occasional periods of stock market malaise, which can last for a few years, stocks remain the preferred long-term investment.

3. ❑ **Foreign investment markets will outperform U.S. stocks.** Numerous foreign countries are rapidly becoming engines for worldwide economic progress. You can take advantage of these attractive investment opportunities by investing in both U.S. companies with substantial overseas operations and foreign companies. The latter will likely offer more investment return potential than domestic companies.

4. ❑ **Inflation will remain benign.** Low inflation and low interest rates will benefit both stock investors and borrowers. Since companies have difficulty raising prices in a low-inflation environment, investors should opt for companies that can increase profitability by reducing costs through technology, acquisitions, and other means. While you may grouse about low interest rates for your short-term savings in CDs and money market accounts, we're a lot better off overall with low inflation and low interest rates than with the alternative of high interest rates and high inflation.

5. ❑ **Autopilot investments will become dominant.** Index and exchange-traded funds and, particularly target funds and lifestyle funds, will revolutionize the way individuals invest. Target and lifestyle funds offer the added advantages of diversification and automatic rebalancing within a single fund.

6. ❑ **Congress will continue to improve tax incentives for retirement savers.** Partly in response to the slow demise of the traditional private-sector pension plan, but mostly just to get Uncle Sam off the hook for supporting retirees, you can look forward to even better tax incentives to save for retirement. Retirees are currently socked with income taxes, but tax relief for retirees may be on the way.

7. ❑ **Competition in the financial-services industry will benefit consumers.** Lower costs, greater choice, and easier access to timely information will benefit investors, borrowers, college

savers, persons seeking insurance coverage, and just about everyone else who has a financial life.

8. ❑ **Technology will revolutionize the way you manage your financial life.** Not only will the Internet become the dominant means of obtaining financial information and guidance, but it will also ease the chore of managing your investments and other family financial matters. Online banking will also considerably ease the chore of paying bills and organizing tax records.

9. ❑ **Those approaching retirement age will enjoy unprecedented opportunities to delay retirement or retire gradually.** New attitudes toward retirement will alter the retirement landscape. Employers will welcome those who opt to work beyond normal retirement age, and many workers will oblige them, whether motivated by financial needs or, more common, because they aren't eager to retire.

10. ❑ **Longer, healthier lives will present both opportunities and challenges to retirees.** Many retirees will spend more years retired than they did working. Enjoying an active and healthy retirement will become the norm. But a long period of retirement poses challenges to retirees as well as younger-generation family members. It will be common during the twenty-first century for middle-aged individuals to have both parents and grandparents who are in some measure dependent on them.

You will benefit greatly from taking advantage of the many investment and financial-planning opportunities that will arise in the future.

■

Have more than thou showest,
Speak less than thou knowest.
—WILLIAM SHAKESPEARE

IDEA 101

It's Time to Indulge Yourself

It's easy to conclude that getting serious about creating a better financial future is filled with "don'ts." Don't overspend, don't speculate with your investments, don't go without insurance, don't borrow. The financial planning "dos" aren't much better. Do save more, do diversify your investments, do your will and other estate-planning documents. No wonder so many people ***don't*** want to be bothered with the drudgery of financial and investment planning. But the last thing I want is for you to slink off with shoulders slumped, flummoxed by the many financial tasks ahead. So the last Idea is to indulge yourself. You work hard for your money, you are (or will be) prudent in your financial life, so you deserve to be rewarded. Total deprivation may be good for some souls, but not for you and me. We already deprive ourselves enough just to secure the future for ourselves and our loved ones.

What's Your Preference? The following checklist will let you identify the splurge that best floats your boat. Several are listed and space is provided for you to add your own. After all, self-indulgence is a tradition in our society. The challenge, of course, is to limit your self-indulgences. If you find it tempting to check them all off, please reread Idea 57, "Big-Ticket Items Tell a Lot," on page 186. But once you have identified your own financial indulgence, don't look back. You deserve it.

- ❏ Nice home
- ❏ Vacation home
- ❏ Expensive furnishings
- ❏ Late-model car
- ❏ Exotic vacations
- ❏ Fancy clothes and jewelry

❑ _____

❑ _____

$ $ $ $ $ $

This is a great time to plan your financial future. Financial security may still be a long way off, but as you begin to take control of your financial future, you'll reap many rewards along the way. If you are well along in your financial life, making the necessary midcourse corrections will further improve your financial well-being. Be sure to refer back to the checklists in the introduction to help you identify important matters requiring your attention. Don't feel overwhelmed. Instead, identify two or three items in your to-do list and address them over the next week. Also, remember to refer regularly to the special reader Web site described on page xliii for up-to-date information and guidance.

Best wishes for a wonderful financial future.

Don't let the many things you may need to do to improve your financial status get in the way of some self-indulgence.

■

Life should not be a journey to the grave with the intention of arriving safely in a pretty and well-preserved body, but rather to skid in broadside in a cloud of smoke, chocolate in one hand and a martini in the other, thoroughly used up, totally worn out, and loudly proclaiming, "Wow! What a Ride!"
—ANONYMOUS

Grow Your Money!
To-Do Calendar

This calendar highlights important to-do matters that may require your attention at various times during the year. Growing your money requires that you leave no stone unturned. The purpose of this calendar is to remind you of items that need at least your cursory attention each and every year.

> ■
>
> *All work and no play makes jack. With enough jack,*
> *Jack needn't be a dull boy.*
> —MALCOLM FORBES

January

❏ **Organize your tax records.** You'll probably receive a lot of mail in January and February that you'll need to complete your tax return. So this is a good time to get organized by setting up a file where you can put all your mail and other tax-related documents. Don't wait until the last minute to assemble the necessary items. The better organized your tax records, the less taxes you'll pay and the better prepared you'll be if, perish the thought, you're audited. (See Idea 97, on page 317.)

❑ **Review the performance of your investments for the prior year.** Once you have received all of your statements, ascertain how your money has fared over the past year. In order to evaluate your overall investment standing, be sure to combine all of your investment accounts, whether you and/or your investment adviser are responsible for them. (See Idea 44, on page 143.)

❑ **Rebalance your investments.** If the stock or bond markets experienced large gains or losses last year, check to see if you should rebalance your investments to get back to your target allocation. (See Idea 40, on page 129.)

❑ **Consider increasing the percentage you contribute to your retirement plan at work.** The beginning of the year is the best time to increase the percentage that you're contributing to your retirement savings plans at work. Even if it's only a 1 or 2 percent increase, that's a step in the right direction. (See Idea 23, on page 76.)

February

❑ **Nag your high school or college student to start looking for a summer job.** The early bird gets the worm—or, in this instance, the job. A summer job not only inculcates good work habits, but also helps the family finances survive the summer.

❑ **Pay off any credit card balances run up over the holidays.** Don't let any credit card charges from holiday excesses accumulate.

March

❑ **Begin making plans and reservations for summer vacation.** The cheapest vacations are typically those that are planned either well in advance or at the last minute. If you're not willing to wait until the last minute, start firming up your plans now.

❑ **Prepare a projection of your expected retirement income and expenses.** This is an important task that should be performed annually. Find out where you stand so that you can devise a plan to eliminate the inevitable gap between what you have now and what you're going to need to have by the time you retire. It won't be as challenging as you think, I promise you. If you're retired, you still need to prepare annual projections to make sure you're on track for enjoying a long, healthy, and wealthy retirement. (See Idea 89, on page 283.)

April

❑ **Speak with your spouse or significant other about money matters.** Set aside one day each year (April Fool's Day?) to discuss the status of and plans for the family fortune. While couples may disagree on day-to-day financial matters, they usually concur on the more significant longer-term goals. It's a lot easier to get where you want to go when you both agree what's important and at least achieve détente on any areas of contention. (See Idea 83, on page 263.)

❑ **If you haven't done so yet, max out on your retirement contributions for the prior tax year.** You can still make last year's IRA contribution up until the April tax-filing deadline. Other plans may allow you to delay prior-year contributions until even later if you file an extension.

May

❑ **Begin planning strategies to reduce this year's income taxes.** Many worthwhile tax-saving strategies can't be put off until the last minute. Plan now on ways to cut this year's tax bill. (See Idea 67, on page 208.)

❏ **If you received a sizable tax refund, adjust your withholding allowances to increase your take-home pay.** There's no reason to give the federal government an interest-free loan, which is what a tax refund amounts to. If you have been receiving refunds, put a stop to it by increasing your withholding allowances. (See Idea 70, on page 218.)

❏ **If you had difficulty coming up with your IRA contribution in April, begin setting aside enough to fund this year's contribution.** If you had to scrounge around for enough money to fund last year's IRA contribution by the deadline, you should put your current-year IRA contribution on the monthly installment plan. Simply instruct your mutual fund or brokerage company or bank to take enough money out of your checking account each month to fund your IRA by next year's deadline. As a bonus, your IRA money will be invested gradually throughout the year, which is a good idea. The sooner in the year you get money into your IRA, the more tax-advantaged growth you will enjoy.

❏ **Time for an annual estate-planning checkup.** Make sure your estate-planning documents are up to snuff. Many adults don't yet have a will and other basic estate-planning documents, in which case: DO IT NOW! If it has been a while since your estate-planning documents were prepared, you should ask your attorney if they're still up to date. Chances are they're okay. But it's better to find out now that they're outdated rather than to wait until it's too late—because when it comes to estate-planning documents, if it's too late, it's really too late. (See Idea 79, on page 247.)

June

❏ **Increase contributions to retirement savings plans.** If your budget can stand the shock—and a pleasant shock it is—ratchet up your contributions to retirement savings plans during the last half of the year. (See Idea 15, on page 54.)

❑ **Evaluate the quality of service provided by your advisers.** This is a good time to decide if you're getting your money's worth from your financial advisers, which may include your tax preparer, attorney, insurance agent, and investment adviser/financial planner. (See Idea 82, on page 258.)

❑ **Improve your personal record-keeping system.** If getting your taxes ready and paying your bills has been an unpleasant chore, you should take some time to spiff up your personal record-keeping system. A little upfront effort can save both time and annoyance later on. (See Idea 97, on page 317.)

July

❑ **Review the performance of your investments over the first six months of the year.** Find out how all of your investment accounts have fared over the first six months and make any midcourse corrections that may be necessary. If your analysis indicates a large deviation from your diversification target, it may be time to rebalance. (See Idea 44, on page 143.)

❑ **Evaluate loans to find better deals.** Look at your overall debt situation with an eye toward finding lower-interest loans or loans with better terms if they're available. (See chapter 4.)

August

❑ **Donate furniture and clothing to a worthy charity.** Rather than waiting until the last minute, do some summer cleaning and give unneeded furniture and clothing to those who can benefit from them—and benefit yourself with a tax deduction.

❑ **Update your files that support the cost basis for your nonretirement-account investments and your home.** While most of your financial records don't need to be kept forever, those that substantiate the cost basis for your nonretirement investments and your home are necessary. Make sure you have past records in hand and have a system for retaining them in the future. (See Idea 97, on page 317.)

September

❑ **Review your insurance coverage to make sure no changes need to be made.** This is a good time of the year to spend some time reviewing your insurance coverage. Your insurance agent should help. If you think income taxes are expensive, they're nothing compared with the cost of an uninsured or underinsured loss. (See chapter 11.)

❑ **Employee benefits checkup.** Find out if you are taking maximum advantage of the benefits offered by your employer. If you're offered a menu of health plan choices, be particularly careful about finding the best option for you and your family.

October

❑ **Pay off any credit card balances run up over the summer.** If the livin' was particularly easy for you last summer, you may have the credit card bills to prove it. If so, try your best to pay them off before the holidays.

❑ **Avoid late-year purchases of mutual funds in taxable accounts.** If you buy a mutual fund late in the year, you risk buying just before the fund company makes a big distribution. Most of them distribute capital gains over the last quarter of the year, and those gains can be particularly large if the stock market had a banner year. This is not a concern with your retirement accounts, since you don't pay taxes on them until you begin making withdrawals. But you could risk an unwanted tax bill if you buy a mutual fund for your taxable brokerage account late in the year.

November

❏ **Make sure enough money has been withheld to pay taxes.** Check to see if enough taxes have been withheld to avoid any underpayment penalties and interest. If not, you may have time to ask your employer to increase the taxes withheld from your pay for the rest of the year. This could avoid any unwelcome assessments when you file your tax forms next year.

❏ **Plan your holiday spending in advance.** Well, the holiday shopping season has begun and with it the temptation to overspend. There are a couple of things to keep in mind: First, strange as it may seem, retailers still accept cash in exchange for any items you wish to purchase. Second, the sooner you complete your holiday shopping, the less you're likely to spend during the late November and December shopping frenzy. You know you've got your financial act together if you spend the same percentage of your income between Thanksgiving and New Year's as you spend between New Year's and Thanksgiving.

December

❏ **Set up self-employed retirement plans.** If you have income from full- or part-time self-employment, you can wait until next year to fund a self-employed retirement plan, but most such plans (the SEP IRA is an exception) must be set up by the end of December to be effective this year. (See Idea 30, on page 93.)

❏ **Sell losing investments in taxable brokerage accounts.** If you have any losses in your taxable brokerage account holdings, this is a good time to sell some of those losers to reap some tax benefits from your misfortune. (See Idea 72, on page 226.)

❏ **Consider a Roth IRA conversion.** If you qualify and have the money to pay the taxes, a Roth IRA conversion could be one of the smartest financial decisions you can make. But the traditional IRA money must be transferred to a Roth account by the end of December. (See Idea 28, on page 88.)

❏ **There's still time to make charitable donations.** As long as your charitable contribution check is dated this year or you pay by credit card this year, you're entitled to a charitable contribution deduction this year. Don't forget any last-minute donations of usable clothing or furniture. (See Idea 72, on page 226.)

Other Events

These events could arise at any time during the year and will probably require some action on your part.

❏ **Pay raise.** When deciding about the many ways you can spend your pay raise, consider investing some of it for posterity, rather than using it all to prop up the economy. (See Idea 15, on page 54.)

❏ **Change in family circumstances.** The arrival of children or grandchildren or changes in your marital or financial status usually require revisiting your will and other estate-planning documents and a review of the beneficiary designations on your retirement accounts. (See Idea 79, on page 247.)

❏ **Financial windfall.** A financial windfall, like an inheritance or the proceeds from the sale of a home, requires due deliberation to decide how it will be invested or spent and what changes, if any, are required in the areas of tax and estate planning and insurance, among others. (See Idea 16, on page 55.)

■

Learn from the mistakes of others; you can't live long
enough to make them all yourself.
—ELEANOR ROOSEVELT

Index

accelerated death benefit, 238
accidental-death benefit, 238
adoption tax credit, 211
advance directive, 247
age-based investing, for college costs, 191–192
aging family members, 253–256, 280–281
alimony tax deduction, 211
Allen, Woody, 111
allowance, for child, 272
annuity, 86, 309, 311–312
appliance service contract, 179–180, 246
April tasks, 339
Aronstein, Michael, 121
assets, 60–61
attorney, 259–260
August tasks, 341–342
Austin, Henry Willard, 327
auto service contract, 180, 246
automatic dollar-cost averaging, 109
automatic premium loan provision, 238
automation of investments, 96–97, 125–127, 320, 332
automobile. *See* car
average returns, 121–125

balanced funds, 118
bank accounts, limiting, 319

bank interest, 110
banking, online, 320–321, 333
bankruptcy, personal, 72
Barrymore, John, 72
Baruch, Bernard, 144
basics, financial, 321–322
Berra, Yogi, 235
Bierce, Ambrose, 163
big-ticket items, 185–206
Billings, Josh, 62
Bombeck, Erma, 205
bond (definition), 9
bond funds, multisector, 137
bonds
    contrarian investing, 130
    individual, 139–143
    taxation, 215, 216
    types, 104–105
    when to sell, 149–150
borrowing
    building wealth, 63–65
    education, 60–61
    home, 60
    home equity loan, 65–66
    home improvement, 61
    investment, 61
    start business, 61
brokerage account, 110–111, 117, 195–196
budget, 51, 70, 285
Buffett, Warren, 125

business ownership, 30–33, 40–41, 61, 210
business plan, 32

Cameron, William J., 33
capital gain (definition), 8
capital gains tax, 38–39, 196, 215
capitalization, business ownership, 31
capitalization rate, real estate, 154–155
car
  buying, 200–206
  insuring, 234
  maintaining, 205
  reducing expenses, 203–205
  selling, 204–205
car loan, avoiding, 205–206
career
  changing, 26–28
  investment in, 17, 19–36
  retirement, 35–36
  sabbatical from, 23–25
  success in, 20–23
Carnegie, Andrew, 115
cash
  gifts to children, 272
  investing, 110–111
cash-value life insurance, 236–237
CD, 81, 117, 223
certificate of deposit. *See* CD
charitable contributions, tax saving, 210, 226, 341, 344
child-care tax credit, 211
children
  IRAs for, 274–278
  money education, 271
Churchill, Winston, 59, 231
Clarke, Edward, 180
cohabitation, 263–267, 330, 339
college costs, 17, 190–192, 198–199
college saving, 191–192, 195–197
  vs. retirement saving, 199–200
college scholarships, 199
college tuition, 211
commercials, impact on children, 271
commodity funds, 136–137
common sense, 326–327
compound growth, 5–9
computer, avoiding scams, 279–280
Confucius, 20, 93
Congress, tax rules, 212–214

contract, appliance service, 179–180
contractor, home improvement, 176–178
contrarian investing, 129–132
Coolidge, Calvin, 53
corporate bonds, 104, 216
coupon codes, online, 53
coupons, use with children, 271
Coverdell Education Savings Account, 196
credit, 17, 62
credit cards
  educating children, 272
  limiting, 319
  paying off, 56, 66–68, 291, 338, 342
  secured, 74
  tax-deductible payments, 227–228
credit counseling, 71–72
credit rating, 73–75
credit-report-monitoring services, 246
credit union, interest paid, 110
creditors, relationships with, 70, 71
critical-illness insurance, 245
custodial accounts, for college, 192

Day, Edward, 43
dealer's "extras," car, 204
debt
  advantageous use, 59–75, 341
  consolidation loans, 70–71
  eliminating, 10
  management, 13
  problems, 69–72
  recidivism, 71
  in retirement, 291
December tasks, 343–344
defined benefit plan, 94–95
defined contribution plan, 98
dependent-care tax credit, 211
Dickens, Charles, 101, 270
diet, balanced, 328
disability income rider, 238
disabled tax credit, 211
diversifying investments, 105–107, 109, 118, 122–123, 152, 331
dividends, taxation, 215
Do Not Call Registry, 280
dollar-cost averaging, 109
double indemnity benefit, 238

down payment
   home ownership, 163–165
   investment real estate, 155–156
   vacation home, 181
dual-career parents, 269–271
durable power of attorney, 247, 304

early retirement, 287–290
earthquake insurance, 232–233
education
   borrowing for, 60–61
   career advancement, 30–31
   value of, 13, 25–26
education savings account, 196
elderly family members, 253–256,
   280–281
elderly tax credit, 211
emergency, financial, 82–83
emerging-market stock funds, 135–136
employer benefits, 210, 342
employer plan
   changing jobs, 98–101
   match, 84
   unmatched, 84
employer stock purchase, 87–88
empty-nester, insurance, 239
enjoyment, aspect of financial
   planning, 188, 334–335
equities (definition), 9
equity, in home, 63–64
estate planning, 17, 247–249, 255, 303,
   340
estate taxes, 248–249
exchange-traded funds, 121–125, 215
exemptions, withholding, 218–220,
   340, 343
exercise, 328
expenses, reducing, 46–50
experience, in business ownership, 31

fads, teenage, 272–273
failure, use of, 12, 13
fake valuables, 279
family circumstances, changing, 344
family members
   aging, 253–256, 280–281
   encouraging, 12
   money decisions, 257–281
   retired, 330

family rider, 238
family trust, 249–252
Feather, William, 25, 135
February tasks, 338
Fields, W. C., 281
financial basics, 321–322
financial common sense, 326–327
financial emergency, 82–83
financial future, enjoying, 316–335
financial independence. *See* financial
   security
financial navigation system, 2–4
financial opportunities, 331–333
financial planner, 57, 261–262
financial scams, 278–281
financial security, 16–18, 323–326
financial services industry,
   332–333
financial windfall, 55–58, 344
fixed income investment
   (definition), 9
flexible-spending accounts,
   taxation, 227
flood insurance, 233
Flynn, Errol, 46
focusing, in career advancement, 22
forecast, retirement, 283–286
foreign investments, 332
Francis, Brendan, 256
Franklin, Benjamin, 49, 63, 79, 198
fraudulent communications, 278–279
free lunch, sales ploy, 278
Friedman, Thomas, 138
friends, in retirement, 330
fringe benefits, tax saving, 210
Frost, Robert, 50, 82, 184

gain (definition), 8
Galbraith, John Kenneth, 326
getting rich slowly, 76–78, 322
Getty, J. Paul, 147
gift cards, theft, 279
Glickman, Louis, 158
goals, financial, 1–18, 12
Godfrey, Arthur, 212
government bonds, 104–105, 216
grocery coupons, use with children,
   271
Grow Your Money! to-do calendar,
   337–344

guaranteed insurability rider, 237
Gurney, Edward J., 218
Guthrie, Thomas, 97

Half, Robert, 240
hard work, 21, 32
health
    age-related declining, 254–255
    investment in, 327–331
health checkups, 328–329
health insurance, 234
    aging family members, 254
    in retirement, 292, 303
home
    borrowing for, 60
    buying, 10–11, 159–165
    equity in, 63–64
    improving, 57, 61, 171–174,
        176–178, 225
    owning, 159–184, 209
    selling, 173
    tax records, 225
    vacation, 180–184
home equity loan, 65–66
home safe, 252
homeowner's insurance, 232, 234
Hoover, Herbert, 277
household inventory, 318–319
housing, aging family members, 254,
    304
housing costs
    future, 64–65
    in retirement, 293–295
    vs. saving for future, 186–187
Humphrey, Hubert, 14–15
hurricane insurance, 232–233

identity theft, 289
identity-theft insurance, 246
income
    annuity, 309
    increasing, 10
    present, vs. pension plan, 34
    relation to wealth, 13
    in retirement, 293–297, 305–307
income tax, 207–229, 256
    reducing, 208–212, 207–229, 339
    in retirement, 292
    returns, 220–224

index funds, 121–125, 215
inflation, effect on retirement, 284, 332
inflation risk, 308–309
inheritance, irrelevance of, 13
inspection, house, 162
insurance
    adequate, 10, 16, 230–246, 342
    agent, 258–259
    aging family members, 253
    car, 204
    comparison shopping, 234, 239
    discounts, 234
    life, 234, 235–240, 304
    long-term-care, 242–244
    private mortgage, 175–176, 234
    property, 231–233
    unnecessary, 233–235, 244–246
    waiver of premium, 238
interest, taxation, 215
international stock, 104
Internet
    avoiding scams, 279–280
    shopping, 53, 280, 319
    researching investments, 109, 333
inventory, household, 319–320
investment(s)
    allocation, 16
    automatic, 96–97, 125–127, 320, 332
    borrowing for, 61
    comparing returns, 133–138
    contrarian, 129–132
    education as, 25–26
    education for, 116–117
    gains, effect on retirement, 285
    high-yielding (warning), 278
    vs. insurance, 239
    interpreting statements, 143–144
    long-term, 152
    monitoring, 323–326
    performance, 143–144, 338, 341
    portfolio, 102–106
    predicting market, 120
    real estate, 40, 61, 153–156
    rebalancing, 131–132, 338
    retirement, 302–303
    risk, 308
    vs. saving, 78–79
    selling, 147–150
    short-term, 56, 80–82
    starting out, 115–119
    supercharging, 128–158

taxation, 209–210, 214–217, 225, 226
terminology, 8–9
wise, 17, 57, 102–127
investment accounts, limiting, 319
investment adviser, 260–261
investment newsletters, fraudulent, 179
investors, types, 111–115
IRA, 75, 340
  children, 274–278
  college plus retirement, 197–198
  deductible nontraditional, 85–86
  deductible traditional, 85
  early vs. late start, 6
  qualifications for, 92–93
  Roth, 85, 88–92, 223, 343
irregular expenses, 193–195

January tasks, 337–338
Jefferson, Thomas, 36
job. *See also* work
  changing, 98–101
  finding, 24–25
  leaving, 29–30, 34–35
  retirement, 36
  summer, 338
July tasks, 341
June tasks, 340–341

land, undeveloped, 156–158
large-company stock, 103
Lehman Brothers Aggregate Bond Index, 124
letter of instructions, 247–248
liability insurance, 231–232
liability risk, 308
life events, preparation for, 16
life expectancy, effect on retirement, 284
life insurance, 234, 235–240, 304
lifestyle funds, 118, 126
living trust, 247, 249–252
loan(s)
  car, 205–206
  debt consolidation, 70–71
  from IRA, 75
  reviewing, 341
  student, 68–69
Long, Russell, 229

longevity risk, 309
long-term goals, vs. short-term purchases, 3–4
long-term-care insurance, 242–244
lottery, advice, 79

March tasks, 338–339
market, predicting, 120
market decline, surviving, 151–153
marriage, 263–267, 330, 339
May tasks, 339–340
McCoy, Mary, 217
medical insurance, 234
  retirement, 292, 303
  self-employed, 211
Medicare prescription drug plans, fraudulent, 278
Mellon, Andrew, 143
mental sharpness, 329
mentoring, in career advancement, 21
mid-sized-company stock, 103
millionaire success secrets, 11–15
money market funds, 81
money
  personal control over, 16
  wasting, 45–46
Morgan Stanley Capital International Europe, Australasia, and Far East Index, 124
mortality risk, 309
mortgage foreclosure scam, 278
mortgage insurance, 245
  private, 175–176, 234
mortgage
  choosing, 162
  paying, 57
  paying early, 165–169
  retirement, 291
  reverse, 303, 312–315
moving expenses, job-related, 211
MSCI EAFE Index, 124
multisector bond funds, 137
Mumford, Lewis, 190
municipal bonds, 105, 216
Murphy's Law, 244
mutual funds, 107–109, 117
  plus individual securities, 139–143
  taxation, 215–216, 227, 32
  types, 118–119, 121–127
  when to sell, 147–149

Naomi, 274
Nash, Ogden, 55, 165
National Do Not Call Registry, 280
Nelson, Willie, 4
nest egg, 16, 303, 307–311
non-medical life insurance, 246
November tasks, 343
"number" for retirement, 101, 290–293

October tasks, 342
online banking, 320–321, 333
online coupon codes, 53
online shopping, 53, 280, 319
overhead, business ownership, 31

papers, unnecessary, 318
parents, dual-career, 269–271
part-time work, 36, 289
passions, following, 12
Patton, General George S., 29
pay raise, 54–55, 344
payments, on-time, 73
pension plans, 33–35
personal bankruptcy, 72
personal information, guarding, 278
personal liability insurance, 231–232
Peter, Irene, 110
Peter, Laurence J., 58
plan, business, 32
planning, career, 20–23
Pond, Jonathan, 52
Ponzi schemes, 278
Powell, General Colin, 323
premium waiver, 238
prenuptial agreement, 265
prescription drug plans, fraudulent, 278
priorities, 2–4, 16
    debt management, 70
private mortgage insurance, 175–176,
    234
professional financial planner, 57,
    261–262, 341
professional reading, career, 20
projections, retirement, 283–286
promissory note, high-yielding
    (warning), 278
property insurance, 231–233
property tax, 169–171
purchase-and-sale agreement, 162

Rabelais, François, 249
Rags to Riches (Liberman & Lavine), 11
raise, saving, 54–55, 344
Reagan, Ronald, 208
real estate mutual funds, 119, 136
real estate, investment, 40, 61, 86,
    153–156
record-keeping, 17, 255–256, 303,
    317–319, 337–338, 341
    by children, 273
recreation, in retirement, 292
Redford, Robert, 195
rent multiplier, 154
rental-car insurance, 245
renter's insurance, 232, 234
replacement cost, insurance, 232
resume, gaps in, 23–24
retirement
    borrowing toward, 63–65
    career during, 35–36, 289
    cost of, 101, 290–293
    delayed, 295–296, 333
    early, 287–290
    financial changes, 302–305
    income, 293–297
    irregular expenses, 195
    life insurance, 239
    long, 333
    minimizing taxes, 221–224, 303,
        332
    phased, 296–297, 333
    planning, 76–101, 282–315, 339
    to vacation home, 183
retirement investment, 10, 78–79, 83
retirement plans, 17, 83–86, 87,
    116–117, 338
    reducing income tax, 208–209, 211,
        221–223, 228, 303, 332, 339
retirement projections, 283–286
retirement saving, 54–55, 56, 76–79,
    306–307, 340
    vs. college costs, 190–191,
        199–200
    vs. home ownership, 163–165
    tax credit, 211, 226–227
returns (definition), 8
    comparing, 133–138
    mutual fund, 108, 121–125
reverse mortgage, 303, 312–315
revocable living trust, 249–252
riders, insurance, 237–238

risks
  career advancement, 22
  mutual funds, 107–109
  retirement, 308–309
  value of, 12
Rivers, Joan, 176
Rogers, Will, 107, 206, 263
rollover, retirement plan, 99–100
Roosevelt, Eleanor, 193
Roth IRA, 85, 88–92, 343
  for child, 274–278
  reducing income tax, 209, 223, 227
Rothschild, Baron, 132
Russell 2000 Index, 124
Russell, Bertrand, 26

sacrifices, in goal achievement, 12
safe, home, 252
safe-deposit box, 232, 252, 255, 317
Saikaku, Ihara, 30
salary raise, saving, 54–55, 344
sales skills, 12
saving
  house vs. retirement, 163–165
  regular, 16, 76–78
  retirement, 287–290
  starting early, 5–9, 267–268
  vs. investment, 78–79
  vs. spending, 41–43
savings bonds, for children, 272
scams, financial, 278–281
scholarships, college, 199
Schopenhauer, Arthur, 23
sector funds, 119, 144–147
securities
  individual, 139–143
  out-of-favor, 132
Seinfeld, Jerry, 171
self-education, 12–13
self-employment
  401(k), 94, 95
  medical insurance, 211
  retirement plan, 85, 92–95, 227, 228
senior citizens, 253–256, 280–281
SEP, 93–94
September tasks, 342
service contract, appliance, 179–180
Shakespeare, William, 333
shopping, educating children, 271, 272

short-term investment, 80–82
short-term purchases, vs. long-term goals, 3–4
Simplified Employee Pension plan, 93–94
skills
  for business ownership, 32
  speaking, 22
  writing, 22
small-company stock, 104
social relationships, 329–330
Social Security, 297–301, 305–306
software, tax-preparation, 220–221
speaking skills, in career advancement, 22
specialization, in career advancement, 21–22
spending
  reducing, 10, 17
  vs. saving, 41–43
splurging, 56
Standard & Poor's 500 Stock Index, 124
Steele, Michael B., 150
Stettinus, Edward R. Jr., 246
Stevenson, John, 86
stock(s)
  contrarian investing, 129–130
  individual, 86, 119, 130–143
  vs. mortgage prepayment, 166–167
  ownership, 39–40, 331
  purchase, employer, 87–88
  taxation, 215
  types, 103–104
  when to sell, 149
stock funds, emerging-market, 135–136
Stout, Rex, 38
stress reduction, 328
student loans, 68–69, 211
summer job, student, 338

target funds, 118, 126–127
tax changes, futility of predicting, 212–214
tax-deferred annuities, 86
tax records, organizing, 228, 337–338
tax returns
  keeping, 224–226
  preparing, 220–221

tax(es)
    credits, 210–211
    deduction, mortgage, 167
    deferring, 43–45
    estate, 248–249
    home-based business, 31
    income, 207–229
    minimizing, 17, 207–229, 217–218
    property, 169–171
    reducing, 208–212, 339
    refund, 218–220
    retirement, 292
    Roth IRA, 90
    time to file, 228
teenagers, money education, 272–273
telemarketers, 280
television, impact on children, 271
term life insurance, 236, 240–242
Thoreau, Henry David, 35
time
    devoted to finances, 18
    financial value of, 4–9
timing, tax-related transactions, 211
to-do calendar, 337–344
total return (definition), 8
Toynbee, Arnold, 274
travel, in retirement, 292
travel insurance, 245
Treasury bills, 81
trip-cancellation insurance, 245
Tucker, Sophie, 41
Twain, Mark, 15, 18, 268
twentysomethings, financial advice,
    267–268
two-paycheck family, 269–271

U.S. government bonds, 104–105
U.S. government bonds,
    taxation, 216
undeveloped land, 156–158

unexpected events, 16
universal life insurance, 237
unplanned expenses, 193–195
used car, 201, 203

vacation home, 180–184
vacation planning, 338–339
valuables
    fake, 279
    insuring, 232
variable annuity, 311–312
variable universal life insurance, 237

waiver of insurance premium, 238
wealth
    accumulating, 9–15, 37–58
    borrowing to build, 63
    creating, 38–43
    display of, 13
Web sites, tax-preparation, 221
West, Mae, 242
whole life insurance, 236–237
will, 247, 252–253
Wilshire 5000 Index, 124
Wilson, Earl, 65, 75
windfall, financial, 55–58, 344
withholding exemptions, 218–220,
    340, 343
work. *See also* job
    in business ownership, 32
    in career advancement, 21
    part-time, 36, 289
work expenses, in retirement, 291
work-at-home schemes, 279
writing skills, in career advancement,
    22

yield (definition), 8

Special Reader Offers

The special reader Web site that can be accessed through www.jonathanpond.com (*see* page xlii) will help you keep up to date on the information and suggestions presented throughout *Grow Your Money!* In addition, you can take advantage of special offers and discounts that Jonathan makes available to help you achieve your financial dreams, including:

✓ Discounts on Jonathan's products and services, including his weekly Smart Money Tips and flash reports

✓ *Your Lifetime Financial Planner:* personalized analysis of your financial status and needs

✓ *Your Investment Road Map:* customized investment guidance and recommendations

✓ Newsletter offers

✓ Invitation to become a member of Jonathan's *Financial Freedom Alliance*

To find out more and to be kept informed of special reader offers in the future, visit:

www.jonathanpond.com/specialoffers.html